CIVILITY IN THE CITY

JENNIFER LEE

Civility
in the City

Blacks, Jews, and Koreans
in Urban America

HARVARD UNIVERSITY PRESS

Cambridge, Massachusetts, and London, England

2002

Library of Congress Cataloging-in-Publication Data

Lee, Jennifer, 1968–
Civility in the city : Blacks, Jews, and Koreans in urban America /
Jennifer Lee.
p. cm.
Includes bibliographical references and index.
ISBN 0-674-00897-9 (cloth)
1. New York (N.Y.)—Race relations.
2. Philadelphia (Pa.)—Race relations.
3. Retail trade—Social aspects—New York (State)—New York.
4. Retail trade—Social aspects—Pennsylvania—Philadelphia.
5. Courtesy.   6. African Americans—Relations with Jews.
7. African Americans—Relations with Korean Americans.
8. African American consumers—Social conditions.
9. Merchants—New York (State)—New York—Social conditions.
10. Merchants—Pennslyvania—Philadelphia—Social conditions.
I. Title.

F128.9.A1 L44 2002
305.8′0097471—dc21   2002024259

To my family

Contents

Acknowledgments

This book reflects long-standing personal and intellectual interests, and like all projects that take years to complete, it owes manifold debts. I first conceived of this project at Columbia University, I developed the manuscript during my brief stay at the University of California, Los Angeles, and I completed the book at University of California, Irvine. Hence, I owe much to the generosity of three fine institutions.

First and foremost, I thank Herbert Gans, my advisor at Columbia. Herb urged me to take a comparative approach in my research, a message that I now pass on to my own students. Moreover, he tirelessly read drafts of my work, and provided fair and well-deserved comments that made for a richer, more nuanced project. I could not have asked for a more evenhanded critic and attentive advisor. While at Columbia I also had the good fortune to work with Kathryn Neckerman, who pushed me to think critically about the intersections of race, class, immigration, and opportunity. I was also privileged to work with Katherine Newman both before and after her departure to Harvard. Her pointed question, "What's really new here?" pressed me to think hard about how my work contributed to the literature on race and ethnic relations.

There are two professors at Columbia who deserve special mention. Harriet Zuckerman first took notice of me as a young, impressionable undergraduate. She encouraged me to apply to graduate school, and as it turned out, several years later I became her research assistant. I was also a research assistant for Robert K. Merton, who, following the

Columbia tradition, taught me to begin with a theoretically interesting problem, an important question, and patterned behavior that needed explanation, and then to inquire how I could empirically test my theory. His unparalleled demand for logic, coherence, and eloquence in both his work and mine constantly challenges me. Words cannot express my sincerest gratitude to and infinite admiration for both of these professors.

After leaving Columbia, I had the fortune of landing at UCLA, where a University of California President's Postdoctoral Fellowship allowed me two precious years to do additional research and develop the framework for the book. My first order of gratitude goes to Roger Waldinger, who agreed to serve as my mentor. As busy as he was, Roger gave freely of his time, his knowledge, and his books, and he offered thoughtful criticism on early drafts of the manuscript. Min Zhou also gave generously of her time and provided insightful comments and advice. Others at UCLA who offered helpful comments along the way include Rogers Brubaker, Steve Clayman, Ivan Light, David Lopez, Bill Roy, and Abel Valenzuela.

The project crystallized after I arrived at the University of California, Irvine. I am grateful to the Department of Sociology and the Center for Research on Immigration, Population and Public Policy for allowing me the time and support to complete the book. While I am indebted to all of my colleagues at UC Irvine for providing an intellectually vibrant and congenial environment, a few deserve special mention. First, I thank Frank D. Bean, who is an exceptionally supportive, caring, and committed mentor. While Frank has many competing demands on his time, he always manages to carve out enough to help me think through analytically and theoretically vexing problems. I only hope that he feels that he benefits from our conversations as much as I do. David S. Meyer and Cal Morrill helped me at critical junctures when I felt I was at a theoretical impasse. Philip Cohen and Matt Huffman helped me gather useful census figures and provided much encouragement throughout the writing of the book. Susan Wierzbicki joined our faculty just as I completed the book, and her moral support and willingness to listen to various quandaries helped me get through the final stages of writing and editing. I also thank the superb support staff at UC Irvine, who helped me assemble the manuscript, and, more important, greet me with warm smiles every day: Linda Cleland, Jan Meza, Carolynn Bramlett, Sandra Cushman, and Monique Bihm.

There are a number of colleagues who read and commented on all or portions of the book. Philip Kasinitz, John Lie, John Skrentny, Paul Sniderman, and Mary Waters read the entire manuscript and provided critical comments that helped strengthen the book's overarching argument. Others who read portions of the manuscript and provided invaluable insight include Nancy Foner, Rubén Rumbaut, Steve Gold, Loïc Wacquant, Lynn Rapaport, Prudence Carter, Miliann Kang, Sara Lee, and Rhacel Parreñas. I also benefited enormously from the feedback I received when I presented my research to colloquia participants at UC Berkeley, UC Davis, UC Irvine, UCLA, UC San Diego, the University of Illinois Urbana-Champaign, the University of Pennsylvania, and the University of Southern California. Of course, not everyone agreed with me, but I learned a great deal from our disagreements, and I take full responsibility for the mistakes that remain. I am also grateful to Michael Aronson, my editor at Harvard University Press, whose keen eye saw merit in a very early draft of the manuscript; to Benno Weisberg, who helped to steer the book along; and to Julie Hagen, whose meticulous copyediting made the book more readable.

This research was made possible by generous funding from the International Migration Section of the Social Science Research Council, the Andrew W. Mellon Foundation, the National Science Foundation (SBR-9633345), the University of California President's Office, and UC Irvine's School of Social Sciences. In a time of diminishing financial assistance for social science research, I feel very fortunate to have been supported so well. The funding allowed me to hire four wonderful research assistants, Marlene Pantin, Gloria Gadsden, Bambi Aldridge, and Claude Crudip, who conducted the rich, in-depth interviews of the customers in the sample. Even more critically, the Social Science Research Council and the Andrew Mellon Foundation introduced me to leading immigration and race/ethnicity scholars who have since become close friends and colleagues.

There would have been no book to write, of course, had I not succeeded in finding people willing to answer my many and often inconvenient questions. I am truly grateful to the merchants, managers, vendors, employees, and customers who gave so freely of their time. I promised that I would not reveal their real names or the names of their businesses, but I hope that they feel that I have painted an accurate portrait of merchant-customer life in their communities.

Finally, I am indebted to my family. My parents, Sangrin and Wonja, emigrated from South Korea because my father intended to pursue a graduate degree in religion. A professional visa given to my mother, who was trained as a nurse, enabled our family to immigrate to the United States. However, soon after arriving here, my parents calculated that a nurse's salary and a graduate student's stipend could not adequately support a family of four, so they took an economic detour and opened a business, which was located in a low-income black neighborhood. After seven years of operating their business, my father, determined to finish his dissertation, returned to graduate school and received his Ph.D. My mother, the nucleus of our family, supported all of us. She continues to amaze me with her extraordinary strength and endless encouragement. Undoubtedly I have benefited from my parents' determination, focus, and "just do it" attitude. Their love and strength remain the cornerstones of my life.

My sister, Jeena, is a source of inspiration, laughter, and infinite enthusiasm. She is my greatest confidante and lends her ear whenever I need to discuss a problem, no matter how trivial. Ernesto Halim rounds out my nucleus of support. All who know me know how influential he has been in my life. He helps me to think logically and to construct coherent arguments in my work, but more important, Ernesto's unending patience, humor, and ability to put everything into perspective help me to achieve a balanced and happy life. To the four who provide unconditional love and support, Mom, Dad, Jeena, and Ernesto, I dedicate this book as my best, if barely adequate, form of gratitude.

CIVILITY
IN THE CITY

CHAPTER 1

Introduction

The final decade of the twentieth century proved to rival the 1960s as one of the most tumultuous in black communities—one fraught with boycotts, urban riots, and firebombings. The decade opened with an eighteen-month-long boycott of a Korean-owned fruit and vegetable market in the Flatbush section of Brooklyn, New York.[1] Much of the media coverage of the event focused on the individual-level differences between Korean merchants and black customers, pointing to cultural and linguistic misunderstandings between the two minority groups.[2] The relationship between black customers and Korean merchants was quickly popularized and exploited by the media with splashy newspaper headlines that read "Will Black Merchants Drive Koreans from Harlem?" "Blacks, Koreans Struggle to Grasp Thread of Unity," "Cultural Conflict," and "Scapegoating New York's Koreans."[3] "Black-Korean conflict"—as it quickly became framed and labeled by journalists and scholars—was featured in mainstream and ethnic presses alike and spilled over into other forms of popular culture. Spike Lee's poignant film *Do The Right Thing*, Albert and Allen Hughes's film *Menace II Society*, and Ice Cube's controversial lyrics in the rap song "Black Korea" brought black-Korean tension and conflict to the fore in both African American and Korean communities. In fact, the film *Menace II Society* opens with the murder of two Korean merchants in Los Angeles by a black teenage customer.

Frictions increased on March 16, 1991, when in the South Central district of Los Angeles, Korean storeowner Soon Ja Du shot and killed an African American teenager, Latasha Harlins, over an allegedly stolen bottle of orange juice. Racial tensions climaxed in South Central on April 29, 1992, after an all-white jury in the white suburb of Simi Valley acquitted four white Los Angeles police officers of beating twenty-five-year-old African American motorist Rodney King. The "not guilty" verdict sparked the 1992 Los Angeles riot—the first multiethnic riot in U.S. history. The nation remained paralyzed as it witnessed buildings in South Central and Koreatown set aflame while inner-city residents looted neighborhood stores, taking everything from televisions and VCRs to food and diapers. Who can forget the media image of Korean merchants armed with 9-millimeter handguns during the riots, attempting to protect their property from looters? The LA riot proved to be the worst domestic uprising in the twentieth century, ending with a count of 16,291 arrested, 2,383 injured, 500 fires, and 52 dead.[4] Korean merchants suffered almost half of the property damage, amounting to more than $400 million and affecting more than 2,300 Korean-owned businesses in Los Angeles.[5] The nation was stunned. While many ethnic groups were involved, by some media accounts the riot was framed as the pinnacle of black-Korean conflict.

Several years later, on December 8, 1995, an African American man named Roland Smith walked into Freddy's, a clothing store on Harlem's 125th Street, with a .38 caliber gun and a can of paint thinner.[6] Four male employees—three white and one Guyanese Indian—dashed for the door, and Smith shot each of them, critically wounding two. Moments later the police arrived, but it was too late. Smith had set Freddy's ablaze and then made his way to the back of the store where he shot himself. Unable to escape, the remaining seven nonblack employees of Freddy's were trapped in the store and died in the flames. The firebombing of Freddy's made the front page of the *New York Times,* with caustic headlines that read, "In Nightmare of Anger, Store Becomes Flaming Madhouse" and "Death on 125th Street: A Scene of Carnage."[7]

The firebombing of Freddy's marked the end of a bitter three-way dispute between Fred Harari (the Jewish owner of Freddy's clothing store), Sikhulu Shange (Harari's subtenant, the African American owner of The Record Shack), and the United House of Prayer for All People (the African American church that owned the building). When Harari initially entered into a lease agreement with the African American church, he inherited Shange as a subtenant. However, when

Harari decided to expand his business, he decided to evict Shange at his lease's end. The African American church (the property owners) stood behind Harari's decision to expand and offered Shange an alternate location. But Shange refused to move and pleaded with Harlem's African American community leaders for help. Black nationalists immediately organized a boycott of Freddy's clothing store to protest Harari's decision. When word on the street got out that a Jewish landlord would soon evict an African American storeowner, community leaders and some of Harlem's local residents joined forces and began picketing outside of Freddy's for Shange's cause.

It was easy enough to ignore the protestors at first, but when racial and ethnic taunts began to permeate the discourse—remarks like "Kill the Jew bastards" and "This block is for niggers only, no whites and Jews allowed"—Harari decided that it was time to file for a restraining order. By the time the order was granted, however, it was too late; Roland Smith had already set Freddy's ablaze. What few Harlemites knew at the time, and even to this day most still do not realize, is that the African American church that owns the property fully supported Harari's plan to evict Shange. In fact, to visibly demonstrate his unwavering support of Harari, the African American pastor at United House of Prayer for All People marched his congregation through Freddy's picket line during the boycott.

Regardless of the African American church's central involvement, the conflict among property owner, tenant, and subtenant was immediately framed as racially charged warfare between blacks and Jews—a framework that had a history, pushed buttons on all sides, and was easily adopted by the media and the public alike. This economic dispute took on collective proportions and led African American customers to ask, "How can you move blacks out of 125th Street when that's all we have?" And when the protestors realized that Fred Harari was not in the store at the time of the fire, one regretfully commented, "The wrong people got killed, and the one that should have got killed—the nasty one—got away."

Clearly, the final decade of the twentieth century was tumultuous in black communities across the country. The 1992 Los Angeles riot, the boycotts of immigrant-owned businesses in major cities, and the 1995 firebombing of Freddy's clothing store in New York's Harlem, brought race and ethnic relations in inner-city neighborhoods to the fore. Journalists and scholars alike turned the nation's attention to communities like Harlem, South Central Los Angeles, West Philadelphia, and Chicago's South Side—where the customers are predominantly black and poor, and the storeowners, immigrant newcomers. Images of urban riots, "bloodsucking" Jewish and Korean storeowners, picket lines, and firebombings have seared into the public's consciousness the idea that racial warfare is a fact of life in black communities. Because few people living outside of them have firsthand experience of the commercial life in these neighborhoods, journalistic accounts become a major means of defining reality. However, the following anecdote challenges the prevailing image of racial strife.

On February 3, 1999, two robbers shot and killed a beloved storeowner outside her business in South Central Los Angeles. The community was outraged and demanded that the two men who took her life be found and brought to justice, prompting the Los Angeles City Council to offer a $25,000 reward for any information leading to the arrest and conviction of the killers. At her funeral, eight days after the shooting, hundreds of South Central residents mourned the death of this popular merchant, affectionately known as "Mama." The African American and Latino residents of this low-income neighborhood remembered the many small favors that Mama had done for them. She had often given credit to customers who fell short in covering their grocery bill, refusing to let a couple of dollars allow her customers to go hungry between checks. Nor could her customers forget the storeowner who recognized them on sight and knew their children by name. These small acts of kindness and respect made up part of the daily fabric of merchant life in this predominantly black, low-income community.

At the time of Mama's death, nearly seven years had passed since the Los Angeles riot erupted in the very same neighborhood. Then, while South Central residents had raided and set many of the community's businesses ablaze, Mama's business had been left untouched. The fact that her business remained unscathed after the riot would not have been surprising if Mama were African American. Many black shop owners had placed "Black Owned" signs in their windows, in the hopes that rioters would think twice before vandalizing one of their own. However, Mama was not black. She was Korean; her name was Mrs. Chung Hong. One year after her death, a memorial service held in

Mrs. Hong's honor drew in more than one hundred Koreans, African Americans, and Latinos. The *Los Angeles Times* prominently featured Mrs. Hong's memorial service with a caption that read, "Mourners Remember Beloved 'Mama.'"[8]

Mrs. Hong stands in stark contrast to the rigid stereotype of the brusque, ethnocentric Korean merchant who treats black customers with little respect. And South Central's residents—who came out to pay their last respects to Mrs. Hong—seem a far cry from the jaded welfare recipients and cold-hearted criminals that we are told inhabit the nation's inner cities. Was Mrs. Hong simply a rare exception, a Korean merchant who was able to transcend race, ethnicity, and nativity to forge positive relations with her black customers? Or are merchant-customer relations in black communities—and race and ethnic relations more generally—characterized by something other than racial animosity, prejudice, and violence?

Based on in-depth interviews and ethnographic research, I seek to answer these questions by dissecting interethnic conflict and cooperation among African American, Jewish, and Korean merchants and their black customers in five predominantly black neighborhoods in New York City and Philadelphia. Media accounts often depict interethnic relations in black neighborhoods as fraught with animosity, with immigrant merchants pitted against African American customers. Past scholarly research also focuses on intergroup conflict, highlighting language and cultural barriers, class differences, interethnic competition, inner-city poverty, prejudice, and the media's construction of conflict. However, I argue that media accounts and past research have been biased toward conflict and controversy and do not reflect the full range of commercial life and merchant-customer relations in black communities. Conflict may be raw material for newspaper headlines, television leads, and even scholarly research, but there is a wide gap between the true nature of merchant-customer relations in black communities (and race and ethnic relations more generally) and the public image of these relations.

Civility in the City

I believe that the prevailing image of racial warfare is inconsistent with most merchant-customer interactions. An important untold story is the mostly quotidian nature of commercial life in neighborhoods like New York's Harlem and West Philadelphia. The everyday interactions between Jewish, Korean, and African American merchants and their black customers are not antagonistic, but rather positive, civil, and routine. The ordinariness of these merchant-customer relations is perplexing because it contradicts both media accounts and the past scholarly research that highlight intergroup conflict in urban communities.

In this volume I examine the ways in which social order, routine, and civility are negotiated and maintained through hundreds of daily interactions between merchants and customers. I demonstrate that while merchant-customer relations are in no way uniform, the majority are civil because merchants actively work to manage tensions and smooth out incidents before they escalate into racially charged anger. Civil relations prevail because merchants make investments to maintain the day-to-day routine, recognizing that failing to do so can have dramatic consequences.

Although merchants actively work to maintain civility, small events can still trigger anger, with race polarizing the simplest interactions. Race is never absent, and it inflects merchant-customer interactions in diverse and sometimes conflict-ridden ways. In extreme cases, race is mobilized in violent ways, becoming the source of protest motivations that lead to boycotts and firebombings. The Los Angeles riot, the firebombing of Freddy's clothing store, and the boycotts of Korean-owned markets make it evident that everyday routine can break down—that under the surface of civil relations lies the potential for conflict.

Let me state at the outset that this is not a book about the LA riot, the firebombing of Freddy's, or the boycotts of Korean-owned fruit and vegetable markets. Those are certainly topics in their own right. However, I have chosen to study merchant-customer relations through an ethnomethodological lens, meaning that my focus is on the everyday and the local, rather than on larger events like riots or boycotts that erupt only rarely.[9] Ethnomethodology's main theoretical proposal is that "there is a self-generating order in concrete activities," and its principle task is to identify the mechanisms by which social order is locally produced.[10] I wish to examine the interactions between merchants and customers to learn how social order, routine, and civility are maintained each day.

While highlighting civility, I also illustrate how race can nuance merchant-customer relations in conflict-ridden ways, and demonstrate how the potential for conflict is embedded in the structure of day-to-day life in poor black communities. Conflict motivations emerge as racial and ethnic groups jockey for position in America's stratified society. As Jewish merchants have moved up and out of black neighborhoods and new immigrants, such as Koreans and Middle Easterners, have moved in, the African American residents have watched these new groups realize the American dream of success. The image of immigrants coming into black communities, buying up the businesses, and leaving with the profits in their pockets is a provocative one for poor African Americans. They may not object to immigrants per se, but African Americans do object to the notion that the foreign-born of all types are moving ahead of them, presumably with the help of government aid, and seemingly at their own expense. Who owns the stores in black neighborhoods is a subject laden with symbolism, which translates into far more importance than what the businesses generate in profits. It reflects blacks' sense of collective identity and group position—that is, where they feel they *ought* to stand vis-à-vis Jews and Koreans.[11] Most critically, the predominance of nonblack-owned businesses in black communities is a symbol of black economic subordination to other groups.

Rather than stating that the structural context allows few options beyond conflict, or that the merchants and customers freely choose their behavior without constraints, I wish to avoid either-or explanations. In examining the interactions between merchants and customers in black communities, this volume does not lose sight of the less visible structures and processes that produce certain modes of interaction.[12] While the day-to-day commercial life may be routine, conditions such as poverty, joblessness, rising immigration, and extreme inequality can certainly tip the balance in favor of conflict. Hence, conflict and civility are not mutually exclusive, and conflict motivations can emerge against the backdrop of prosaic routine.

Theories of Service Providers and Customers

This book draws from and bridges two strands of literature: the literature on service workers and their clients more broadly and past studies of merchant-customer relations in urban neighborhoods. The relationship between service providers and customers is one in which personal attitudes should come secondary to the role relationship. However, as previous research shows, ample scope exists for individual attitudes to affect these interactions. For example, in their study of customer-clerk encounters, Albert McCormick and Graham Kinloch reveal that race affects service interactions, with intraracial encounters generally characterized as friendlier than interracial ones.[13] Black clerks are more likely to smile at, make eye contact with, and initiate conversation with black customers than white, and correlatively, white clerks are friendlier to white customers. Therefore, we should expect African American merchants to have friendlier and more positive relations with black customers compared to their Jewish or Korean counterparts.

Experience on the shop floor also matters, affording service providers two distinct advantages. First, as William Foote Whyte noted in his classic study of the restaurant industry, more seasoned service providers know how to deal better with unreasonably demanding or rude customers.[14] Second, as Robin Leidner noted in her study of service workers in the fast food industry, time and experience build a steady flow of regular customers, allowing for service interactions to go beyond impersonal, perfunctory, and utilitarian exchanges.[15] The length of time a merchant has been in business, therefore, should be positively correlated with positive service interactions. In other words, merchants who have been in business for a longer time are more likely to have better relations with their customers compared to the newcomers on the street.

In addition, the nature of the business niche affects service interactions. In her study of service workers, Barbara Gutek makes a useful distinction between "relationships" and "encounters."[16] In relationships, customers and service providers spend a fair amount of time together, getting to know one another as individuals as well as role occupants, whereas encounters are typically fleeting interactions, marked by high turnover, speed, and efficiency. A customer may have a relationship with her hairstylist, with whom she may spend several hours, but an encounter with her local grocer, with whom she spends only a few seconds.[17] Whereas success in a relationship is based on how much time a customer spends with the service worker, success in an encounter depends on how little time is spent completing the transaction. Accordingly, merchants whose businesses foster relationships are more likely to have positive interactions with their customers than those who engage in encounters, since service relationships allow for prolonged interactions that go beyond anonymous exchanges.

Other research on service interactions highlights the potential for conflict that stems from the subordinate status of service providers in relation to their customers.[18] In service positions, workers must often endure mistreatment at the hands of supposed "social betters" because they often lack what Arlie Hochschild refers to as a "status shield."[19] Furthermore, when providers find themselves serving customers who are lower in class and status, they find it exceedingly difficult to adjust to this type of subordination. As William Foote Whyte noted more than fifty years ago, "It is hard to be pushed around by those of higher status, it is doubly hard to be pushed around by one's equals or inferiors."[20]

What makes the merchant-customer relationship in poor black neighborhoods unique is that middle-class storeowners serve the minority poor, reversing the status hierarchy for the duration of the interaction and within the spatial confines of the store. Middle-class merchants find themselves taking orders from low-income black customers they deem inferior in class and status. Boas Shamir's research on service providers underscores this point, demonstrating that in subordinate service roles, the higher the status of the customers, the lower the level of conflict.[21] Therefore, we should expect lower levels of conflict to emerge between storeowners and middle-class customers compared with low-income customers.

While the literature on service providers and customers identifies some of the variance in service interactions, this line of research gives scant attention to the way in which the structural context of poverty and inequality may affect individual interactions. The service provider–customer literature does not link individual interactions with the community context but examines them apart from structural conditions that may affect the interactions.[22] It is also important to note that because blacks, Jews, and Koreans do not regularly come in contact with each other outside of the merchant-customer relationship, their interactions in the store have implications for race and ethnic relations more generally. For example, of the black customers we interviewed, 83 percent claimed that they do not know Koreans who are *not* storeowners, and 72 percent said the same of Jews. Among those we interviewed in low-income neighborhoods, the percentages are even higher; 89 percent and 78 percent of the black customers claim that they do not know Koreans or Jews, respectively, who are not storeowners. Because blacks, Jews, and Koreans often interact within the limited roles of merchant and customer, the way in which they perceive one another in these roles will have a direct bearing on the way they perceive one another as members of their respective racial and ethnic groups. Therefore, it is germane to locate merchant-customer interactions in the literature on race and ethnic relations in urban communities more generally.

Merchant-Customer Relations in Urban Neighborhoods

Research on merchant-customer relations in poor urban neighborhoods focuses on points of contention, stressing that disagreements between merchants and customers frequently arise over faulty merchandise, high prices, and exchange policies.[23] Past research also emphasizes the structural context in which Jewish and Korean merchants come into contact with black customers, highlighting that nonblack merchants often serve black customers in urban neighborhoods where poverty, unemployment, and inequality are extreme. The structural context, in turn, creates ripe conditions for the emergence of racial conflict in the form of boycotts, protests, and riots.[24] Other researchers emphasize Jewish and Korean merchants' role as middlemen who provoke resentment because they are caught between the elites who manufacture products and the poor consumers who buy them.[25] Moreover, customers often believe that middlemen minorities compete with native-born groups and take opportunities away from them. Others underscore the media's role in constructing and reifying interracial conflict among minority groups.[26]

However, what this body of past research has failed to reconcile is that boycotts, violent protests, and riots are anomalous events in inner cities, while structural conditions such as poverty, unemployment, and inequality are ever present. By focusing only on the structural context, past researchers have allowed few options beyond conflict and, in essence, overpredicted the level of conflict between merchants and customers in urban neighborhoods. These researchers have also failed to examine how variations in class may affect merchant-customer relations. Conversely, by examining service interactions without embedding them within a structural framework, theories of service providers and customers ignore how the structural context may affect merchant-customer interactions.

A fuller understanding of merchant-customer relations in black neighborhoods requires examining these interactions through an ethnomethodological lens. This approach is particularly fruitful because, apart from dramatic and contentious events such as boycotts and riots, we know little about the nature of merchant-customer relations in black communities. What previous research has overlooked is how nonblack merchants make investments to abate tensions and socially embed their businesses in black communities, in order to maintain civil relations under conditions of extreme inequality. Nonblack merchants recognize that maintaining civility and thwarting conflict are important goals, especially because the failure to do so can have dramatic and conflict-ridden consequences.

Research Strategy

Because merchant-customer relations have been cited as a source of animosity and a catalyst to conflict, I focus on these interactions as the site of interracial contact and possible tension. I set out to study merchant-customer relations in black communities by interviewing merchants who have businesses in black neighborhoods and interviewing the customers who patronize them. I chose to interview Jewish and Korean merchants because both groups have experienced mobility through self-employment, and both have prospered by serving the black community.[27] Korean immigrants today are achieving rates of socioeconomic mobility that parallel the experience of Jewish immigrants in earlier decades. The media, the politicians, and the public have touted both groups as "model minorities" who have battled discrimination and achieved success through hard work and determination.[28]

However, Jewish and Korean merchants' economic success has come with social costs. Black customers have charged both groups with disrespectful treatment, prejudice, and exploitation of their communities.

Black nationalists have accused Jewish and Korean business owners of buying all of the stores in black neighborhoods, draining residents of their resources, and failing to "give back" by hiring local people.[29] Furthermore, black nationalists charge that immigrants take away business opportunities from African American entrepreneurs and residents. Jewish and Korean merchants have also been the targets of boycotts, strikes, and riots. Clearly there are parallels between the Jewish and Korean entrepreneurial experiences. I decided to compare black-Jewish and black-Korean merchant-customer relations in black communities, and then to interview African American merchants and compare their experiences with their Jewish and Korean counterparts. Adding African American merchants to the study enabled me to examine merchant-customer relations when race is held constant—that is, when merchants and customers are both black.

This book is based on interviews with seventy-five African American, Jewish, and Korean merchants and seventy-five black customers. Interviews took place in five predominantly black neighborhoods in New York City and Philadelphia. Of the five neighborhoods, three are low-income, with median household incomes under $20,000 (East Harlem and West Harlem in New York, and West Philadelphia), and two are middle-income, with median household incomes slightly over $35,000 (Jamaica, Queens, and Mount Airy, Philadelphia). I chose to compare low-income and middle-income black neighborhoods in order to see the effect of class on merchant-customer relations. Table 1.1 illustrates the various characteristics of the five research sites, and Table 1.2 shows the variety of industries in the sample of merchants.

Each of the five neighborhoods has bustling commercial strips lined with small businesses that offer a variety of merchandise and services, some of which are geared specifically to a black clientele, including wigs, ethnic beauty supplies, inner-city sportswear, soul food restaurants, beauty salons, and barbershops. There are a variety of other businesses as well, that offer furniture, sneakers, jewelry, fruits and vegetables, fresh fish, electronics, and discount household supplies. Noticeably missing on these shopping strips are the large retail chains and department stores that are nearly ubiquitous in white, middle-class neighborhoods and suburban shopping malls. The absence of large retail chains has created a niche in which small-scale entrepreneurs can set up shop in these communities.[30] The retailers in these

Table 1.1 Characteristics of research sites

Characteristic	New York			Philadelphia	
	West Harlem	East Harlem	Jamaica, Queens	West Philadelphia	Mount Airy
Total population	55,142	28,448	53,127	48,672	27,675
Median household income ($)	16,767	11,348	35,224	18,394	35,152
Households receiving public assistance (%)	22	42	8	21	8
Households below poverty line (%)	34	46	13	27	8
Race (%)					
Black	60	54	28	93	95
White	26	18	39	5	4
Other	14	27	33	2	1
Nativity (%)					
Native-born	81	90	51	96	97
Foreign-born	19	10	49	4	3
Gender (%)					
Male	44	46	49	44	45
Female	56	54	51	56	55
Employment (%)					
Employed	48	40	61	46	67
Unemployed	7	9	6	8	7
Not in labor force	45	51	33	46	26
Education (%)					
Completed high school or more	64	42	72	58	70
Completed college or more	27	4	26	8	17

Source: 1990 Census of Population and Housing Summary.

Note: West Harlem, East Harlem, and West Philadelphia are low-income neighborhoods; Jamaica, Queens, and Mount Airy are middle-income neighborhoods.

Table 1.2 Types of businesses in the sample

Product or Service Offered	Jewish Ownership	Korean Ownership	African American Ownership	Total
African cultural products	0	0	1	1
Apparel				[17]
Army and navy/industrial	2	0	0	2
Inner-city sportswear	1	4	0	5
Ladies' dresses	0	3	1	4
Ladies' better casual	0	0	1	1
Men's and ladies' better casual	0	0	2	2
Men's dress apparel	2	0	0	2
Men's better casual	0	0	1	1
Auto repair	2	0	0	2
Baked goods/coffee shop	0	0	1	1
Barbershop	0	0	1	1
Beauty salon	0	0	3	3
Bookstore	0	0	1	1
Cards and gifts	1	0	1	2
Carry-out food	0	1	1	2
Dry cleaning	0	2	0	2
Electronics	1	0	0	1
Ethnic beauty supplies	1	4	0	5
Eyeglasses	1	0	0	1
Fish	0	2	0	2
Furniture	7	1	2	10
General merchandise	0	1	0	1
Groceries	0	4	0	4
Hardware	0	0	1	1
Jewelry	1	1	0	2
Lingerie	1	0	1	2
Music	0	0	1	1
Pawnshop	1	0	0	1
Pharmacy	1	0	1	2
Shoe repair	0	1	0	1
Sneakers	1	2	0	3
Thrift store	0	0	1	1
Variety/household supplies	1	0	0	1
Wigs	1	3	0	4
Total	25	29	21	75

neighborhoods include Koreans, Jews, Asian Indians, Middle Eastern-ers, Latinos, African Americans, and West Indians, while the customers are primarily black.

I spent a great deal of time observing merchant-customer inter-actions in all of these businesses, since I visited each store at least twice. Because I interviewed the storeowners during business hours, we were routinely interrupted when customers needed to make pur-chases, which provided opportunities for me to act as a nonparticipant observer. In addition, I benefited from working as a bag checker in a clothing store on 125th Street in West Harlem and as a cashier in a sneaker store on 52nd Street in West Philadelphia. Acting as a partici-pant observer allowed me to be at the field site in an inconspicuous way and provided rich data that would have been missed had I relied on interviews alone. These positions were invaluable to my research, because I was able to observe the daily activities of the merchants and their interactions with customers.

To get a complete understanding of the merchant-customer rela-tionship, I hired African American research assistants to conduct the interviews with black customers, which no study has done to date. All of the customers are local residents who reside and shop in these com-munities, and they were asked specifically about their shopping experi-ences in Jewish-, Korean-, and black-owned stores in their neighbor-hoods. Table 1.3 illustrates the various status characteristics of the sample.

New York and Philadelphia provide a fascinating comparison of two eastern cities that are similar on a number of dimensions, such as the self-employment rate, the proportion of service-sector employment, the rate of unemployment, and the percentage of residents living be-low the poverty line. However, the two key dimensions on which these cities differ remarkably are the rate of immigration and the number of race riots. New York City leads the country in the percentage of for-eign-born inhabitants, with 28.4 percent of its residents having been born outside the United States, whereas Philadelphia lags far behind, ranking thirty-seventh among U.S. cities, with only 6.6 percent of its residents being foreign-born.[31] As I will demonstrate, immigration is a key variable that shapes and constructs race, ethnicity, and opportu-nity in diverse and unforeseen ways. The second point of divergence I note is the number of race riots that each city has experienced. Al-

Table 1.3 Characteristics of black customer sample

	New York			Philadelphia		
	West Harlem	East Harlem	Jamaica, Queens	West Philadelphia	Mount Airy	All Sites
Mean age	39	44	36	39	42	40
Mean years of education	13	12	13	13	14	13
Gender (%)						
Male	53	27	33	40	53	42
Female	47	73	67	60	47	58
Occupational status (%)						
Employed	53	53	53	47	53	52
Uemployed	20	47	20	27	7	26
Retired	7	—	27	13	27	9
Student	20	—	—	13	13	13
Ethnic identity (%)						
African American	87	93	60	100	87	85
West Indian	13	7	40	—	13	15
Number of black customers	15	15	15	15	15	75

Note: West Harlem, East Harlem, and West Philadelphia are low-income neighborhoods; Jamaica, Queens, and Mount Airy are middle-income neighborhoods.

though the northeast has been a common site of racial unrest, New York experienced nearly four times as many black race riots as Philadelphia in the second half of the twentieth century. From 1960 to 1993, there were twenty-two black race riots in New York, compared with only six in Philadelphia.[32] (Complete details about the research design and the methodological issues raised while I was in the field are provided in the Appendix.)

Organization of the Book

To understand how civil relations prevail between merchants and customers in communities characterized by poverty and gross inequality, and to reveal the implications that merchant-customer relations have for race and ethnic relations among blacks, Jews, and Koreans in black communities, this book examines four closely related research questions.

The first is the much-debated question of whether immigrant entrepreneurs compete with and inhibit opportunities for African Americans. Chapter 2 provides a history of the ghetto merchant, describes the ethnic succession of ownership of these retail shops, and explains how Koreans have come to dominate the inner-city retail niche. In Chapter 3 I show that competition is far more likely to be *intra*ethnic rather than *inter*ethnic in nature, because retail niches are segmented along ethnic lines. However, this is not the end of the story. Retail niches are segmented in the first place because ethnic networks not only help coethnics move into similar niches but also work to exclude outsiders. Nonetheless, it is precisely the segmentation of the retail niches that places Koreans—and other immigrant entrepreneurs—in lines of business that are more susceptible to customer conflict.

The second question is, What are merchant-customer relations like on an interpersonal level in black neighborhoods? Moving away from simplistic images of antagonism and racially charged warfare, Chapter 4 demonstrates the wide variance in merchant-customer interactions, which range from routine and friendly to brusque and antagonistic. However, more significant than the race, ethnicity, or religion of the merchant in shaping customer interactions are such variables as the length of time a merchant has been in business, the age of the customers, the merchant's gender, and the class composition of the clientele.

The third question I examine is how and why small economic disputes between merchants and customers escalate into racially charged arguments. As "out-group" merchants, Jews and Koreans realize that seemingly trivial arguments can quickly take on powerful racial overtones. In Chapter 5, I demonstrate that when customers are black and poor and have faced oppression and discrimination in other realms, merchant-customer arguments can easily be interpreted within a racialized framework. Some Jewish and Korean merchants attempt to thwart altercations by hiring black employees to act as "cultural brokers" to keep day-to-day tensions from erupting into racially charged conflict. Black employees also serve another critical function: they socially embed nonblack-owned businesses in black neighborhoods. "Black," however, is a generic category, masking differences in ethnicity and nativity. Merchants may indeed hire blacks as cultural brokers, but this does not necessarily mean that they hire African Americans.

African American merchants are not immune to racialized disputes with their black customers, as Chapter 6 reveals. One of the deepest sources of contention within the black community is the coethnic disadvantage of serving one's own. On a collective level, blacks may object to the presence of out-group merchants such as Jews, Koreans, and other immigrant newcomers, yet blacks remain the most critical of each other. African American businessowners complain that their customers fail to patronize them as frequently as they do nonblack businessowners and also hold them to an impossibly high standard. At the same time, black customers complain that black storeowners deliberately charge higher prices and offer inferior merchandise and service. Despite this internal criticism, most African Americans say they would like to see the majority of the stores in their community owned and operated by coethnics. The contradiction reflects the paradox between the realities of black business ownership and the symbolism behind black control over black communities.

The fourth and final question is, What are the implications of merchant-customer relations for race and ethnic relations more generally? In Chapter 7, I demonstrate that positive merchant-customer relations do not preclude the possibility of conflict. Although merchant-customer interactions are routinely civil, protest motivations emerge as groups compete for better positions in America's racially and ethnically stratified society. As African Americans witness a continuous stream of newcomers moving up and out of their communities, they begin to question exactly who is American, and who makes up the rules to the mobility game. In black communities, the categories of race, ethnicity, opportunity, and Americanism are locally constructed, and it is here that these minority groups define one another and struggle to secure their group position in the system of ethnic stratification. The symbolism behind black business ownership and group position is the ideological tool that transforms prosaic routine into racial conflict.

As a further point of comparison, in Chapter 8 I look at black customers' shopping experiences within their communities versus those in predominantly white neighborhoods, and show that blacks are treated far *worse* when they shop outside of their own neighborhood. Although black customers may be treated better in black neighborhoods, protests have turned from white establishments to immigrant-owned shops in black communities. This chapter seeks to uncover why boycotters have focused on the local Mom and Pop, immigrant-owned shops in black neighborhoods instead of the larger, well-established chain stores in white neighborhoods.

Each chapter of the book informs one aspect of merchant-customer relations. Taken together, they provide a complete picture of merchant-customer relations—and relations more generally among blacks, Jews, and Koreans—in black neighborhoods. Chapter 9 engages and synthesizes the theoretical debates and comes back to the people who make up the daily life in these communities. It concludes with some modest policy recommendations that I hope will work to avert protest motivations in the future.

CHAPTER 2

The Ghetto Merchant
Yesterday and Today

When it came down to the nitty-gritty you could always go to Mister
Ben. Before a Jewish holiday he'd take all the food that was going to
spoil while the store was shut and bring it over to our house. Before
Christmas he'd send over some meat even though he knew it was going on the tablet and he might never see his money. When the push
came to the shove and every hungry belly in the house was beginning to eat on itself, Momma could go to Mister Ben and always get
enough for some dinner.

       —Dick Gregory, in *Nigger: An Autobiography*

It is bitter to watch the Jewish storekeeper locking up his store for
the night and going home. Going, with your money in his pocket,
to a clean neighborhood, miles from you, which you will not be
allowed to enter.

       —James Baldwin, in "Negroes are Anti-Semitic Because
       They're Anti-White"

Over the past few decades, the growing number of immigrant entrepreneurs has made a distinct and consequential presence in many
large U.S. cities, most notably in the inner cities. Today, Jewish, Korean, and other foreign-born merchants dominate the inner-city retail niche. Walk along East Harlem's Third Avenue, and you find a succession of large furniture stores that have been in the community
for more than four decades. Peer through the windows, and you see
crowded displays of sofas, living and dining room sets, washers and
dryers, and coffee tables. Walk further north on Third Avenue, and
you come across a smattering of stores that cater to East Harlem's residents—a fish store that sells an array of seafood from deep-fried crab
cakes to fresh salmon steaks; a variety store that offers bargains on pa-

per towels and laundry detergent; a public laundromat; and a grocery store that carries the usual fruits and vegetables along with some ethnic specialties such as dried fish and beans.

Now walk to 125th Street and head west. After crossing Fifth Avenue, one enters West Harlem—also characterized as "the heartbeat of black America" or, as Claude McKay once described it, "the Negro capital of the world" and the "queen of black belts."[1] Walk further west and you see jewelry shops displaying chunky gold chains and a medley of the enormous gold hoop earrings that adorn the local teenagers. Look across the street at the wig store and you will find dozens of dark-skinned mannequin heads displaying wigs ranging in price from $19.99 for synthetic hairpieces to more than $300 for real human hair. Walk farther west on Harlem's 125th Street and you stumble upon the infamous Apollo Theater, where amateur and veteran artists still perform for New York audiences. Continue walking and you come across several urban sportswear stores that sell knock-offs of Polo designer T-shirts at two for $20; the latest Nike Air Jordon's, which retail for $140; and the costly Timberland boots that are popular among today's youth. Sprinkled among the immigrant-owned retail shops are beauty salons, barbershops, and record stores owned and operated by African Americans.

Signs of black entrepreneurship are not limited to these businesses. On some street corners one finds African women dressed in kenta cloth, asking passersby if they would like to have their hair braided. African American vendors offer books and magazines ranging from *The Autobiography of Malcolm X* to Terry McMillan's *Waiting to Exhale* to the latest high-fashion magazines. But 125th Street in Harlem is more than a shopping strip; it is also a social scene, particularly on Saturdays, when residents and visitors come to check out what's happening on "1-2-5." Dressed in the latest fashions, teenagers and young adults walk the strip with the intent to shop and socialize. On the residential side streets during the warm spring and summer months, one finds neighbors, young and old, hanging out on the steps of their brownstones with their children and their dogs, exchanging the latest gossip. The scene evokes a sense of community that seems to have been lost in the upper-middle-class white neighborhoods further downtown.

The hustle and bustle of Harlem's 125th Street is mirrored in the energy of Jamaica Avenue in Queens, New York, and 52nd Street in West Philadelphia. One crucial difference, however, is the number of black street vendors along these other shopping strips. While most of the street vendors have been removed from West Harlem's 125th Street, they are ever present on Jamaica Avenue and in West Philadelphia. The vendors include African Americans, West Indians, and Africans. Not having the capital, or the access to it, to open a shop of their own, the vendors take advantage of the foot traffic on these shopping strips and offer an assortment of merchandise that the stores do not typically carry. Many sell scented oils and incense, not only because these items are popular but also because they are inexpensive to stock. Other vendors offer hair clips, bootleg tapes, batteries, scarves, hats, gloves, handbags, inexpensive apparel, silver rings, and earrings. So long as the vendors do not carry the same merchandise as the store-owners, merchant-vendor relations are just fine.

Although the shopping strips in Harlem, West Philadelphia, and Jamaica Avenue resemble one another, the retail strip in Mount Airy stands apart from the rest. Tucked away in a more middle-class section of Philadelphia and far from the city's subways, Mount Airy's stores attract far less foot traffic and cater to a more middle-class clientele. Instead of urban sportswear stores, one finds shops that sell moderately priced ladies' dresses and offer Afrocentric products. In lieu of jewelry stores and ethnic beauty supply shops, one finds video rental stores, restaurants, and a car dealership. The check-cashing outlets and pawnshops that are viable businesses in low-income neighborhoods are nowhere to be found in Mount Airy. The one constant is the plethora of beauty salons and barbershops owned and operated by African Americans.

This chapter looks at the history of commercial districts such as these. It provides an overview of merchant life in black communities throughout the twentieth century, examines some of the causes and consequences of the tumultuous urban riots that struck the nation in the 1960s, and depicts the succession of ethnic business owners in these black urban communities. Finally, the chapter describes how Korean, Jewish, and African American storeowners set up shop today. It illustrates the different resources available to these groups and explores why African American businessowners find themselves at a comparative disadvantage.

Jewish Merchants' Historical Presence in Black Neighborhoods

The Jewish population in the United States increased dramatically between the tail end of the eighteenth century and the beginning of the twentieth. In 1790, there were about 1,200 Jews in the United States, and by the mid-1920s, the figure had jumped to more than 4 million.[2] While political and religious concerns determined the timing of Jewish emigration, economic reasons were the primary motivations. Since Jews were prohibited from owning land in eastern Europe, many became merchants and traders.[3] When Jewish immigrants arrived in the United States, discrimination did not cease at America's doorstep. American unions excluded Jews from jobs in existing firms, and so Jewish immigrants chose self-employment because it offered the only viable avenue to upward mobility. Furthermore, Jewish immigrants arrived in the United States with training and education that were well-suited to mercantile-related occupations. And unlike native whites, Jewish immigrants were willing to ignore the prevailing racial codes that censured contact between whites and blacks and serve black consumers. Jewish immigrant entrepreneurs found little competition from native whites in selling to black consumers in black neighborhoods.[4]

By the 1920s, the merchants in New York and Philadelphia were predominantly Jewish. But by the mid-1920s, socially mobile German Jews began to leave the city for the suburbs, and their places of residence were taken over by the more recent Russian Jewish arrivals. In 1924, when the U.S. Immigration Act closed off further European immigration, African Americans—who migrated to northern cities such as Philadelphia and New York during the First World War—began moving into Jewish residential neighborhoods.[5] During the 1920s, Jewish merchants were the model for African American entrepreneurs to follow, but by the time the Great Depression struck the nation in the early 1930s, Jewish storeowners—once esteemed as role models for black businessowners—increasingly became targets of rancor.[6]

Large department stores, such as Blumstein's on 125th Street in Harlem, symbolized Jewish domination of commercial entrepreneurship and greatly overshadowed the black-owned neighborhood barbershops, beauty salons, and funeral parlors. The pawnbrokers, who regularly deal with customers in despair, were also Jewish, as were the landlords who often charged exorbitant rents for substandard housing. Under the climate of economic duress during the Depression, anti-Semitic stereotypes began to circulate, depicting Jews as "dollar crazy" people who were always prepared to invade black communities and milk the ghettos of millions.[7] Making matters worse was that while the Jewish storeowners earned their living selling to blacks, they refused to hire them in sales or clerical positions. The racial discrimination in hiring practices aroused the indignation of such black activists as Marcus Garvey, Adam Clayton Powell, Jr., Arthur L. Reid, and Ira Kemp, who launched the "Don't Buy Where You Can't Work" campaign. So deplorable was this situation that blacks took to the picket lines in New York, Baltimore, and Chicago to boycott Jewish storeowners who refused to hire black sales clerks.[8] The "Don't Buy Where You Can't Work" strategy of 1934 began the successful drive to force Blumstein's Department Store, among others, to hire blacks as sales associates.

This campaign not only urged blacks not to buy where they could not work but went a step further and advised black customers to "buy black." Ira Reid, a former lieutenant of Marcus Garvey's, urged his supporters to shop at black-owned stores, encouraging blacks to patronize their own on the basis of racial loyalty. Catchphrases such as "patronize your own" and "sustain Negro enterprise" soon became part of "Negro business chauvinism." Moreover, not only did Negro business chauvinism seek the support of black consumers through its emphasis on racial loyalty, but it also directed intense antagonism toward white—and particularly Jewish—businessmen, who were considered the obstacle to black business ownership, black economic independence, and black social mobility.[9] For instance, in their classic study of life in black Chicago, St. Clair Drake and Horace Cayton noted that most black storeowners sincerely believed that they were victims of a "Jewish conspiracy" that made it virtually impossible for their businesses to thrive.[10]

By 1940, black entrepreneurs still owned comparatively few businesses in their communities. In Harlem, for example, blacks operated less than 19 percent of the businesses, largely dominating retail niches that required little capital.[11] The lack of black economic progress, particularly vis-à-vis Jews, heightened anti-Semitic stereotypes, and by the early 1940s, black neighborhoods like West Philadelphia and Harlem were characterized as "hotbeds of Negro anti-Semitism."[12] In Harlem, black frustration boiled over in the riot of 1943, and from Sunday night, August 1, to Monday afternoon, black Harlemites took to the streets in a wave of fury and smashed store windows, looted goods, and burned down Jewish-owned stores.[13] By the time the looting and arson subsided, 5 blacks were dead, 565 were injured, and 500 were arrested. The property damage amounted to $5 million, with 1,234 stores severely damaged in the riot.[14] Along 125th Street—Harlem's main commercial thoroughfare—and up and down Seventh and Lenox Avenues, rioters had taken armloads of goods, including food, liquor, clothing, jewelry, furnishings, and radios. While rioters had smashed and looted Jewish-owned stores, blacks shopkeepers had kept rioters at bay by placing "Colored" signs in their windows. What no one could have predicted at the time was that the Harlem riot of 1943 foreshadowed events to come twenty years later.

In the 1960s, Jewish entrepreneurship was still firmly implanted in black neighborhoods like New York's Harlem and the north and west sections of Philadelphia. Although Jews owned about 40 percent of the stores in these neighborhoods, they tended to operate in the high-end, most profitable retail niches, such as furniture, appliances, apparel, hardware, food, liquor, and pharmacies. In contrast, black entrepreneurs owned a mere 10 percent of the capital invested in the community, and their businesses were still confined to beauty parlors, barbershops, funeral homes, and small restaurants. Compared with black-owned shops, the bigger and more glamorous businesses remained in the hands of Jews, reinforcing the notion that black communities were "colonies" exploited by Jewish businessowners and landlords.[15]

Lenora Berson vividly describes the feelings that Jewish ownership often engendered among African Americans: "The landlord, too, is likely to be Jewish, as is the grocer and the man who owns the appliance store on the corner. All too often the Negro sees himself as a victim of their exploitation, and the contrast between himself and the more affluent businessmen of the community generates bitterness and resentment."[16] Newspaper accounts also recorded the antagonism that black residents felt toward Jewish merchants. For example, the *Wall Street Journal* in August 1966 reported that "the most frequently heard complaint by Negroes was that the white storekeeper, 'treats us like animals.' Negroes in many other ghettos display antagonism against white merchants."[17] Fostering even greater resentment was the fact that the businessowners and landlords lived elsewhere and thus took their profits out of the black communities. The novelist James Baldwin described the bitterness for poor blacks of watching a successful Jewish storekeeper lock up for the night and go home to his clean white neighborhood.[18]

Fleecing and the Easy Credit System

Jewish merchants were also criticized for "fleecing" their customers—selling inferior merchandise, such as stale bread, tainted meat, over-ripe fruit, secondhand furniture advertised as new, and second-class dresses, at exorbitant prices. Groceries that typically cost one dollar in other parts of New York City cost one dollar and fifteen cents in Harlem.[19] Add to this the complaints about dishonest weighing and short-changing, and one had a community of irate customers.[20] Overcharging the poor, who make a marginal living—and for what amounted to second-rate goods—seemed particularly egregious.

Spelling more trouble for poor black consumers was the introduction of so-called easy credit plans that allowed them to purchase big-ticket items by making a small down payment and then paying off the balance and interest a little each week. In *The Poor Pay More*, David Caplovitz vividly describes the way in which bait advertising lured customers into stores and high-pressure salesmen pushed untagged merchandise for whatever price they could get. Customers who came with the intent to pay cash for a moderately priced item often found themselves purchasing much more luxurious, more costly merchandise on an installment plan at usurious interest rates, just shy of unlawful.[21] What poor customers often failed to understand at the point of purchase was that they would be burdened with heavy credit payments for years to come. And when a buyer was unable to make the regular monthly payment, he or she would accrue penalties. In severe cases, if the buyer stopped making payments altogether—perhaps due to unemployment or illness—the merchant would repossess the merchandise, and all the money already paid off was simply lost.[22] In a vivid description of the frustration that often resulted from such installment plans, author Roi Ottley explains, "The Negro's inability to meet regularly any kind of payments creates irritability; and, if pressed for payment, he is stirred to anger, which is expressed in hostility to the merchant."[23] The easy credit system, however, served a valuable function for the poor: it allowed them to lift their standard of living, partake in the consumerism of American culture, and benefit from some of the goods enjoyed by the middle class.

Fleecing and easy credit may have characterized the business practices of some Jewish merchants, but certainly not all. Jewish store-owners in the ghetto were not all exploitative, nor was the merchant-customer relationship universally hostile. In an illustrative exposition of merchant-customer relations, novelist Dick Gregory describes his family's relationship with the local Jewish grocer. While the grocer sold them three-day-old bread, rotten peaches, and green butter, since that was the only kind of merchandise the grocer would sell on credit, Gregory adds that "when it came down to the nitty-gritty you could always go to Mister Ben."[24] Gregory's characterization of his family's relationship with Mr. Ben suggests ambivalence rather than antagonism.

While anti-Semitic stereotypes may have abounded, Gary Marx's study of black-Jewish relations in the mid-1960s confirms that merchant-customer relations were not normally conflictual. Marx reveals that, contrary to the prevailing image of Jewish merchants' exploitation of black customers, only 21 percent of black New Yorkers claimed to receive unfair treatment from Jewish storeowners.[25] Unfair business practices may not have been uncommon in the ghetto neighborhoods of the past, but clearly, their prevalence was overstated.

Perhaps more important to note is that black customers frequented the retail shops in their neighborhoods because they had little or no choice. Blacks did not have the luxury of shopping outside the ghetto, since many stores in white neighborhoods simply refused to serve them. Moreover, blacks were spatially isolated from the large downtown and suburban shopping centers. While whites could shop where they pleased for basic items such as apparel, furniture, and food, blacks were denied this privilege.[26] Such were the conditions of black consumerism in the 1960s.

The Urban Riots of the 1960s

Racial violence in the United States may be as old as the nation itself, but in no single period of the twentieth century was there anything that approached the chain reaction of race riots that began on July 18, 1964, in Harlem. The Harlem riot of 1964 began the prolonged urban protests that raced through black neighborhoods in seven major cities before finally dying down in Philadelphia on the last day of August of the same year.[27] During the riots, participants of all ages dashed through the commercial thoroughfares, broke windows, and looted merchandise from white-owned businesses. They worked over small and large businesses alike, taking groceries, liquor, furniture, appliances, clothing, drugs, and items held in pawnshops. Rioters generally looted stores whose merchandise they could drink, wear, or readily sell, and what they could not carry, they threw into the streets. Credit records in pawnshops, furniture stores, and grocery markets were consistently destroyed, providing evidence that there was some method involved in the frenzy and fury of the riots.[28]

While Jewish merchants—and white merchants more generally—were the targets of attack, black storeowners were spared, so long as they made it to their shops in time to place identifying insignia outside of their store. They placed signs that read "Blood Brother," "Colored," and "Poor Working Negro" in their windows, in the hope that rioters would bypass their establishments. Even the owners of a Chinese restaurant displayed a sign reading, "We Are Colored Too," which spared them from the rioters.[29] Black businessowners who lived further away and were unable to make it to their stores in time were not as fortunate; their businesses, too, were ransacked. Service-oriented businesses such as beauty salons and barbershops—typical black retail niches—received the least amount of damage during the riots, partly because they tended to be black-owned and partly because they offered looters little to take. When the riots died down, the toll was 112 damaged stores in Harlem and 726 damaged stores and offices in Philadelphia.[30]

Social scientists argued that the riots of the 1960s were not merely acts of uncontrolled frenzy but, rather, a manifestation of the deeper grievances of black residents in urban ghettos—against racial discrimination, economic deprivation, involuntary residential segregation, and consumer exploitation.[31] The riots characterized widespread desperation that resulted in the release of mass anger and rebellion against the social and economic system that placed blacks on the outside. They reflected the failure of American society to address the glaring gap between blacks' subordinate position and the ideals of American democracy.

Looting symbolized a bid for redistribution of property. It was the have-nots hitting back at the haves, and it was a way of showing hatred for America's economic and class system.[32] One of the deepest frustrations for poor blacks was life in the ghetto and their inability to be part of America's "have" society. The Kerner Commission recognized that unemployment, limited education, poor jobs, poverty, and, beneath all, racism had caused the outbursts of the 1960s. In essence, the problem was one of securing full rights of citizenship for black Americans.

After the riots of the 1960s, Jewish merchants in black neighborhoods faced a quandary—to stay or to leave? The decision was complicated because, following the riots, there were few buyers interested in succeeding Jewish storeowners. Closing up shop without selling the business would have resulted in financial ruin, yet 50 percent of Jewish storeowners wished to sell their businesses.[33] Following the wave of riots, the overall mood was one of desperation and fear, and most Jewish merchants expressed panic at the thought of being looted, robbed, or personally harmed. Their fears were not unwarranted and prompted many of them to carry weapons, reduce their inventory, close up shop early, and place barricades on all windows and doors.[34]

Convinced that they had not seen the last of the violence, and certain that police protection was inadequate, many Jewish merchants in black neighborhoods decided to set up shop in distant suburbs or simply retire. Those who owned smaller businesses found it easier to liquidate them or find potential buyers, and if they could not, they had less to lose than businessowners who operated department stores and large-scale furniture shops. Some Jewish intellectuals argued that it was time for Jews to move out of neighborhoods like Harlem. For instance, Max Geltman in the *National Review* maintained that "Jewish storekeepers who remain today in Harlem or in Watts, encamped as it were in enemy territory, can expect future forays into their business establishments when the next riot breaks out. For them a process of disengagement should suggest itself, away from Harlem and away from Watts and away from other such volatile neighborhoods in other cities."[35] Faced with rising crime, the cancellation of insurance policies, decreasing profitability, and customers who questioned their legitimacy in neighborhoods in which they did not reside, some Jewish merchants simply boarded up their stores.

Project Transfer and the Merchants' Program

While Jewish retailers were anxious to leave, black leaders indicated that blacks wanted to own the community businesses but lacked the capital to purchase them. The lack of capital within the black community was a severe handicap for potential entrepreneurs and one that was exacerbated by discriminatory lending practices. When Eugene P. Foley, administrator of the Small Business Administration, convened a meeting in August 1964 to encourage economic investment among minorities, he confessed, "I am ashamed to admit that my agency had made seven loans to Negroes in ten years."[36] After the Small Business Administration opened a field office in Philadelphia in that year, the situation improved dramatically. Six months later, fifty-five loans had been granted to blacks and sixteen new businesses had opened. Soon thereafter, new field offices opened in Harlem and Washington, D.C.[37]

It was in this economic and social climate that Jewish and African American community organizations, the Small Business Administration, and local banks developed an innovative plan. In 1969 and 1970, the American Jewish Congress and the Interracial Council for Business Opportunity sponsored a program called Project Transfer, which facilitated the turnover of Jewish-owned businesses to interested African American buyers. In each transaction, the buyer had to be familiar with the business before settlement, often through working as a paid employee for the businessowner for several months before the transfer of ownership. This was an important feature of Project Transfer, because it gave the new buyer the experience and expertise needed to manage the day-to-day business operations.[38]

In Philadelphia, the process was executed under the direction of the Jewish Community Relations Council (JCRC) and was called the Merchants' Program. It provided African Americans who had long dreamed of owning a business the opportunity to purchase a Jewish-owned businesses.[39] To help finance the transition from Jewish to black ownership, the JCRC worked in conjunction with local banks and the Small Business Administration. The Jewish seller was required to take approximately 20 percent of the purchase price in the form of notes, to reduce the total loan needed by the buyer. In addition, for one year after the transfer of business ownership, the seller was required to serve as a business consultant at no cost to the buyer. In total, the Merchants' Program successfully turned over fifty stores to African American buyers throughout the Philadelphia area. However, within a few years all fifty of the African American merchants had closed down the businesses or sold them to other buyers.[40]

Jewish old-timers who witnessed the turnover of the stores attribute the closing of the businesses under African American ownership to cultural characteristics. The veteran business owners stated quite unabashedly that they believed African Americans did not have the skills required to run a business successfully. For example, a third-generation Jewish merchant in West Philadelphia frankly asserted, "Blacks are incapable of running a store. They lack discipline. They lack knowledge. Their work ethic is poor. None of them could run a store." He was not alone in holding negative cultural stereotypes of African American businessowners. Another Jewish merchant in West Philadelphia echoed these sentiments in telling the story of an African American merchant who benefited from the Merchants' Program but whose business went under within a year after the transfer of ownership.

> I can tell you a story of a friend who had three stores, three businesses, in different sections of the city, mostly in black areas. He had a black man there who worked for him for twenty years. And I guess this was in the late sixties, and he wanted to get out and the banks were bending over backwards to loan money to black entrepreneurs. And here was a going business—a men's clothing business—and [the Jewish merchant] was giving him some generous terms. And the bank poured the money in and gave [the black merchant] eighty or a hundred thousand dollars, which is a lot of money, through the stock and the business and all that.
>
> And my friend told me that he would call periodically and stop in to see how this guy was doing. He seemed to be doing great. The guy was dressing well, he said. He came in the day before Christmas, and he said, "Where's the boss?" An employee said, "He's in New York." The day before Christmas in a men's clothing store! He was having a good

time in New York! The business went under within a year. He wasn't paying his bills and he couldn't get merchandise. Look, if you're not paying your bills, if he's doing business, then he's spending the money. And I'm sure the bank went over this with him, and they were baby-sitting with him and all that, but they don't have that business sense.

Many other Jewish merchants whose businesses have survived for decades or generations expressed similar opinions, relaying stories of African American businessowners who benefited from the Merchants' Program and bought new cars, clothing, jewelry, and furs instead of re-investing their profits in their business. Others told of African American merchants who opened their stores late in the morning and closed early in the evening, consequently losing a significant portion of their clientele. However, when I interviewed a member of the JCRC who was as director of urban affairs and social action for the Merchants' Program, he said that limited business experience combined with the lack of capital in African Americans' business networks were the main reasons behind the failure of the Merchant's Program. The lack of capital made it difficult for the businesses to survive a slow business cycle and thrive under the new ownership.

The future of small business in the United States seemed bleak by the early 1970s. The consequences of the riots were disastrous for a large minority of the retail shopowners. African Americans could not sustain the businesses, and few white ethnics were interested in setting up shop in inner-city black neighborhoods. Furthermore, the rising cost of insurance and upkeep seemed to make small business owner-ship an unattractive option compared with steady salaried work for a large corporation. The riots affected both the objective and subjective situation of inner-city retailers.[41]

While African American–owned shops were going under and Jewish merchants were moving out, a new group of immigrants was posi-tioned to enter the inner-city retail niche. What nobody predicted in the early 1970s was that this retail niche would soon become vibrant and profitable with the entrance of these newcomers. Although Jews still retain a hold on some of the largest and most lucrative retail busi-nesses, such as appliances and furniture, ethnic succession has altered the face of inner-city retailing from Jewish to African American to Korean.

Koreans' Entrance into Black Neighborhoods

In 1965, when the United States liberalized immigration laws, the Asian immigrant population grew exponentially. While the reforms favored immigrants with kinship ties to U.S. citizens, it also created opportunities for highly skilled immigrants, such as doctors, engineers, nurses, and pharmacists. This created the opening for the first wave of Korean newcomers to the United States. Although Koreans constitute a relatively small portion of New York and Philadelphia's immigrant stream—rarely more than 3 percent of the legal immigrants who come to these cities each year—they play an important and visible role in the cities' economies.[42]

Korean immigrants are largely middle class and were motivated to emigrate because of limited opportunities for social and economic mobility in South Korea. Because the supply of college graduates in South Korea far exceeds the demand for such a highly educated workforce, the average rate of unemployment in Korea for male college graduates is 30 percent.[43] Professionals who are fortunate enough to secure professional employment in the Korean economy must endure fierce competition, delayed promotion, underemployment, and job insecurity. In addition, favoritism in the workplace based on kinship, region of origin, and school ties make mobility nearly impossible for those who are not immersed in these networks. Given the limited prospects for advancement in South Korea, middle-class Koreans view immigration to the United States as a means to mobility in an open opportunity structure, not only for themselves but also for their children.

In the 1970s Korean immigrants began setting up shop in inner-city neighborhoods and soon created a profitable niche for themselves. Initially drawing on their import connections to Korea and capitalizing on the wig craze of the 1970s, Korean immigrants' first foray into the inner-city retail niche was through selling wigs made in Korea.[44] Taking over retail businesses that Jews had abandoned and African Americans could not sustain, Koreans began with wig shops and fruit and vegetable markets and then expanded to other retail niches, such as fish stores, liquor stores, handbags and accessory shops, and dry cleaning establishments. Today, one-third of the Korean families in the United States are self-employed. African Americans, by contrast, are extremely underrepresented, exhibiting a self-employment rate of only 4.5 percent.[45] Clearly African Americans have not been able to take full advantage of the retail self-employment opportunities in their communities, reflecting their divergent networks and resources.[46] Even today the process of setting up shop reflects the differential resources available to Koreans, Jews, and African Americans.

Setting Up Shop

Korean Merchants

Korean immigrants choose self-employment as a quick route to upward mobility. Their relatively poor English language skills, inability to transfer their education credentials, and unfamiliarity with U.S. corporate culture and customs lead Koreans to choose self-employment as their most viable and lucrative option. Koreans use a variety of class and ethnic resources to set up shop, drawing upon loans from kin and coethnics and turning to Korean-language newspapers to locate businesses for sale. However, unlike the previous literature on ethnic entrepreneurship that stresses Koreans' reliance on rotating credit associations *(gae)*,[47] my research indicates that few Korean immigrant merchants use this resource at the start-up phase. In fact, only 7 percent of the Korean merchants in my sample acquired capital to open their business through a rotating credit association. Instead, the majority relied on a combination of other resources: personal savings, loans from family members, and credit from the previous coethnic storeowner.[48] Seventeen percent bought their business from a family member—usually a brother, sister, or in-laws—who had immigrated to the United States several years before them.

When Jews and Koreans purchase businesses from fellow ethnics, rather than going through a third financial party such as a bank, the buyer will normally pay the seller one-third of the value of the business as a down payment and the remaining two-thirds in monthly payments over a period of two to four years. Economist Timothy Bates notes that Koreans use this debt source more frequently than do other groups because they are likely to purchase retail firms that are already in operation, rather than starting from ground zero.[49]

Although the use of rotating credit associations may not be as prevalent at the start-up phase, this resource is highly utilized in later stages of business. Rotating credit associations range in both membership size and value, with participation extending from only a few people to more than thirty, and the value of loans ranging from $100 to over $100,000 or more. Korean merchants report that the average *gae* includes ten to twenty people, with each member contributing $1,000 to $2,000 monthly into a pot totaling $10,000 to $40,000. Every member contributes to the fund, and each receives his or her share according to a predetermined schedule. For example, one Korean merchant belonged to a rotating credit association that had twenty members. Each member contributed $2,700 a month, so the first who received the pot got $51,300 ($2,700 × 19). After receiving the money, the individual had to contribute $3,100 monthly until the rotation was complete. In this way, the member who received the pot first got only $51,300 while the one who received the pot at the end of the rotation was rewarded with $58,900—the surplus accounting for interest and appreciation. Sociologist James Coleman offered the rotating credit association as a prime example of the manifestation of social capital, because it is based on a high degree of mutual trust, obligation, and expectation among its members.[50]

Unlike previous research that underscores the importance of the *gae* at the start-up phase, I found that the use of rotating credit associations is far less important at the beginning. However, it is considerably more important after Korean merchants have already established their businesses. Koreans use this capital for business purposes such as buying new merchandise or equipment, remodeling, purchasing seasonal merchandise in bulk, or pulling though a slow business cycle. Although the use of *gae* varies among the Korean merchants interviewed, all said that the rotating credit association is a resource they could draw upon if they needed to accumulate capital quickly. The facility with which Korean immigrants can tap into this financial resource attests to their command of social capital as well as their access to economic capital.

Koreans are not the only ethnic group to benefit from social capital. In fact, first-generation immigrants of many ethnic backgrounds— such as West Indians, Asian Indians, and the Vietnamese—draw upon their own versions of rotating credit associations.[51] Dense coethnic ties, based on a shared immigrant experience, a common language and lifestyle, and involvement in coethnic institutions, provide a firm basis for intraethnic cooperation.[52] But as these groups acculturate into the American social structure, they utilize this resource far less frequently. For example, whereas first-generation Jewish immigrant entrepreneurs formerly used mutual loan associations, later generations have long since discarded the tradition.[53] Second-generation Koreans, like the second- and third-generation Jews before them, have also abandoned the practice.

Korean merchants explain that the benefit of using *gae* over more traditional means of financing—such as bank or government-agency loans—is the facility and guarantee of the *gae* system. A Korean sportswear merchant in Harlem explains why Koreans prefer using rotating credit associations to institutional loans:

> I looked into it, but from a Korean's standpoint, it's such as hassle. So much paperwork. You have to give them two years' financial records. You have to give them a business plan of what you want to do for the next three to four years. You have to give them business projections. And it's a lot of things that Koreans don't want to hassle with because there are other avenues to get money, other avenues that are 100 percent guaranteed that you get it instead of going through the Small Business Administration. There's, number one, a language barrier, and number two, you lack the expertise in getting the proper information to them. I've looked into them. Next year, we'll qualify to enter into some of their programs. It's a resource that people need to utilize more, but they don't know about it. And if they do, it's too much of a hassle, and they don't want to do it.

In addition, because small businesses are generally cash-based businesses, entrepreneurs often underreport their income, thereby making their businesses appear less profitable—and reducing their taxes. But this also diminishes the probability that they will receive a bank loan.

Some Korean merchants are now wary of using rotating credit associations because of the risk involved. An inordinate amount of trust is required for such a system to operate. Many I spoke with could recall recent *gae* failures when one person took the pot of money and left the country. However, although there are no legal ramifications for defaulting, since the members do not sign written contracts, Korean merchants explain that the social sanctions—such as loss of standing in and exclusion from the immigrant community—are strong enough to prevent such losses on a regular basis. Another problem is the costly interest payments, which can be as high as 30 percent, surpassing the legal limit in New York state, for instance, where interest charged must be less than 25 percent. Rotating credit associations may help those who need to acquire cash very quickly, but they also function as financial investments for the affluent, who benefit from exploiting fellow ethnics with exorbitant interest payments.

Not all Korean merchants have participated in *gae*, yet all in this study have borrowed funds from their family or coethnic friends, either at the start-up phase or later when cash flow was tight, often accepting tens of thousands of dollars in loans. Their high degree of social and economic capital remains the most valuable resource for Korean immigrant entrepreneurs; the importance of this cannot be overemphasized. The availability of and access to cash resources can determine whether a business will be able to withstand an emergency such as a break-in or robbery or pull through a slow business cycle.

Jewish Merchants

Today's Jewish entrepreneurs in black neighborhoods are primarily second- and third-generation European immigrants who have taken over retail shops from their predecessors. More than half of the Jewish retailers in the sample bought their business from their parents or other family members, making Jewish-owned stores the longest lived in black communities, with an average tenure of forty-two years. While the majority of the Jewish-owned shops were passed down from family members, one-fourth were purchased from nonfamily coethnics with personal savings. Finally, 16 percent of the current owners benefited from coethnic "training systems," having bought out the previous coethnic owner for whom they once worked. In this case, the buyers had generally worked out a plan for monthly payments over a period of years rather than putting down an enormous initial payment.[54]

Neither the first-, second-, nor third-generation Jewish storeowners used bank or government-agency loans to start their businesses. The Jewish merchants I interviewed attribute their families' ability to set up shop to a simple formula of hard work, thrift, and family participation. For example, a second-generation Jewish owner of a large and profitable furniture business in East Harlem explains that his parents immigrated to the United States penniless, yet through hard work, delayed gratification, and perseverance, they succeeded in opening and maintaining a successful operation.

> My parents came to this country penniless. They worked hard, and they didn't spend because of the insecurity of knowing what it's like to be poor. When they worked hard and put money in the bank, that gave them happiness. My father started the business with two uncles and then my father bought them out. It was a family business. Everybody would work here. My family was very frugal. My father was such a hard worker. My mother saved and saved, and she wanted to buy the building someday from the landlady. Would you believe the landlady lived until she was ninety-nine? My parents were very hard working. My mother was a simple woman, she wasn't frivolous. She never bought anything really fancy.

When asked whether his parents received a business loan, the storeowner immediately barked at the idea, reiterating the formula of "hard work," "innovation," and "building slowly," and pointing to today's Korean immigrants who have followed suit,

> No loans, my God! It was just hard work and savings. My father used to go and knock on people's doors when they didn't pay for their furniture like they said they would. And then some people would say that they couldn't pay for everything now, but they promised to pay him, and he just had an instinct about them. My father worked so hard, just like the Koreans now. They're hard working people. You see them in the winter, in the cold, with nothing but plastic to protect them in the cold. I would say that you have to be innovative, not lazy. If they really wanted to, they could do it too, but in time. You have to build it slowly, and show people that you're not a fly-by-night business. You have to be here all the time.

Similarly, when asked whether he received a bank or government loan for his businesses, a Jewish owner of a clothing store on Jamaica Avenue quickly became defensive and retorted,

> Ridiculous! Ludicrous! Absolutely moronic! That's ridiculous! That's stupid! It's a fantasy. Everybody knows how a Korean starts a business.

They borrow money from their family or their friends and they don't spend any of the money they make. They wear sandals and eat rice. They do things the way people did things long ago, just like the original people [Jewish immigrants] did long ago. So just the way the original people did it many, many years ago, the Koreans are doing when they come along.

The ethnic succession from Jewish to Korean ownership leads many of the Jewish merchants to note parallels between the Jewish and Korean immigrant experience. Jewish merchants underscore their belief that every individual—regardless of race or ethnicity—has the opportunity to open a business if he or she so chooses. Implicit in statements such as "You have to be innovative, not lazy," "If they really wanted to, they could do it too," and "Don't spend money that you make" is the opinion that, were African Americans simply not lazy, if they were more ambitious and willing to delay gratification, they too could be just as successful as Jews and Koreans. Jewish merchants are not unique in this regard. Korean retailers, too, subscribe to the ideology behind the American dream and equality of opportunity—that, in essence, all it takes to succeed in business is hard work, grit, and frugality.

African American Merchants

Unlike Jewish merchants, who rely primarily on family resources, and Korean merchants, who receive loans from kin and fellow ethnics, African Americans use a combination of resources to accumulate sufficient capital to start their businesses. Of the sample studied, 33 percent started their business with personal savings and 14 percent purchased their business using a combination of personal savings and capital borrowed from their retirement or insurance plan. Another 14 percent started their business with a partner, and 19 percent received a loan from a bank or the Small Business Administration. Five percent bought their business from the former Jewish owner, and the final 14 percent did not need start-up capital because their businesses are based on consignment—meaning that they sell used furniture, clothing, or appliances without having to purchase the stock beforehand. In some cases, people donate merchandise, such as clothing and appliances, to these store owners and expect no profit in return. Others, who give costly furniture or antique pieces to consignment shop owners, expect to split the profits with the owner after the merchandise is sold.

African Americans are more likely than Jews or Koreans to look for external sources of funding, such as bank loans, to help finance their businesses. The foreign-born, by contrast, rarely rely on external loans—particularly at the start-up phase—because they entail lengthy, bureaucratic processes, and, more important, because there exist immediate, guaranteed alternatives within their coethnic networks. For African Americans, this option is closed, since their ethnic networks tend to be far less affluent.

Another crucial difference between African American entrepreneurs and their Jewish and Korean counterparts is that self-employment is not simply a means to achieving the end of upward mobility but the end in itself. While the Koreans and most Jews interviewed were likely to describe self-employment as a stepping stone to upward mobility, the African Americans were much more likely to describe owning a business as their "passion" or "dream." Others took a more political stance, subscribing to the ideology behind African American economic autonomy. Moreover, whereas Jewish and Korean storeowners do not wish their children to follow in their footsteps, African Americans view retail self-employment as an attractive career option for the next generation.

Some African Americans firmly believe that small businesses are the "backbone" of the economy and offer individuals the opportunity for economic growth and upward mobility, as one storeowner in Queens conveys,

> I believe that Mom and Pop stores are the backbone that keeps American society going. One of the guys I graduated with, this Italian fellow, I asked him, I'll never forget, "What are you going to do?" He said, "I'm going to work for my father's cleaners. I'm going to run that business." And he's walking out of school with a degree, and they were telling black people that they should take that degree and try to get a job in corporate, and go into a lower level and work your way up. And this is different thinking. Hey this guy is going to work for his father's cleaners, and eventually he can have a chain of cleaners.

In the early 1900s Booker T. Washington extolled self-employment for African Americans as a means to developing wealth and power. Historically, the African American self-employment rate has remained low, especially compared with immigrant groups such as Jews and Koreans. One of the main reasons for the underrepresentation of African Americans among entrepreneurs is that their networks have led them into different occupational niches, primarily in the public sector. Another is that African Americans are less likely to have access to the large sums of capital needed to open and maintain a business. Finally, as I will discuss further in Chapter 6, there are disadvantages associated with serving one's own, particularly for African American businessowners.

Divergent Networks and Outcomes

The majority of the African American merchants in the sample are the first among their families and friends to set up shop. In fact, only two of the twenty-one African American business owners interviewed have ties to friends or family members who are also self-employed. By far, the majority established their businesses with no guidance from fellow ethnics. For instance, a beauty salon owner in Mount Airy explains why African Americans are much less likely to choose self-employment as a career option:

> A lot of them [other ethnic groups] had stores, or relatives that owned maybe candy stores or furniture stores, or some type of small business. Whereas in an African American community, it was very rare, so I didn't have like an uncle or a grandfather to pass it down from generation, just that mentality of being an owner.

The African American businessowners revealed that while they were growing up, their families never guided them into self-employment but instead directed them toward landing a "safe" and "secure" job in the public sector. For example, another retailer in Mount Airy explains,

> You know when I was coming up, the safe thing was to get a government job. My father's a mailman, a postal worker. Or get a city job; you'd have job security. But we were always taught, you have to work for

someone. I never heard around the house, you can do your own thing. I never heard that! But if you talk to a little Jewish child, you ask them what they want to be, they'll tell you, doctor, lawyer, or I want to own my business like Daddy, because they see it in the home, they hear it.

Ethnic social structures create networks that have a "fateful effect," which pulls members of those ethnic groups into certain occupational niches. Sociologist Roger Waldinger describes the way in which the separate ethnic networks of African Americans and immigrant groups led to disparate occupational outcomes. Whereas immigrant groups have turned to self-employment, African Americans' search for opportunity has led them into the public sector. Waldinger explains how, in New York, "once African-American networks became implanted in government jobs, those networks transmitted signals that led other black New Yorkers to converge on public employment. By contrast, burgeoning business activity among groups like Koreans or Chinese sends out a different type of signal, suggesting to newcomers that they set up shop on their own."[55]

Furthermore, the absence of economic capital poses severe consequences. Since African Americans' kin and coethnic friends tend to be less affluent, their ethnic networks cannot supply them with the large amounts of financial help often needed in business. When asked whether he could borrow money from his family for his business, an African American hair salon owner in Mount Airy replied, "My family, I have kind of a middle-class, working family, and we don't really have large incomes. Everyone is mainly just trying to maintain their own homes. Maybe I could have gotten $500 here, but not really more than that." By contrast, Jewish and Korean storeowners often borrow as much as tens of thousands of dollars from family or fellow ethnics for business purposes. Because this option, which Korean and Jewish storeowners regularly utilize, is closed to African Americans, they are cut off from even the possibility of employing social capital.

The Importance of Capital

The importance of economic and social capital in small business should be underscored. Capital is needed to make renovations, to buy new equipment, to order seasonal merchandise, and to respond to un-

foreseen emergencies. As a Jewish pawnshop owner in West Philadelphia explained, "If you're undercapitalized and you're in business, you
can't stand a slow period because you have to pay your suppliers. If you
don't pay your suppliers, you can't get merchandise." Access to capital
is also essential after emergencies such as robberies and break-ins,
which are not uncommon in low-income neighborhoods like Harlem
and West Philadelphia. In such cases, Jewish and Korean merchants often turn to coethnics for loans, but, again, African Americans are unable to tap into this ethnic resource. By illustration, a Jewish, Korean,
and African American storeowner each explain the importance of capital in coping with emergencies such as fires or break-ins. All three
merchants were able to keep their businesses afloat after the crises, but
each turned to different sources, thereby experiencing different outcomes.

After a fire that ravaged a large Jewish-owned variety store in West
Harlem more than ten years ago, the merchant drew from his own capital and a bank loan to quickly rebuild the business. He explains,

> The bank that we used at that time gave us some money, but that was
> based on our own long-term relationship with them and based on
> collateral, and it wasn't a tremendous amount of money. A lot came
> strictly out of cash flow. We were way underinsured, because in the late
> seventies when things were a little tough, insurance was very hard to
> get up in Harlem, and very, very expensive. So we weren't insured for
> everything that we had, so there was a little bit of insurance money that
> kicked in, but it was a lot of hard work.

The combination of his savings, money from insurance, and a bank
loan enabled him to go back into business a few months after the fire.

A Korean storeowner in Queens had experienced a similar catastrophe that ruined his business. Prior to setting up shop on Jamaica
Avenue, he had owned an ethnic beauty supplies business in Brooklyn. When the business adjacent to his caught on fire, his store also
burned. After the fire, with the money that he acquired from a *gae,* the
Korean storeowner opened his second business, on Jamaica Avenue.
Although he emphasized the enormous difficulty of keeping up with
monthly *gae* payments while running a newly formed business, he was
able to keep his business afloat and avoid bankruptcy because of his

access to financial help within his coethnic network. In short, he was able to gain access to resources by using his social capital.

Unfortunately, many retailers in low-income black neighborhoods go uninsured because they cannot afford the exorbitant rates that insurance companies demand from businesses located in such "high-risk" zones. Weighing the high rates against the probability of an accident, many storeowners choose to gamble and remain uninsured. Others explain that they choose not to carry insurance because companies will cover only a small fraction of the business's overall value, making their insurance policies virtually worthless.

In contrast to the Jewish and Korean storeowners, who turned to coethnics or received loans from financial institutions to rescue themselves from financial disaster, an African American merchant in West Harlem explained how his lack of access capital had created a web of misfortune. After a few minor break-ins, his insurance company had cancelled his policy at the contract's end. While he was searching for another insurance company, robbers broke into his store once again, but this time they stole the entire inventory. The robbery then snowballed into an even larger financial catastrophe. Because the owner could not secure capital from family, friends, or financial institutions, his only alternative was not to pay his business taxes. Consequently, because he failed to pay his taxes, he was disqualified from all types of government or bank loans. He regretfully describes the sequence of events:

> They came in through the roof, and they cleaned out the store and stole everything. No insurance because they cancelled the policy. No way to really get credit because we were mostly on a cash basis with our suppliers, and we were in a very bad condition. We tried all the lending agencies and none of them wanted to lend. So as a result, what we did is we didn't pay our sales tax. We hadn't paid the IRS. We borrowed money from them, but borrowing from the government is like borrowing from a criminal. Number one, they penalize you for taking their money. And for argument's sake, if you borrow $5,000 from them, with interest and penalties you owe them $10,000. So as a result, I got behind very badly on my taxes; I didn't pay the taxes and the IRS.

When asked how not paying his taxes affected his business, he elaborates,

It's extremely hard trying to get back together because I wasn't able to get funded. If I were able to get funded, I would have been able to put the store back together and go on with my business, making money and paying back the bills. But trying to do it little by little, you're always a pound short and a day late with the merchandise coming in. You're late with so many things that as a result, cash flow is bad. Whenever cash flow is bad, you can't make money. So anyway I have agreements with the IRS, the state, and I pay back a certain amount of money monthly.

The retailer adds that "minority businesses" often struggle with this "tax problem," which creates an "awful circle" of disadvantage.

I have tried everything, and the biggest problem most minority businesses have is the tax problem, and the tax problem is not always of their making. That tax problem can materialize from many different acts, like my situation, and as a result when you apply for a loan, the tax looks like a red flag, and they're not going to give it to you. A lot of times, development and money that's supposed to be coming to our community, small people like myself do not even see any of that money because we don't fit the criteria because we have a tax problem. You see, they're not going to lend you city money if you owe the city money. And they're not going to lend you government money if you owe government money. It's an awful circle. So in other words, you're actually forced to stay in the position you are because to be able to break the circle, to get out of the position, that's not made available for you.

While the Jewish and Korean storeowners immediately acquired capital through savings, bank loans, or loans from coethnics, the African American merchant found himself desperately searching for funding from a variety of sources and coming up empty handed. The merchants' different avenues and outcomes reflect the disparity in social and economic capital between Jews and Koreans, on the one hand, and African Americans, on the other. As early as 1969, David Caplovitz noted in his study *The Merchants of Harlem* that 40 percent of African American entrepreneurs reported that raising capital for their business is a major problem.[56] Although capital is important at the start-up phase, it is often just as significant in the maintenance of a business.

Entrepreneurs who have access to capital more readily than others have a distinct advantage over those whose channels are limited.

Immigrant entrepreneurs have made great inroads in many large U.S. cities. By the 1920s, Jewish entrepreneurship was firmly implanted in black communities such as Harlem and West Philadelphia, with Jews operating the largest, most profitable, and most glamorous businesses. In stark contrast, African American entrepreneurship was confined to such traditional black retail niches as barbershops, beauty salons, soul food restaurants, and funeral parlors—not only niches that relied on coethnic tastes but also those that other ethnic groups did not want to enter.

The urban unrest and riots of the 1960s affected both the objective and subjective positions of Jewish merchants in black communities. Having suffered a disproportionate amount of damage during the riots and ready to retire, many Jewish storeowners sought a way out. It was in this economic and social climate that the American Jewish Congress and the Interracial Council for Business Opportunity joined forces with the Small Business Administration and local banks to sponsor Project Transfer, and the Merchants' Program, the goal of which was to facilitate the turnover of Jewish-owned businesses to interested African American buyers from the community. Under the new ownership, however, many of the businesses failed to thrive. Fifty businesses were turned over in the Philadelphia area alone, yet within a few years all fifty had been closed down or sold to other buyers.

Shortly thereafter, Korean immigrants began setting up shop in inner-city neighborhoods, and they soon created a profitable niche for themselves. Today, approximately one-third of Korean families in the United States are engaged in small business, a figure that parallels the rate of self-employment of Jewish immigrants in the early twentieth century. Touted as "model minorities," Jews and Koreans are seen as proof of the American dream—that if an individual works hard, perseveres, and delays gratification, he or she can make it. For some merchants, the fact that the African American–owned businesses did not thrive under Project Transfer reinforces negative cultural stereotypes of African American businessowners as a whole. However, as this chapter underscores, the underrepresentation of African Americans among the self-employed should be understood as the result of their divergent employment networks, which pull them into the public sector, as well as differential access to economic and social capital, both of which are crucial for success in retail self-employment.

Business ownership has historically played an important role in the upward mobility of some American immigrant groups—including Italians, Jews, Koreans, Asian Indians, and Middle Easterners—which is one main reason that the low rate for African Americans is cause for concern. Nathan Glazer and Daniel Patrick Moynihan recognized that small business ownership holds a significance that goes far beyond the dollars that these businesses generate. Business ownership offers the potential for the accumulation of wealth, political influence, and upward mobility. As Glazer and Moynihan write,

> The small shopkeepers and manufacturers are important to a group for more than the greater income they bring in. Very often, as a matter of fact, the Italian or Jewish shopkeeper made less than the skilled worker. But as against the worker, each businessman had the possibility, slim though it was, of achieving influence and perhaps wealth. The small businessman generally has access to that special world of credit and finance and perhaps develops skills that are of value in a complex economy. He learns too about the world of local politics, and although he is generally its victim, he may also learn how to influence it, for mean and unimportant ends, perhaps, but this knowledge may be valuable for an entire community.[57]

Business ownership in African American communities is significant because it serves as a real and symbolic construction of the cultural hierarchy in black communities and black control over black communities.

CHAPTER 3

The Significance of Small Business
and the Nature of the Niche

Small businesses are very important. I subscribe to that 100 percent. If you believe in America and what they have done businesswise, you find that in every community, it's run by a group of small businesses. And small businesses are not just the local candy store. It's the fruit stands, the bakery, it's the small store that's making, maybe, hats. They're all there and they're employing people, and those businesses carry on.

—African American merchant in Queens

I don't have the type of store that leaves me open to a tough customer or a group of kids. I don't have that. At one particular point in time, I did have a lot of sneakers and jeans in the store. And these kids would come running in ten at a time, grab a leather jacket and grab a pair of jeans, and run out of the store, try to start trouble, be very antagonizing. And I didn't want that, so I went back to the original, what we did. I get a working-class customer coming in here, a guy that needs a suit for church. My customer base is different now. It's not the arrogant, hotshot, crazy kid on cocaine or that needs money for crack. I don't really have much of that, and I'm very happy with that.

—Jewish merchant in Queens

One chief source of tension between immigrants and African Americans is the notion that immigrant entrepreneurs who set up shop in black neighborhoods take business opportunities away from native-born blacks. Given the prevalence of immigrant-owned businesses in black communities, one may readily presume that immigrant entrepreneurs do compete with African Americans, thereby inhibiting African American small-business development. Because business ownership is a visible indicator of opportunity, social mobility, and economic success, the question of immigrant–African American competition is a much-deliberated one in the fields of sociology, economics, and political science.[1]

Although, gauging from the ubiquitous presence of Jewish and Korean entrepreneurs in black communities, it might seem logical to deduce that immigrant entrepreneurs take opportunities and profits away from African Americans, my research reveals a more complex and nuanced story. First, because Jewish, Korean, and African American entrepreneurs tend to cluster and occupy different retail niches, there is less interethnic competition than there is competition within the ethnic groups.[2] In other words, immigrant groups enter and dominate retail niches different from those of African Americans, and because the business niches are segmented, competition is far more likely to be intraethnic in nature. For instance, Koreans dominate the fruit-and-vegetable retail niche and Jews the furniture niche, while African Americans dominate in hairstyling, barbering, and restaurants. Previous quantitative studies have showed immigrant entrepreneurs did not, in fact, increase competition for black small businesses but instead entered economic niches that were previously unfilled.[3] However, this is not the end of the story.

Large-scale, quantitative studies cannot always capture the subtle ways in which immigrant entrepreneurs may affect African American small business development, but qualitative studies can sometimes fill in the missing blanks.[4] There are both intended and unintended consequences of retail niche domination—what sociologist Roger Waldinger aptly refers to as "the 'other side' of embeddedness."[5] Entrepreneurship is embedded in ethnic networks that act as coethnic advantages for some and blocked opportunities and exclusion for others. Ironically, while there may be no direct competition between immigrant and African American entrepreneurs, it is precisely the segmentation of the retail niches that places Koreans—and other immigrant entrepreneurs—in businesses that are more susceptible to situations that may produce conflict with customers.

Identifying and Occupying Retail Niches: An Evolutionary Chain

As I have noted, immigrant entrepreneurs often choose self-employment as a means of quick upward mobility because mobility in the primary labor market may be blocked for them, owing to their relatively poor English language skills, their inability to transfer educational credentials, and their unfamiliarity with the American corporate structure and culture.[6] Many immigrant entrepreneurs set up shop specifically in low-income black neighborhoods because there is little competition there from larger chain corporations and small businesses can thrive in these underserved communities. The slight competition also means that rents are relatively inexpensive compared with those in middle-class white neighborhoods, so launching a new business becomes financially feasible, even for recent arrivals.

Additionally, immigrants claim that running a business in a middle-class white neighborhood is more difficult because they do not have the language fluency or know the middle-class mannerisms that help merchants deal with a more affluent and more educated clientele. For example, when asked why she opened a business in a low-income black neighborhood as opposed to a middle-income white neighborhood, the owner of a Korean take-out restaurant in West Harlem replied,

> Because easier. First of all, you don't have to have that much money to open up the store. And second of all, easier because you don't need to that much complicate. White people is very classy and choosy, and especially white people location is not like this, mostly they go to mall. Here they don't have many car, so easier, cheaper rent. When you go to white location, Second Avenue, Third Avenue, rent is already cost $20,000 [per month], you know, and they don't have any room for us. But black people area, other people hesitate to come in because they worry about crime and something like that, so they got a lot of room for Koreans.

Because they have comparatively low levels of education and few shopping alternatives, poor blacks are perceived to be a less "difficult," less "picky" clientele base.

However, the type of businesses that the foreign-born choose to enter is not random. The newest immigrant groups tend to locate in physically exhausting, labor-intensive businesses that require relatively little start-up capital and have low profit margins, such as fruit and vegetable markets, take-out restaurants, and fresh fish stores. The long hours and physically demanding labor often ensure that first-generation immigrants will be the ones to occupy these lines of business. Ko-

reans presently dominate these niches, but they are merely the succes-
sors in the line of immigrant groups that have occupied these retail
niches. Immigrant entrepreneurs cluster in vacant business niches,
and the process of retail niche domination can be best described as
"an evolutionary retail chain."[7]

Jewish storeowners are the veterans in black neighborhoods, and
most are second- or third-generation merchants whose businesses have
remained a part of these communities for more than forty years. Jewish merchants have moved up the retail chain and now occupy the
most profitable and least labor-intensive business niches. Their retail
mobility, coupled with their mobility out of retail altogether, has left
room for newer immigrants to penetrate the less desirable niches that
Jews and other white ethnic groups have abandoned. Jewish retailers,
like the Korean immigrants, began with businesses requiring low capital investments. For example, a Jewish merchant today who sells industrial apparel explains how his father acquired his first business: "My
father sold ice cream from a pushcart and sold secondhand dishes in
front of Macy's to make a living, and when he accumulated enough
money, he could afford to go into business."

The Jewish- and Korean-owned businesses that line the major avenues in black inner-city neighborhoods are thus often not the immigrants' first businesses. Like the Jewish merchant whose father once
sold ice cream from a pushcart, most immigrants begin on a smaller,
less capital-intensive scale. Once they have amassed enough capital
from their first business, they move toward larger, more costly businesses. One Korean merchant in West Philadelphia owned three businesses prior to purchasing her fourth and final business, a profitable
sneaker store. She began by opening a grocery store with her brother
and worked there for three years, seven days a week. When she grew
tired of working such long hours every day, she sold the grocery business and bought a discount variety store. After several years in that
business, she sold the variety store for a profit and bought a clothing
store, which she later also sold for a profit, and she eventually bought
the sneaker store she currently owns. In each successive move, the Korean business owner made a profit by selling her former business and
also made the shift to a less physically demanding business that required more economic capital.

In this way, retail niche domination is an evolutionary process—as immigrant entrepreneurs gather experience and capital, they penetrate more capital-intensive businesses, leaving room for newer arrivals to occupy the abandoned retail niches.[8] Korean immigrants have largely succeeded the Jewish immigrants, and today, newer immigrant entrepreneurs are already beginning to succeed Koreans. For example, Asian Indian and Middle Eastern immigrant groups have entered such retail niches as delicatessens, discount variety stores, and perfumeries, becoming a notable presence along these inner-city shopping strips. So long as the second and third generations find better opportunities in the mainstream labor market, retail self-employment (particularly businesses that cater to a low-income clientele) will remain a protected occupational niche among immigrant groups, who will continue to succeed one another.

While new immigrants replace the old in certain types of businesses, African Americans tend to dominate different retail niches altogether, such as barbering, hairstyling, full-service restaurants, and music— niches that are protected by the distinct tastes of their coethnic clientele and that require little start-up capital. Traditional lines of black enterprise, such as the hair service industry, form a protected market for blacks because they rely heavily on coethnic tastes and preferences and also because other ethnic groups are unable or unwilling to enter these markets. For instance, a former Jewish beauty salon owner candidly admits that when the racial makeup of West Philadelphia changed, he switched his line of business from hairstyling to hair products such as wigs and synthetic hairpieces. He explained, "In 1975, it was no longer a hair salon. By 1975, we were strictly selling hair products—wigs and hair accessories. I didn't feel like doing hair any more. I don't want to do black hair. I don't want to offend them, but I just don't want to do it." Moreover, beauticians and barbers need to acquire licenses in order to service clients, and this is an additional deterrent for immigrant ethnic groups who choose self-employment strictly as a means to upward mobility.

Also, given their capital constraints, African American retailers in black neighborhoods are more likely to enter service-oriented industries, most notably the hair service industry.[9] The capital needed to open a modest beauty salon or barbershop is minimal. Typically, African American salon owners begin with one hair station and gradually expand the number of stations and the services they can offer their clientele. Due to disparities in capital, very few African American–owned businesses overlap with Jewish- or Korean-owned businesses in these neighborhoods, and because the three groups occupy separate retail niches, business competition is more likely to be *intra*ethnic in nature.

Ethnic and Economic Exclusion

Ethnic clustering and retail niche domination can have positive consequences for coethnics but negative consequences for outsiders.[10] Ethnic clustering facilitates the entry of fellow ethnics into similar social structures but at the same time may disadvantage other groups, who are excluded from those business opportunities simply by virtue of their nonmembership in the ethnic networks. To illustrate how advantage for one group can translate into disadvantage for another, an African American pharmacist in Philadelphia describes how she is excluded from business networks and reveals the difficulties of being one of very few black pharmacists in a predominantly white field. Since she opened her own business, other pharmacists in the community will no longer communicate or work with her, even though they had worked with her in the past when she served as a manager for a Jewish-owned pharmacy in the same neighborhood. She explains,

> When I worked for the Jewish guy, I used to call Gary [another Jewish pharmacist in the neighborhood] and say, "Gary, I need such and such [medication]. Can I buy it off you? Can I borrow it?" "Sure." He'd call and say, "Do you have such and such?" He'd come and we'd swap [medication], and we'd send our drivers over there. As soon as I moved over here [and opened my own business], no more. Pharmacy is a closed-network field.

Favors—such as swapping medications and transferring patients' drug histories—that pharmacists normally do for one another out of common professional courtesy in the interest of the patient, ceased when the African American pharmacist decided to branch out on her own. Articulating her astonishment at the other pharmacist's unprofessional behavior, she remarks, "I just can't understand it. And I think if someone asked him why he don't speak to me, he's going to say because she's my competition. That's the only reason why I can think he's not speaking to me anymore." Yet competition cannot be the only reason for this type of exclusion, since she once worked for another Jewish pharmacist in the same neighborhood who also served as his competition. Now that she can no longer rely on neighboring pharmacists to exchange favors, she finds herself at a disadvantage compared with those who are willing to work together. She responds with disbelief in the face of their apparent grave concern over her newly established business: "See, that's what I can't understand. Why ya'll worried about me? You're already established. You already put your kids through college. You already got your boat and your house down at the shore. Why you worrying about me?!"

Michael Woodard's study of African American businessowners finds, similarly, that one of the greatest external barriers to their success is their exclusion from markets and distributor networks. An African American entrepreneur who owns a commercial furniture business regretfully comments,

> We are often excluded from opportunities . . . It's not because minority businesses don't reach out, but they're not competitive because they've been excluded from the distributor network. And the companies who exclude offer a thousand reasons why minorities can't be a part of their network, such as financial strength and other factors they manage to get around with our white counterparts. The biggest obstacle is that we don't know how it's done and we've never seen it done, since we're not even in the loop. There are too many industries that exclude us that we don't even look at—food service, sports equipment. Consequently, we're not in those industries.[11]

Coethnic embeddedness thus works to exclude other ethnic groups from deriving business advantages or even gaining entry into certain lines of business. Regardless of the ways in which exclusion operates—whether subtle or blatant—it can have deleterious social and economic consequences for those who are outside these networks.

Hence, while it may initially appear that interethnic competition does not exist, since Jews, Koreans, and African Americans occupy separate niches, retail niche domination often precludes the possibility of interethnic competition altogether. Like Waldinger, who studied black-immigrant competition in Los Angeles, I found "little evidence of competition strictly defined."[12] However, interethnic competition is far more nuanced and is better depicted as a combination of blocked opportunities, constraints, and exclusion from business networks—ultimately resulting in niche segmentation and exclusion from certain retail niches. Business communities are embedded in ethnic networks that have dual reinforcing functions: helping coethnics and excluding outsiders. Ethnic retail niche domination has made it virtually impossible for African Americans to compete effectively with immigrant entrepreneurs on a level playing field.[13] Were African Americans equally able to penetrate all retail niches, interethnic competition would undoubtedly take a different form.

Mass Marketing a Once Exclusive Product

Based on the industries in which immigrant entrepreneurs concentrate, some succeed in those in which they are able to "mass market" a once exclusive product. In other words, they take a luxury product and make it available more cheaply, thereby making it more accessible for a wider population. For instance, before Korean-owned manicure salons opened on virtually every block in New York City, manicures were available only in full-service beauty salons. In these salons a manicure would cost about $20, making this service affordable only to an elite group of people, namely upper- and upper-middle-class white women. Korean manicurists took this luxury service out of the beauty salons, charged women only $7, and made the manicure a mass-market service.[14] Today in New York, women from a broad range of social classes and occupations—from executives to secretaries to fast-food workers to students—can easily afford to get their nails done. Koreans are able to compete with full-service salons because mass marketing means concentrating more on volume and less on service. From the customers' perspective, they "negotiate a tradeoff between the kind of service received, the price, and the convenience, and they calculate the Korean nail salons as an overall better bargain than the full-service beauty salon."[15] Moreover, given the working woman's schedule and her need to balance work with her second shift at home, few women have the free time to spend hours in a salon indulging in a full-service beauty treatment.[16] Instead, many opt to squeeze in a manicure when they can, typically during a lunch or afternoon break, traveling no further than to the local Korean-owned manicure salon on the corner.

Koreans have also used the strategy of mass marketing to sell fresh flowers, once available only at florist shops and now readily available at corner delis. These businessowners have successfully adapted to the changing demands of the service economy by bringing small, convenient, full-service retail shops close to both high- and low-income consumers.[17] Korean-owned nail salons and delis have become ubiquitous in New York City, as evidenced from a recent article in the *New York Times* by a woman who had moved out of the city. She complained, "There are no Koreans. Which explains why you can never find flowers and why manicures cost $15."[18]

Korean immigrants have used the same strategy with ethnic beauty supplies, which includes both hair- and skin-care products for an ethnic clientele. These products were once only available through beauty salons, but immigrant entrepreneurs have mass marketed these goods by offering them to the general public on a retail level, thereby making them available at a much lower price. Interestingly, retail ethnic beauty supplies is a relatively new business, dating back only ten years, and of the 300 beauty supplies stores in New York City, 80 percent are Korean-owned. Ethnic clustering like this leads to advantages such as the ability to pool orders with neighboring storeowners, form business associations, and negotiate with manufacturers to receive cheaper wholesale prices.

The strategy of mass marketing, which transcends industries, also explains immigrants' success in lower-line apparel. According to the U.S. Department of Labor's 1993 *Consumer Expenditure Survey,* blacks spend a greater percentage of their income on apparel and services than whites.[19] Fashions for certain types of clothes and accessories among African Americans in inner cities have created a demand for what people in the business call "ethnic urban sportswear" or "inner-city sportswear." Inexpensive designer knockoffs form a large component of urban sportswear, and Koreans have capitalized on this trend, as evidenced by the large number of Korean-owned businesses that sell this merchandise in the neighborhoods under study. An African American employee of a Korean-owned store illustrates the immense demand for the less expensive, imitation designer clothing as he explains the difference between the Korean-owned store in which he works and the more expensive Jewish-owned sportswear stores on 125th Street in West Harlem:

For example, you have this Ralph Lauren look-alike. JJ [a Jewish-owned clothing store] is too expensive, so people that are, quote, drug dealers, hustlers, they can afford JJ and DJ. Welfare recipients, people who just receive money twice a month, or maybe once every month, they want that look. So what they do is they'll come in, and we'll cater to their needs.

Since low-income blacks cannot afford to purchase designer clothing, Korean-owned businesses that sell designer imitations prosper in poor neighborhoods. Although Korean merchants currently dominate this market, they were not the first to identify it. Jewish retailers once predominated in the lower-line apparel industry, but they have departed this niche and have instead entered the more exclusive niche of higher-priced apparel, dress wear, and authentic designer sportswear.

Compensatory Consumption

Immigrant-owned shops that sell designer knockoffs in low-income black communities thrive because there is a high demand for the apparel in what is essentially a captive market. Unable to achieve status through the conventional avenues of prestigious jobs, high salaries, or higher education, poor blacks' spending on imitation designer clothing, expensive sneakers, and jewelry is a form of "compensatory consumption." In other words, some poor blacks use clothing and costly accessories as a means of rebuffing their low-income status. In fact, merchants and store managers openly state that their business success rests on blacks' excessive spending on apparel, as the African American manager of a Jewish-owned clothing store on Jamaica Avenue notes:

Blacks buy even more [than other groups] because they got to match. You know blacks match things more than other people. They don't care what it costs, it's got to match, right on down to the sneakers and the underwear. So not only do they buy more clothes, but they got to match. And when you're in an area like this, you have the traffic going, and black people are spending money!

Compensatory consumption refers to the act of purchasing items, such as apparel, automobiles, appliances, and other material merchandise, to compensate for blocked social and economic mobility. As David Caplovitz noted in his classic study of the East Harlem furniture district, "Since many [low-income consumers] have [little] prospect of greatly improving their low social standing through occupational mobility, they are apt to turn to consumption as at least one sphere in which they can make some progress toward the American dream of success . . . Appliances, automobiles, and the dream of a home of their own can become compensations for blocked social mobility."[20] The concept of compensatory consumption is certainly not confined to African Americans in inner-city neighborhoods. In fact, the idea was first introduced in Robert and Helen Lynd's classic sociological study, *Middletown in Transition*. They observed that the Depression and declining opportunities for occupational mobility shifted the aspirations of working-class individuals toward the realm of consumption. As they perceptively noted,

> Fascinated by the rising standard of living offered them on every hand on the installment plan, they [members of the working class] do not readily segregate themselves from the rest of the city. They want what Middletown wants, so long as it gives them their great symbol of advancement—an automobile. Car ownership stands to them for a large share of the "American dream"; they cling to it as they cling to self respect, and it was not unusual to see a family drive up to the relief commissary in 1935 to stand in line for its four or five dollar weekly food dole.[21]

Americans are trained to consume and to display their consumption, often to win the respect of others or maintain self-respect. Displaying material items and gaining respect from others is particularly important for those who cannot acquire respect through the conventional means of education, occupation, or income. Hence, poor blacks who buy Nike sneakers for $140, or those who spend $200 for a leather jacket or $120 for a gold chain, do so because footwear, clothing, and jewelry are outward symbols of social status and economic mobility. Designer accessories such as handbags, backpacks, hats, and socks, even paper shopping bags that display the names of exclusive department stores, are important outward displays of financial and social status. The success of inner-city retail shops that cater to black consumers thrive in a culture that strongly encourages the display of consumption.

The Nature of the Retail Niche

While retail niches are segmented along ethnic lines, what previous research has failed to point out is that it is precisely this segmentation that places Koreans (and other immigrant entrepreneurs) in niches that are more susceptible customer conflict. Immigrants tend to enter niches characterized by high volume, low profit margins, poorer customers, and fleeting customer interactions—niches that are more vulnerable to misunderstandings and customer conflict. By contrast, the native-born businessowners are more likely to enter niches typified by low volume, higher profit margins, middle-class patronage, and greater specialized attention. Barbara Gutek's distinction between service "encounters" and "relationships" is relevant here.[22] Whereas Jewish and African American merchants enter businesses characterized by "relationships," Korean immigrants deliberately opt to enter businesses characterized by "encounters," specifically because of their loose command of the English language and their unfamiliarity with American customs and culture. As I will illustrate, the nature of the niche structures the interpersonal interactions between storeowners and their customers.

When I first began doing fieldwork, it seemed that Jewish and African American merchants were more sympathetic to their customers than some of their Korean counterparts, but I soon realized that their "Jewishness" or "blackness" has little to do with this. Instead the merchant-customer relationship is largely shaped by the retail niche that the merchant occupies. African American and second- and third-generation Jewish merchants, unlike most Koreans, are not handicapped with a language barrier and are therefore able to enter businesses that require a great deal of communication. Korean merchants—most of whom are first-generation immigrants—are far more restricted by language and consequently choose retail niches that require much less communication or virtually none at all. For example, Jewish merchants today cluster in such retail areas as furniture, apparel, and jewelry, and African Americans tend to predominate in hairstyling and music shops. Korean merchants locate in grocery stores, ethnic beauty supplies, fast-food restaurants, sneakers, and lower-line apparel.

To a certain extent, the merchant-customer relationship is shaped by the interactions that unfold based on the type of merchandise sold or service provided. For example, selling furniture or styling hair requires greater personalized attention from the merchant than selling fruit or flowers at the corner market. In fact for the customer, picking up fruit or vegetables at the corner deli requires almost no interaction at all, and this is one principal reason why immigrants dominate these labor-intensive, self-serve niches. A Korean grocer in Mount Airy explains that speaking fluent English is not a prerequisite to setting up shop: "You don't need much English. You just work, try hard, you know?"

The merchant-customer encounters in one East Harlem grocery store were typical of those at the several greengrocers I observed during my fieldwork. In this case the grocer, Mrs. Kim, had problems understanding the customers due to her limited English, but usually the transactions did not involve much communication at all. I watched as customers bought a basket of strawberries, a cantaloupe, or vegetables. The customer would place the merchandise on the counter, and then Mrs. Kim would total the merchandise and tell the customer how much it cost. Mrs. Kim would then take the money, put the merchandise in the bag, and place the change in the customer's hand. Neither Mrs. Kim nor the customer would say hello, nor would they make direct eye contact during the transaction, but Mrs. Kim always ended each exchange with a "Thank you." Often the customer did bother replying but simply took the merchandise and left the store. That was the end of the transaction.

Immigrants shy away from retail niches that require a great deal of communication with their customers because they fear that they do not have the appropriate language skills. Few Korean merchants dare enter industries that require a great deal of communication; those who do tend to have greater English language fluency and more years of business experience under their belt than the newer arrivals.

African American merchants and nonimmigrant Jewish merchants are native-English speakers and are therefore not restricted from entering businesses that require a great deal of communication. The nature of the Jewish- and African American-owned business is such that the owners have to devote more time and attention to each customer; their work requires a much higher level of skill in interpersonal interaction. Selling furniture or styling hair calls for giving more personal and specialized attention to the customer than does operating a dry cleaning service or selling fresh fish.

The salesmen in the Jewish-owned furniture stores I observed spend an inordinate amount out of time with each customer, showing them the numerous floor displays and a variety of catalogs to help them select furniture for their home.[23] Additionally, because the storeowners offer their own credit and layaway plans to those who cannot pay in full or do not have credit cards, they also take time with the customers to go over their employment status and financial history. And when customers purchase furniture using a credit plan, they must return once a month to make their payment. This type of in-depth and repeated exchange stands in stark contrast to those with immigrant entrepreneurs, whose customer interactions are generally fleeting, perfunctory, and anonymous.[24]

Like the furniture storeowners who spend a great deal of time with their customers, a Jewish pharmacist in Mount Airy explains that he has become very familiar with his customers and their families, because they come in on a regular basis to have their prescriptions filled. While they wait for their medications, he often engages in conversation with them. "You get an idea what children they have, how old they are," he says. "They feel comfortable talking about their family, so you get an idea whether they went to camp this past summer, or if they're going to college or something like that."

By contrast, business in immigrant retail niches thrives on a constant and speedy flow of customer traffic. Whereas Jewish furniture salesmen and African American hairstylists spend anywhere from thirty to forty-five minutes or more with each client, Korean grocery, fast food, and fish market owners generally spend only a few seconds or a minute at most. Exchanges are transitory and nameless in most immigrant-owned shops because the success of their business rests on volume, not service—on getting customers in and out as expeditiously as possible.[25] Who wants to wait in line to pay for a sandwich or can of soda while a Korean deli owner has a conversation with one of her other customers, especially during lunch hour? When a customer stops in at the corner market to pick up a bouquet of flowers on his way home from work, he can quickly lose patience when the line does not move swiftly enough. Most have come to expect and demand quick and efficient service.

However, the customer's expectations are far different when he or she enters a furniture store or a beauty salon. Fast-paced, in-and-out service would be deemed unacceptable and rude within a business context that entails, at the very least, a modicum of personal service. Essentially, the nature of the business in a Jewish-owned furniture store or African American–owned hair salon, for example, lends itself to prolonged contact with customers, whereas Korean-owned businesses require high customer turnover and brief exchanges that are limited to "Hello," "Thank you," and "Come again." Customers' expectations for these exchanges differ sharply depending on the retail niches that the merchants occupy.

It's All in the Service

Businessowners who provide services such as hairstyling are the most likely to spend a great deal of time with their clients and are consequently least likely to experience disputes with them, regardless of the race or ethnicity of the businessowner. For instance, while interviewing an African American beauty salon owner in Mount Airy, I noticed how quickly and easily bonds formed between clients and hairdressers. What makes this relationship particularly unique is that hairstylists stand very close to their clients and physically touch their head and hair. They engage in extensive conversations and spend a great deal of time with each client. Moreover, many hairstylists have come to adopt the role of therapist, as a hairstylist in Mount Airy freely admits: "We're like doctors for hair, and therapists for our clients. A lot of this job has to do with just being here and listening to them." "It's all in the service," chimed in a stylist at the neighboring station.

Service-oriented businesses such as barbershops, beauty salons, and restaurants are often more than just places of business. They provide social spaces where the clientele can spend time, relax, and socialize with the businessowners, employees, and fellow customers. In black urban neighborhoods, they are traditionally social spaces where customers can "disrobe" and code-switch, in a sense, shifting to an ethnic African American interactional style. The spaces are a haven in which blacks can interact almost exclusively with "their own," providing relief from the daily strain of public interactions with whites.[26]

For example, the beauty shop owners I interviewed attest that on weekends, customers spend hours in the salon, reading magazines, sipping coffee, and chatting with other clients while waiting to be served. Some salons have television sets on so clients can catch up on their favorite sit-coms or soap operas while getting their hair styled. Often, the story lines of the actors become the entertaining topic of conversation that brings customers close to one another. Another hairstylist in Mount Airy says that her customers come not only to get their hair styled but also to enjoy each other's company—referring to her clients as a "breakfast club" that looks forward to meeting on a weekly basis.

> The good part about it is that they all mix well—all my clients, they all mix well. They all look forward to coming because there's certain people that come on their day; it's like a breakfast club. So they'll have coffee and tea and they'll chat about what's going on. They basically talk to one another. A lot of times we talk about stars and award shows. The conversation is very general. Like we don't have that whole, "You sleeping with my husband" thing. That doesn't go on. General conversation, funny, light conversation. We have a lot of conversation back and forth.

In an increasingly impersonal world where public banter, civility, and sociability in everyday life are declining qualities in America's cosmopolitan cities, black-owned beauty salons and barbershops are some of the few private social spaces that offer black customers a respite. An African American barbershop owner in Queens points out that, unlike grocery stores, barbershops have "personalities" that attract different types of people to each salon.

> Barbershops have personalities. How a person owns it, runs it, there's a chemistry; it's almost like a team. So it's personality, it's character. There's a lot involved in the hair business. So it's not just like having a grocery store and having somebody pack boxes. You don't have to like the customers to pack the boxes. He makes his $5 an hour. Here you have to like what you do, appreciate what you do, and like making people look good . . . You got to get along [with your customers]; it's like getting along with your girlfriend! No sense being with her if you can't get along with her [laughs]. You don't want to be miserable. You got

to be friendly and cheerful. Your customers are how you're making money.

It should be stressed that the nature of the retail niche is in fact *more* salient than the race or the ethnicity of the businessowner in shaping merchant-customer relations. For example, Korean nail salon owners have better relations with their black customers than do their coethnics in the grocery business because manicures require both extended physical contact and one-to-one conversation in a more private social space.[27] Furthermore, whereas Korean-owned grocery stores have been targets of boycotts, Korean-owned nail salons have been shielded from this type of racial animosity. In short, the greater physical contact and the extended communication required in service-oriented businesses reduce the potential for merchant-customer altercations. Even when holding race and ethnicity constant, the retail niche is a significant factor that determines the nature of the merchant-customer interaction and the potential for interpersonal conflict.

Merchants whose businesses require more extensive customer communication and interaction become more familiar with their customers, often getting to know them personally. Some of the storeowners even know their customers by name and recall details of their personal and family lives, which adds a more intimate facet to the commercial encounter. The merchants do not pretend to create a close sense of community in their stores, but for those whose businesses rest on delivering a service—and not merely a product—it is important for them to interact more extensively with their customers. The Jewish and African American business niches require greater levels of communication, giving Jews and African Americans an organizational advantage over newer immigrant entrepreneurs with respect to positive merchant-customer relations.

Class Matters

Not only does the retail niche define the nature of merchant-customer interactions, but also—perhaps more important—it determines the class of the customer base. Merchants who specialize in men's and women's suits, better apparel, or high-quality furniture have a different clientele than those who sell inner-city sportswear and sneakers—the former attracting working and middle-class customers, and the latter largely drawing in a younger, poorer clientele interested in the latest fashion trends. Retailers who deal with middle-income older shoppers have better relations and fewer altercations with their customers than those who deal with younger, tougher, and less affluent customers.

Jewish merchants—the longest in business and the most financially established of the three groups—are most likely to occupy niches that involve higher-priced items, higher profits, and less customer traffic. By contrast, Koreans occupy niches that attract both poorer and younger customers. And even though most African American–owned businesses are smaller than either Jewish- and Korean-owned stores, they tend to cater to a more middle-class clientele. So within the stratification of a relatively poor community, the best-off residents tend to shop in the Jewish-owned businesses, while the least well-off patronize the Korean-owned stores. Because Korean merchants' customers are likely to be poorer, they may also be more disgruntled to begin with, for reasons that have very little to do with the merchants themselves.[28]

Storeowners of all backgrounds admit that the younger, poorer customers are the most difficult to handle. For example, in an attempt to capitalize on the boom in the ethnic sportswear market in the 1980s, a Jewish merchant in Queens decided to change his business from men's dress wear to inner-city sportswear. The change in his merchandise produced a dramatic shift in his clientele base, which in turn persuaded him to quickly return to his original business. The sportswear business had attracted a young, tough crowd, far more prone to theft and hot tempers, while his current business brings in older, family-oriented customers with whom he feels far more comfortable. His many years of business experience working with middle-class clients had not translated into ease in dealing with younger, more troublesome customers:

When we used to have sneakers, we had different kinds of people. I had people that came in, that I don't know where they got their money from; I don't think they worked for it. But the way we have the business geared now is towards family people. So these people that come in, they're hard-working, conscientious. Most of them are church-goers, so I would say they're the same as anybody else. My customers are family people. They come in with their kids. Their kids come in when they get older.

Similarly, an African American retailer who sells men's better casual apparel on Jamaica Avenue explains that his business draws in a combination of professional and working-class customers. He fully realizes that if he were to change his stock to inner-city sportswear, he would have to deal with younger "brothers" with an attitude, and he admits that similarities in race and ethnicity offer little protection against a young tough crowd.

We always did better men's wear. We always did up and better goods. We did a lot of trendy stuff. I have a mixture of customers. I have doctors, professors, schoolteachers, bankers, regular working blue-collar, technicians. The kind of customers I get, I don't get those customers that has the kind of young mentality. Some stores cater to a lot of younger kids that kind of talk to them with an attitude, and if I buy the sportswear, I guess some of the brothers might act a certain way to me too.

The nature of most Jewish- and African American–owned businesses keeps out the most troublesome customers, namely the teenagers, who *all* merchants agree are more prone to theft and are more generally the most difficult to handle.

Korean merchants do not always cater to poor customers, and those who target middle-class customers have more favorable relations with them. For example, a Korean merchant who specializes in upscale women's dresses—ranging in price from $50 to $500—asserts that she rarely has problems with customer altercations because her clients are "high-class black ladies" rather than low-income shoppers looking for the latest bargains.

This kind of customer I have, they dress nice. Nice dress we selling, party dress. This kind of a very high-class black ladies, they have good jobs. They work for government. It's not a ten-dollar store, so we selling nice suit. They go church and nice business meeting they go, so I have good customers. That's a good thing. That's why I don't have many arguments. Maybe once a year.

Similarly, an African American merchant in Queens also expresses her preference for servicing an older, more sophisticated, middle-class clientele. Specializing in Afrocentric cards and gifts, she keeps out the "riffraff and undesirables" and caters instead to more "mature adults."

> What I attract are people who like this kind of merchandise, which is better for me, because I spend less time with riffraff and undesirables because I'm in the public here, so I don't have to worry. There are people who would never look this way. They beeline when they come through here, not even for tantalizing because they think that this is above them or it's not in their lifestyle, which is fine with me because it cuts the fat. Most of my people are mature adults, into social events among their people that they know. They're gift-giving people, people who remember birthdays, death, and births, and things like that.

A salesman in a high-quality, Jewish-owned furniture shop explains that his business draws in "middle-income" customers and weeds out local welfare recipients who cannot afford the high-ticket items:

> [The customer base] depends on what kind of store that you have and the things that you sell. The things that we sell, nobody can buy if they're on welfare, especially furniture. They can buy furniture, but they're going to buy cheaper furniture somewhere else. We have high-quality furniture, so we deal with middle-income people.

By sharp contrast, an African American merchant in West Harlem who sells used and inexpensive furniture to poor customers in the neighborhood complains that he must regularly deal with customer complaints and disputes. For instance, when customers purchase used furniture "as is" and later find that there are flaws, they immediately return to his store, infuriated by the defect. "If I sell something 'as is,' and something's wrong with it, they come back and want to kill me. Ah man, they want to kill me, beat me up! And that happens all the time, and sometimes for no reason at all." Clearly, customer conflicts emerge with merchants of all racial and ethnic backgrounds, even African American merchants.

Minimizing Theft

Security measures form one aspect of merchant-customer relations, and the nature of the retail niche also determines the kind of security procedures that merchants employ to minimize the likelihood of customer theft. Storeowners who sell sneakers, sportswear, or small items are most prone to shoplifters and in turn have adopted numerous strategies to cut down on theft. For instance, most establishments that sell sneakers in West Philadelphia and Harlem give only one sneaker at a time to customers as they try them on for size. Employees initially provide the customer with only the right sneaker, and if the customer wants to try on the left, he must take off the right sneaker and hand it back to the employee. Very seldom did customers complain about this one-shoe-at-a-time policy; instead, most accepted the practice without raising an eyebrow. Merchandise is also organized in such a way to make theft as difficult as possible: sneakers are located far from store entrances, sensors are placed on all articles of clothing, and sometimes security guards and bag checkers are employed to watch customers and take their bags when they enter the store. Some merchants hire extra employees just to keep a watchful eye out for potential shoplifters, believing that their presence alone deters theft. And employees often use code words or numbers to alert one another to those who have shoplifted in the past.

Perhaps the most surprising measures to prevent theft are policies of not admitting groups of teenagers. A Jewish clothing retailer on Jamaica Avenue posts a sign on his front door that reads "No Food, No Drinks, No Groups," and he stops teenagers who wish to enter in groups larger than four or five. After experiencing numerous incidents of theft by teenagers who entered his store in large groups in order to distract his employees, he implemented his no-groups policy. All merchants claim shoplifting would be significantly more prevalent were these types of social controls not imposed on customers. They maintain that the prevalence of theft, particularly among youths, leads them to be wary of most teenagers, especially those they do not recognize.

While such security procedures are commonplace in many stores in low-income neighborhoods like Harlem and West Philadelphia, these social controls do not exist in businesses that offer higher-priced merchandise like furniture and better apparel. In addition, business-owners who provide services such as hairstyling, barbering, manicuring, and dry cleaning need not worry about shoplifters. "How can you steal a hair cut?" laughs an African American barber, mirroring the Jewish owner of a furniture store who commented, "Well, it's not easy to walk out of here with a sofa. If they can do it without anybody noticing, be my guest." Without the worries of potential theft, merchants drastically reduce their probability of running into disputes with their customers.

Thus, while the retail niche determines the type of interactions that unfold between merchant and customer, more fundamentally it determines the age and class of the clientele itself. Furthermore, some businessowners are immune to theft while others must keep a watchful eye on potential shoplifters. Retailers who carry more expensive, more upscale merchandise and those who provide personal services are more likely to have better merchant-customer relations and less likely to experience disputes with their customers. They are more likely to deal with a better-educated, more affluent customer base, thereby minimizing the possibility of merchant-customer arguments altogether. In stark contrast, storeowners who specialize in merchandise that attracts a largely poor or teenage clientele remain most vulnerable to day-to-day customer altercations.

Immigrants who open businesses in black neighborhoods do so because there is little competition from larger chain corporations, because rent is relatively cheap, and because they feel that they do not have the middle-class mannerisms to serve a more affluent and educated clientele. Because corporations largely ignore low-income neighborhoods like New York's Harlem and West Philadelphia, small, immigrant-owned shops can thrive by providing much-needed services to these under-served communities.

While immigrant entrepreneurs may not directly compete with African American businessowners (since ethnic groups cluster in different industries), the niches in which these groups locate should be understood as resulting from ethnic succession, differential opportunities, constraints, and exclusion. Their inequality of economic and social capital, combined with their exclusion from business networks, leave

African Americans severely disadvantaged in more costly retail markets and in competition with their immigrant counterparts. In fact, inequality of opportunity often precludes the possibility of immigrant and African American competition. However, there remains the prevailing perception in the black community that immigrant entrepreneurs—and the foreign-born more generally—directly compete with and take opportunities away from the native-born, particularly African Americans. Perceptions—whether accurate or not—can have very serious consequences, as we shall see in the following chapters.

The retail niche that merchants occupy affects the manner in which they interact with their customers. By nature, Jewish- and African American–owned businesses lend themselves to extended conversation and contact with customers, with their primary focus on delivering service. The businessowners and their employees spend a great deal of time with each customer, typically anywhere from half an hour to forty-five minutes with each client. The economic character of furniture stores and beauty salons rests on higher profit margins, fewer customer transactions, and fully serving each customer. This is not the case with most Korean-owned shops. Low profit margins, high customer turnover, fleeting "encounters," and general anonymity characterize most immigrant-operated businesses. The in-and-out exchange in immigrant-owned stores allows owners no time to forge "relationships" with their customers.

The nature of the niche is merely one factor shaping merchant-customer interactions. As we shall see in Chapters 4 and 5, time on the street, the age of the customer, the gender of the merchant, and the presence of black employees are other important variables that affect the commercial life in black communities.

CHAPTER 4

Life on the Street:
The Everyday Encounters between
Blacks, Jews, and Koreans

It's not black versus white, or black versus whatever, because you find people who—regardless of who they are—can be very courteous. You can find people who can be discourteous, abrasive, very nasty. So to me, I look at things now in terms more of individuals than when I was younger, and I was one of those guys that I'd be throwing bricks and stuff to help get these Jews out of Harlem.
> —African American resident, West Harlem

So I've been here thirteen years in Harlem; everybody respects me. You see everybody says hello. I've been here thirteen years, and I love these people. I've been here so long, everybody's so nice. I've been stick up three, four times, but it don't mean anything that they are black. They are bad guys.
> —Korean merchant, West Harlem

To be a merchant in New York's Harlem or West Philadelphia is an odd mixture of prosaic routine and explosive tension, of affectionate customers and racial anger. Yet despite the media focus on incidents like the firebombing of Freddy's clothing store in Harlem or the boycotts of immigrant-owned businesses, most striking is the sheer ordinariness of most merchant-customer encounters. Having witnessed hundreds of daily interactions between African American, Jewish, and Korean storeowners and their black customers, I find that the overwhelming majority are characterized by civility, routine, and the simplicity of business as usual. Contrary to popular perception, most merchant-customer interactions are not antagonistic, and are not the source of hostility that gives rise to boycotts and riots.

The civility between merchants and customers is at odds with the prominent media images that feature poor, black communities as bubbling cauldrons of racial animosity, with African Americans pitted against Koreans and Jews. Even much of the scholarly research spawned after the 1992 Los Angeles riot centered on cultural differences, focusing sharply on the prejudicial attitudes of inner-city merchants and the negative treatment that black customers receive. Other research highlights the role of middleman minorities, emphasizing the inevitable conflict of interest between buyers and sellers in a capitalist economy.[1] Unlike past research, however, my findings reveal that most merchant-customer encounters are not characterized by racial prejudice and conflict. Moreover, past studies have not included the views of black customers. Needless to say, focusing strictly on merchants' accounts produces a one-sided argument. This chapter seeks to fill the void by examining merchant-customer relations from both perspectives.

That the majority of merchant-customer interactions are civil and conflict-free may not come as a surprise to ethnomethodologists who understand that "there is a self-generating order in concrete activities."[2] However, what is crucial to note is that the order is not random. The principle task of ethnomethodology is to explain the way in which social order is produced through the recurrent details of everyday practices.[3] Using an ethnomethodological lens to study merchant-customer interactions, I demonstrate how the everyday order of mercantile life is mediated through certain mechanisms and contextual variables.

More significant than race or ethnicity in determining the nature of merchant-customer relations are the contextual variables that shape these interactions. The retail niche that merchants occupy (see Chapter 2), the familiarity and fictive kinship between merchants and customers, the age of the customer, the gender of the merchant, and the presence of black employees (see Chapter 5) are some mechanisms through which the everyday social order is locally produced and maintained. Also important to note is that while both the media and past research have strictly focused on the poor treatment of black customers by Jewish and Korean merchants, I will illustrate that black customers also experience negative treatment from African American merchants, a point never raised in prior research.

One caveat before continuing: this chapter's focus on social order and everyday routine does not mean merchants and customers do not get into arguments or that tempers do not flare from time to time. But civil relations prevail because merchants and their employees work to maintain the normalcy and routine, recognizing that the failure to do so can have dramatic consequences.

The Ordinariness of Merchant-Customer Interactions

While past research emphasizes that disagreements between merchants and customers typically arise over faulty merchandise, high prices, and exchange policies, during my fifteen months of fieldwork I found merchant-customer altercations to be extremely rare.[4] For instance, merchants would greet the customers as they entered their store and ask if they needed assistance. The common answer from the vast majority of the customers was, "Just looking," and they would make their way through the store's displays. The merchants would continue straightening up the merchandise or simply take a seat behind the register. Often, their employees would point out newly arrived merchandise, especially in the case of furniture or clothing. The employees also made small talk with their customers as they browsed throughout the store, commenting about the weather or the latest fashion trends. In some of the businesses, the chatter between employees and customers evoked a sense of community that seems lost in the boutiques found in middle-class white neighborhoods further downtown. When the customer found what he or she wished to purchase, the customer would place the item on the counter, where the merchant would ring up the sale and conclude the interaction with a "Thank you" or "Have a nice day."

The majority of the black customers that we interviewed said they experience positive interactions with the merchants in their community. Fifty-six percent reported consistently positive relations with the merchants in their neighborhood while only 9 percent of the customers reported consistently negative treatment. Customers who reported that they were treated "well," "very well," "fine," or "nice," were coded as having received positive treatment, whereas customers who claimed that they were treated "bad" or "suspiciously," or who complained of being routinely followed, were coded as having received negative treatment.

While the majority of the respondents in the sample maintained that they regularly received positive treatment, 35 percent reported mixed interactions, claiming that they were treated "okay," "alright," or "it depends on how I carry myself." It is crucial to note here that when the customers reported mixed treatment, we probed them to recall specific instances of either positive or negative treatment by a local merchant. Most of the customers readily recalled one negative experience with a particular merchant. Then when we asked whether the negative experience characterized their shopping experiences in general, they revealed that it did not. Instead, they stated that most of their experiences were in fact positive, with positive interactions far outweighing negative ones.

Barbara Gutek's research on service encounters sheds light on this contradictory pattern when she makes the distinction between relationships and encounters.[5] In relationships, customers and service providers spend a fair amount of time together and get to know one another as individuals. Furthermore, she notes that customers readily discuss bad encounters with almost anyone who is willing to listen but rarely praise good encounters. In other words, a customer may readily complain of a negative encounter with the local Korean grocer but fail to mention the numerous positive encounters with others. Such was the case in our interviews. When asked to comment on merchant-customer encounters, some of the customers were quick to mention one negative experience rather than the typical positive ones.

Remarkably, positive merchant-customer interactions vary little according to differences in the race, ethnicity, or religion of the merchants. This point should be underscored. Contrary to previous research that finds intraracial customer-clerk encounters more positive than interracial ones, I find that positive merchant-customer interactions vary little across lines of race, ethnicity, and religion.[6] For example, while 59 percent of the black customers reported routinely positive interactions with black merchants, 53 percent reported routinely positive experiences with Korean storeowners, and the number reporting routinely positive experiences with Jewish businessowners falls in between, at 55 percent. The figures vary more in terms of negative experiences, but not as much as one would expect according to the journalistic and scholarly accounts that highlight racial tension and conflict. Although twice as many black customers reported negative interactions with Korean merchants (16 percent) compared with Jewish merchants (8 percent) and black merchants (7 percent), this variation in black customers' experiences can be explained by other variables. In sum, black customers are not necessarily treated better in African American–owned stores than in Jewish- or Korean-owned stores.

These findings confirm Gary T. Marx's earlier study of black-Jewish merchant-customer relations in New York. Contrary to the prevailing image of Jewish merchants' exploitation of black customers, Marx found that only 21 percent of black customers said they received unfair treatment from Jewish storeowners.[7] Clearly, merchant-customer relations are not uniformly negative or positive. As I will illustrate, the diversity of merchant-customer interactions can be explained by the merchants' length of time in business, their ability to evoke fictive kinship, the age of the customers, and the presence of female retailers who act as "maternal brokers."

Time on the Street

As I noted in the previous chapter, the nature of retail niches largely structure merchant-customer interactions and determine the class composition of the clientele. However, length of time in business, or time on the street, is also crucial. Much of the difference between Jewish, Korean, and African American storeowners has more to do with how long they have been in business in the same neighborhood than with differences in race, ethnicity, or religion. Merchants who have been in business for ten or fifteen years know and recognize their customers, speak with them frequently, feel at ease doing business in the neighborhood, and understand the importance of preserving the everyday routine.

Many Jewish and African American merchants have been in business for decades or, in some cases, generations, giving them an advantage over their Korean immigrant counterparts. In *Streetwise,* sociologist and urban ethnographer Elijah Anderson illustrates the benefits that familiarity affords the Jewish merchants of a community that he calls "Norton," and how this gives them a distinct advantage over their newer Asian counterparts.

On the streets of Norton, race-conscious blacks at times complain bitterly about the recent incursion of Asians and wonder aloud "who helped them out" . . . Yet Jews, who have long run similar businesses there, provoke little hostility; the community is used to Jewish merchants. The hostile reception the Asians get has to do with the way residents perceive them as a new competitive group bent on taking opportunities from blacks and establishing itself within Norton.[8]

What Anderson fails to note is that when Jewish merchants were the newcomers to the scene in low-income black neighborhoods, they too received a hostile reception from local residents. A great deal has changed over the second half of the twentieth century for Jewish storeowners in black neighborhoods. Their length of time in the community has allowed residents to become more familiar, more comfortable with Jewish businessowners, and vice versa. As a third-generation furniture retailer in East Harlem remarks, "We've been around here so long, we're friends with the people. I think it's different for Koreans, because they've only been here a short time. Like the guy next door, he's only been here for two years."

Veterans not only have the advantage of knowing their customers, but they have also developed more finely tuned skills for handling them. By contrast, novices are noticeably nervous doing business in poor black communities—and their nervousness is reflected in their stiff posture, failure to smile, reluctance to speak, and propensity to have little physical and eye contact with their customers. Less adept at taking the initiative and seizing control of business interactions, newer merchants are thus less capable of keeping the upper hand in their service transactions.[9] Experienced merchants understand that taking the initiative means welcoming the customer in a friendly yet confident manner with greetings such as, "Hello there, sir. What can we do for you today?" or "What a nice day. I sure wish I could take in some of that sunshine." Novices are notably more reticent, simply mumbling a quiet "Hi" or giving a mere nod of the head.

Seizing control of the interaction is important in service encounters, as William Foote Whyte noted in his study of waitresses. Whyte explained that when examining the worker-customer interaction, the first question to ask is, "Does the waitress get the jump on the customer, or does the customer get the jump on the waitress?" He vividly described how skilled waitresses seize control of the service interaction:

The skilled waitress tackles the customer with confidence and without hesitation. For example, she may find that a new customer has seated himself before she could clear off the dirty dishes and change the cloth. He is now leaning on the table studying the menu. She greets him, says, "May I change the cover, please?" and, without waiting for an answer, takes his menu away from him so that he moves back from the table, and she goes about her work. The relationship is handled politely but firmly, and there is never any question as to who is in charge.[10]

Veteran storeowners understand that taking control of the situation is paramount to successful merchant-customer interactions—from the initial greeting to making the sale to adroitly handling customer gripes to finally closing the interaction. In contrast, novices are far less attuned to the importance of the extended series of interactions involved in getting off on the right foot and maintaining control of the interaction.

One Korean owner of a fruit and vegetable store in East Harlem, who had been in the United States for only three years and in business for less than one, said she was fearful of her black customers and professed that her Latino employees were equally afraid. Her mix of trepidation and disdain manifested itself in curt, rude, and suspicious behavior toward her customers, provoking young blacks to ask, "Why you disrespecting me like this?" and "Why you doing this to me, man?" In one instance, when two elementary school–aged black boys walked into the store, the woman, sitting behind the register, simply glanced at them and made no further motion to acknowledge their presence. They wanted to buy a kiwi, which sold three for a dollar or one for 35 cents. One of the boys asked, "Why can't I have a kiwi for 25 cents?" By this time the woman's husband had come into the store, and he interjected in an impatient and disparaging tone of voice, "Because it's 35 cents. Get an apple, an apple is 25 cents." The boy replied, "I'm allergic to apples." When neither storeowner responded to the boy, his friend demanded, "Why you doing this to me, man? You know I always come in here." The wife glanced at the boys in disgust and then turned her head away from them, and her husband just walked to the back of the store. Both gestures gave these young customers a clear signal that the merchants were ignoring them—refusing to answer their requests or even acknowledge their presence in the store.

Black customers readily sense the newcomers' nervousness, unease, fear, and disdain. One East Harlem customer explains how the Korean fruit and vegetable merchants changed their attitude from nervous awkwardness to ease once she began frequenting the market on a regular basis, "At first it was a little awkward. I think they were awkward. They weren't trusting, I don't know why. But now I go in there all the time, and I don't have any problems. Now I'm comfortable, and they're just fine." An African American man in West Philadelphia also says that the local retailers treat customers with suspicion until they become familiar with them: "If they don't know you, you're treated with a little suspicion until you go in there regularly enough for them to know you. If they don't know you, I'd say you're treated differently, but once they get to know you, they treat you nice."

In addition to the increased comfort level that comes with years in business in a neighborhood, veterans also have another advantage: a steady clientele. When merchants establish regular customers, they become more familiar with them, often forming long-term and even intergenerational relationships, as a second-generation Jewish storeowner in Queens describes:

> We've been here for forty years, and we've had a pretty steady clientele, which helps us. We have three generations of customers. Going back forty years, we have people that used to shop with their dads, they shop here with their sons. You know, so we have steady, regular customers that are loyal to us. And I think the fact that we've been here so long, I feel very comfortable. I know a lot of people in the area.

Most important, veteran storeowners, regardless of race or ethnicity, have far fewer disputes with their customers. For instance, a seasoned Korean merchant—who previously owned a fruit and vegetable market and now runs a ladies' dress wear store—attributes merchants' arguments with their customers to their inexperience and pettiness. With eight years of business experience under her belt, she has come to realize that small monetary losses are not worth the aggravation of arguing with customers, not to mention the potential conflict that may ensue from trivial disputes. Time on the street has taught her that maintaining a normal business routine and creating goodwill with her customers takes work, and may sometimes even necessitate forfeiting small losses.

Korean owners [of grocery stores] act cheap. Let them [the customers] have it. They argue with fifty cents, one dollar. Let them have it! It's not going to hurt them. Businessowner when they have a grocery store, they have certain amount money coming every month, enough money. I think enough money coming. Let them have it. Let them go with it. They always fight with a dollar. They act too cheap!

Similarly, a Korean dry cleaner in Mount Airy who has been in business for more than five years fully understands that customer service is paramount to running a successful operation and maintaining positive relations with her clientele. When she first started in the business, customers who complained about the stains left on their clothes easily aggravated her, prompting her to argue. However, since she has adopted the American adage that "the customer is always right," she has far better relations with her clientele. In her broken but expressive English, she explains,

Friendship and relationship is good [with my customers]. You know why? First time I'm very angry for customers. Now okay. Money is customer's money, not my money. Customer is king. First time I don't have experience, it's very hard time, but now is no problem, no problem. My service is best. And then everybody I know, I know every customer, and then customer knows me. Before, they say, "This is not clean. Why is there spot?" Before I was upset to customer, but now I say, "Okay, I'm going to try again." Then customer say, "Okay, you did good job. You did try more times, that's it."

Experienced retailers understand that arguing with customers about dry-cleaning stains, incorrect change, or refunds is often not worth it. Time on the street teaches merchants that maintaining ordinariness and creating civility takes work, and may even necessitate succumbing to customers' demands. Constructing and maintaining civility, they come to realize, is well worth the effort, especially because it minimizes the likelihood of customer altercations.

Eroding Rigid Stereotypes

The newest merchants on the street in poor black neighborhoods also tend to be the most recent arrivals to the United States. They have had little or no direct experience with black communities prior to immigrating, yet they hold preconceived prejudices of blacks, just the same. Images of black criminality and poverty plague the U.S. media and films and are easily transported to foreign television, impressing on America's newcomers stereotypes that blacks are poor, violent, uneducated, and dangerous. Thus, even before setting foot in America's inner cities, many new immigrants see blacks as a monolithic racial category, adopting the negative racial stereotypes of the black welfare queen, the black criminal, and the black drug abuser. These negative perceptions of their customers, in turn, affect the way the new merchants interact with them.

Time on the street teaches merchants that their customers are a diverse population with differences in ethnicity, class, and character. As a result, veterans view holdups and robberies as isolated incidents and refrain from making stigmatizing judgments about blacks as a group. For example, a Korean merchant who has been in business for thirteen years in West Harlem reports that she has developed a favorable rapport with her customers. The fact that she has been robbed at gunpoint several times has not led her to adopt the negative stereotypes of black criminality. Witnessing the stream of customers with whom she chatted and whom she recognized by name made it abundantly clear that she was quite fond of her customers, as they were of her. She was at ease with her customers and remarked on everything from their weight loss or gain and stylish clothes to their new boyfriends. She would even chide some of them for failing to pay her a visit if she had not seen them in a while.

Another Korean long-timer in Harlem explains that when she first opened her sneaker store, customers used to steal frequently, making her suspicious of everyone who walked through the door. But as a more seasoned merchant on 125th Street, she is far less wary and recognizes the heterogeneity of her customer population. "First time, I didn't remember anybody. I couldn't tell difference. First time, almost everyday somebody would steal. Now I remember face. I remember good people, I remember bad people." In fact, when she first opened her business in Harlem, she and her husband were handcuffed and forced into the store's basement while their attackers robbed them, cleaning out their stock. But even after such a frightening experience, she avoids blanket generalities based on race.

The refusal to adopt negative racial stereotypes comes with the realization that there are far more decent customers in these neighborhoods than there are bad. Years of experience have taught veteran businessowners that negative experiences—no matter how traumatic—are few and far between. Although newer merchants are nervous, with a few years of experience under their belt, they too begin to recognize the normalcy of even the poorest inner-city neighborhoods, like Harlem and West Philadelphia. Time and experience teach merchants that their customers are not a homogeneous blur of blackness but, rather, a diverse lot. As merchants come to know their customers as individuals, they soon recognize the diversity of their clientele, and this erodes the negative stereotypes of race and class. Furthermore, the process is dialectical; black customers also come to recognize that the merchants are individuals, not just racial and ethnic categories.

To help explain this finding, social psychologists such as Gordon Allport have argued that repeated contact erodes stereotypes and leads to more positive interpersonal relations. More specifically, the contact hypothesis maintains that increased contact reduces prejudice, which in turn reduces the probability of intergroup conflict.[11] However, it underpredicts the probability of conflict. Even long-time Jewish and Korean veterans of poor black communities—who know and get along with their customers—have been targets of conflict. Jewish and Korean merchants fully realize that their veteran status can hold little relevance for hostile customers and boycotters, who recognize first and foremost their "nonblackness." Race and ethnicity can easily inflect merchant-customer relations in conflict-ridden and sometimes even violent ways, regardless of how long a merchant has been in business, a point I will return to in the following chapters.

Fictive Kinship

Although time on the street is significant for Jewish and Korean merchants, it is not as important for African American merchants. With time, African American merchants also become increasingly adept at dealing with their customers and more comfortable doing business more generally. However, even the novices did not express the same degree of nervousness and unease as their new immigrant counterparts.[12] African American merchants immediately recognize the diversity and normalcy of inner-city neighborhoods like Harlem and West Philadelphia, many of whom grew up in similar communities. For instance, one newcomer to Harlem's scene, an African American storeowner, articulates her surprise about the misconceptions that outsiders have of Harlem. She states incredulously, "They have an idea of what Harlem is, but Harlem is a very nice community. It's a community of working people, not basically welfare recipients like some people seem to think."

Time on the street is not as pivotal for African American merchants for two main reasons: first, African American merchants have contact with blacks outside of the merchant-customer relationship; second, they know what it is like to be "on the other side of the counter," having themselves experienced negative encounters while shopping. African American merchants come into contact with blacks in a variety of roles outside of the merchant-customer context, as family members, friends, neighbors, and coworkers. By contrast, Jewish and Korean merchants rarely have contact with blacks outside of the merchant-customer relationship. Jewish and Korean storeowners do not live in the low-income black communities in which they do business, and given the patterns of residential segregation in the United States, it should come as little surprise that Jewish and Korean merchants' social worlds do not include many, if any, blacks.[13] However, it is important to note that African American merchants are not dissimilar with regard to living outside the community in which they work; only two of the African American business owners in the sample actually lived in the low-income community in which they did business.

Although African American merchants may not live in these communities, they come into contact with other blacks in a diversity of social settings and across class lines. For example, black kin networks are often class-heterogeneous, and middle-class African American merchants who have moved out of the inner city often return to visit friends and relatives, to attend church, or simply to experience a black social or cultural milieu. Therefore, middle-class African American merchants have a great deal of experience negotiating interclass relations with poorer kin and coethnics, and consequently have more experience dealing with blacks who reside in poor, inner-city neighborhoods.[14] Because African American merchants are more likely to interact with blacks outside of the merchant-customer context, they, unlike their Jewish and Korean counterparts, are fully cognizant of the diversity within poor black communities long before they set up shop.

Moreover, while African American merchants may also reside in distant suburbs, black customers still perceive them as part of the place and as members of the community. Community membership extends beyond the geographic boundaries of a neighborhood block or zip code. As a young African American female resident of West Philadelphia explains, membership in the community means that "you're still a sista' or a brotha'," not necessarily a resident in a particular neighborhood. Community membership involves a shared sense of fictive kinship, based on the collective experiences of one's racial or ethnic background.[15] African American merchants have the advantage of being able to evoke a sense of fictive kinship with their customers, which is evident not only in their less formal interactional style but also in their use of kinship terms such as *brother* and *sister.*

For example, a young African American customer in Queens explains that black merchants often make her feel comfortable by greeting her as "my sister," evoking an immediate sense of shared experience based on race alone:

> Well with blacks, it's like if you walk in their store or their little booth, it's like, "Hello my sister. Is there anything in particular that you're looking for?" I feel more comfortable when I go to stores that are owned by black people because I feel that we share something, we have something in common. We may not live in the same community, but just by us having the same skin color, I feel that person probably has also experienced racism like I have.

This young woman's statement vividly illustrates that community membership goes beyond the spatial confines of a geographical neighborhood and extends to those who have "the same skin color" and have "experienced the racism like I have." This affinity based on shared experience forms the foundation of collective identity and solidarity.

I Know What It's Like to Be "On the Other Side"

Another reason that length of time in business is not as significant for African American merchants is because they understand what it is like to be "on the other side of the counter"—what it's like as a customer to have others make judgments about them based on race alone. An African American storeowner in West Harlem underscores that the poor treatment he has received in other stores reinforces his commitment to treat his customers with respect.

> I have not always been on this side of the counter. I used to be on that side of people's counters, so I know how I feel if someone doesn't treat me right. I wouldn't come back again. So I learned to treat other people the way I wanted to be treated. Even now if I go to a person's store and they act as if they don't want me there or my business means nothing to them, there's too many businesses today you can go to, to take that type of abuse. So I just thank them and go about my business. I don't give any verbal remark whatsoever, because it isn't worth it. You don't have to go back again. But when you treat people right, they appreciate that.

Most of the black merchants revealed that at one time or another they have felt that other retailers have made negative assumptions about them and treated them unfairly. Several black merchants admitted that they have been stopped in large department stores or businesses located in white neighborhoods so that security personnel could check their bags to make sure that they had not shoplifted. Others have been followed while shopping or have had sales associates ignore or snub them, assuming that they cannot afford to buy the merchandise sold in that store. By illustration, an African American retailer in Queens says that when he enters businesses in predominantly white neighborhoods, "They'll look at me, and I'll say, wait a minute, what did I do?" Because of his negative experiences, he gives his customers the benefit of the doubt. He professes, "If you ever walk into my store, I will never follow you around. I will always trust you . . . unless you prove yourself untrustworthy." Hurtful experiences while shopping have made some African American storeowners fully aware that they should not judge their customers based solely on age, race, class, or neighborhood. However, as we shall see in the following section, young black customers do not necessarily agree with this assessment. Black customers do not feel that they are always given the benefit of the doubt, even from coethnics.

Age and Respect

Age largely determines the way in which merchants *initially* respond to customers when they enter their store, particularly when merchants and customers are unfamiliar with each other. Both young black males and females, but especially males, complain that merchants follow them as they browse in stores, to ensure against customer theft. This creates an uncomfortable environment for many young customers, who feel that they are treated like criminals when they intend to shop. For example, a twenty-five-year-old Jamaican American customer explains that when he shops in Jewish- and Korean-owned stores, he feels that he is "scrutinized" and "monitored." He complains, "I'm followed when I walk in the store to the point of annoyance." Young black women are not immune to this type of treatment, as an eighteen-year-old African American customer reveals, describing her frustration when shopping in a Jewish-owned gift shop in Queens.

> In [the Jewish-owned store] you're followed. I'm telling you, that's why I really don't like shopping in there. I like the quality of the things that they have in there, but the way that they treat the customers when you go in there, it's not worth it.

Although many storeowners may not literally follow customers, merchants who sell small items often perch themselves behind comically high counters or hire employees to sit on tall chairs or ladders so they can observe the customers while they move about the store. This constant feeling of being watched, monitored, and scrutinized creates a sense of distrust, which customers justifiably resent.

Surprisingly, even though young customers expressed their discontent with this type of treatment, some provided explanations for why merchants are wary and may stereotype based on age. Since theft is not uncommon in low-income neighborhoods, the few individuals who steal make it difficult for merchants to trust newcomers on sight, particularly teenagers. A twenty-year-old African American man speculates why inner-city merchants tend to follow him.

> I mean, a lot of stuff they do, I don't necessarily agree with, following me around stores and what not, but I understand there's reasons for all

of this. They follow me around stores because they've been robbed by a black person, and they fall into the stereotype that all black people are criminals, thieves, hoodlums, so therefore, I'm just a representative of them.

Whereas the younger customers interviewed sense that merchants discriminate based on age and treat them poorly as a whole, older customers assert that they are treated very cordially in all of the businesses in their neighborhoods, regardless of the merchants' race or ethnicity. In stark contrast to teenagers who feel that they are "scrutinized," a sixty-two-year-old African American woman who shops regularly on West Harlem's business strip explains that in Korean-owned stores, "I'm treated very good. They come up to me, and they ask me how may they help me, and what would I like to buy. And if I tell them I'm just shopping around, they say okay. They treat me nice and say, 'ma'am.'" Elderly customers pose no threat to the merchants, so storeowners in black neighborhoods treat them affably. Moreover, these merchants also treat older customers more cordially because age deserves respect.

Although young black customers complain that Jewish and Korean merchants follow them, they adamantly assert that African American businessowners do *not* treat them differently in this regard. Despite what coethnic merchants may claim, African American storeowners in low-income neighborhoods also follow their younger clientele, reacting to the stereotypes of age, race, class, and space. For example, when asked how he is treated when he enters black-owned stores, a twenty-two-year-old African American man in West Harlem admits,

> I tend to have problems in black-owned retail stores, where items are readily available to be pilferaged. So that creates a climate or the perception of thieves. And I think as a businessperson, that's a legitimate concern. That's a major problem in any business, theft, so I don't hold that against them. I would venture to say that maybe for some, especially if they've been robbed and they've dealt with their own people in that situation, they tend to follow you. It may just be the reality of doing business in the inner city.

This point should be underscored: contrary to popular perception, African American retailers in inner cities do *not* treat their young black customers better or far differently than their Jewish and Korean counterparts do. An African American male customer in West Harlem spells this out: "It doesn't matter, if I walk into a store [whether it's] Korean, black, or Jewish, they all follow me around." However, what is important to distinguish in merchant-customer relations is *treatment* in Jewish-, Korean-, and African American–owned retail stores versus the *comfort level* that black customers often feel while hanging out with "their own" in service-oriented businesses.

Although most customers may not necessarily be treated very differently in retail stores, some feel more comfortable spending time in black-owned shops, particularly service-oriented businesses such as barbershops, beauty salons, and restaurants that have a "down home attitude." These service-oriented businesses are social spaces where African American customers can let their guard down and "chill" with fellow blacks in a relaxed social scene. Moreover, African American businessowners are also more capable of picking up and interpreting interactive, verbal, and nonverbal cues from customers compared with their nonblack counterparts, adding to the comfort of the environment. Hence, while there may be little difference in the manner in which African American, Jewish, and Korean retailers treat individual customers, black shoppers sometimes prefer hanging out in African American–owned service businesses for reasons that go beyond economic exchange.

Maternal Brokers

Scholarship on immigrant entrepreneurship has paid relatively little attention to the role of gender in the economy, particularly the way in which gender shapes merchant-customer interactions.[16] While gendered patterns of work emerge quite differently among Jewish, Korean, and African American businessowners, the role of gender shapes interactions between merchants and customers across lines of race and ethnicity. Men largely operate Jewish-owned stores today, with only a few Jewish women present in these businesses. By contrast, Korean-owned stores tend to be operated by both a husband and wife, and African American-owned stores are usually operated by a man or a woman but rarely both. Despite these differing work patterns, women—regardless of race or ethnicity—are more likely to adopt distinct work roles in which they have more contact with their customers. They are more adept with customer relations because their gender acts as a resource, especially when it comes to performing the "emotional labor" in these businesses.[17] The female retailers in these communities act as "maternal brokers" who work hard to defuse rising tensions and ensure that the day-to-day routine runs as smoothly as possible.

Most prominently, the emotional labor in these retail jobs differs starkly along gender lines. Women are more likely to chitchat with the customers—asking them about their families, their children, or discussing other bits of daily trivia—thereby bringing a more human dimension to the commercial encounter. Women also adopt the role of host, greeting customers as they enter the store. One Jewish owner of a furniture store fondly recalls his mother's role in the business.

> My mother was an amazing judge of character, and she greeted all the customers. She was like a host. She had the greatest memory. She remembered each and every customer. She would ask them, How are your kids? How was your surgery? She had that personal touch.

The division of emotional labor is most obvious in businesses where both men and women are present but the men interact minimally with their customers. In such cases men usually prefer tasks that shield them from direct customer contact, such as ordering merchandise from suppliers, attending business meetings, or simply stocking shelves. For example, in New York it is the Korean men who rise at four in the morning to go to Hunt's Point to buy the fresh fruit and vegetables or get up at the crack of dawn to purchase their daily supply of fresh fish from wholesalers at the Fulton Fish Market downtown. Similarly, it is the Jewish men who negotiate with suppliers, place orders, and attend sales meetings and luncheons. By contrast, the women turn their attention to the customers, helping them select merchandise, ringing up sales, and making certain that the business routine runs as smoothly as possible. As a Korean woman who owns a clothing store with her husband puts it, "I'm the seller; he's the buyer."

Because women are better able or simply more willing to perform the emotional labor in these retail businesses, they are positioned at the "front end" of the business—behind the cash register or on the selling floor—while men assume inconspicuous positions in the background. Women often act as hostesses, welcoming the customers with a smile and a "hello," and making sure that they leave with a "thank you," "come again," or "good-bye." The female merchants feel that it is just "natural" for them to be more congenial, more communicative, and even a bit maternal toward their customers compared with their male counterparts in business. "I guess there's something about a woman. People kind of connect women with nurturing and caring, and being particular about things more than a man would. We handle things different. Our manners are different," says an African American coffee shop owner in Queens. Other female storeowners maintain that women are more intuitive, have more "sense," and are therefore more capable of reading customers' cues and moods.

Most critically, women are better at defusing tensions because their gender makes them less threatening to their customers, who interpret their authoritative voice as maternal scolding or "nurturant mothering" rather than as offensive or confrontational.[18] As a young, African American man in West Philadelphia comments about black female businessowners, "Black ladies, especially older black ladies, I mean, they can say anything to you, and nobody will say anything back to them." This is precisely why Jewish, Korean, and African American female storeowners can be feisty with their customers or even yell, "Get out of my store!" without fear of a violent backlash. Furthermore, female retailers more readily stop shoplifters on site, break up fights, or refute customers who claim that they were given the incorrect change, because their actions are interpreted as nonthreatening.

By illustration, while working as a cashier at a store in West Philadelphia I saw a fight break out between two black male customers outside the store. The middle-aged Korean female merchant immediately ran outside to break up the fight, physically wedging herself between the two young men. They pushed her aside and began brawling once again, yet the Korean merchant persisted and managed to successfully break up the fight, yelling at both of them to stop. After exchanging a few hostile words, the two men went off in opposite directions. Visibly shaken by the encounter, the woman marched back into the store and proceeded to yell at her husband and the three male employees for failing to intervene. When I asked why she decided to risk harm to herself and come between the two men to break up the fight, she indignantly replied, "If they break one of my store windows, that's a big problem! If another customer gets hurt, that's another problem!" Still upset by the fight, she walked to the back of the store to cool off. I then turned and asked her husband why he refused to jump to her aid. He first said, "I don't know," and then paused. After a few seconds, he added, "They could turn around and fight me, maybe. I don't know."

The Korean man had not intervened because he feared that the two black men fighting outside his store would turn their anger on him. He grasped that race and ethnicity could jump to the foreground in a way that they would not for his wife. Fearing that his intervention could be misinterpreted as paternalistic oppression by an outsider, he had opted not to get involved. By contrast, the Korean female merchant's act of breaking up the fight was interpreted as maternalism; her gender made her less of a threat, and what was most salient was her gender, rather than her race and ethnicity. Furthermore, if either male had fought the female merchant—who happened to be middle-aged and petite—he would have lost face and jeopardized his masculine status, especially in the presence of male witnesses.[19]

For Jewish businesswomen, their gender holds another decided advantage. When a white Jewish woman serves a poor African American customer, for the duration of the interaction and within the confines of the store, racial, ethnic, and class hierarchies are overturned. As a Jewish storeowner in East Harlem remarks about his wife, who had recently passed away, "The customers loved my wife. The worst thing that would ever come out of her mouth is, 'Now that wasn't very nice,' and they just loved being served by a white woman." In asserting that his customers had "loved being served by a white woman," he points out how race, class, and gender intersect to shape the service interaction. He recognizes that whereas most contact between white women and African Americans normally takes on a hierarchical dimension—with white women in charge—in the relationship between Jewish business-owners and African American customers, the roles are uniquely reversed. For blacks, to be served by a white woman is symbolically significant, which is precisely why the Jewish women who still work in these retail businesses are artfully positioned at the front of the store, where they can effectively manage customer interactions. In essence, female merchants are not passive agents in the shadows, but maternal brokers who actively attempt to forge better relations with their customers, defuse tensions, and preserve the civility of day-to-day commercial life.

Amid the affection and abrasion, merchants and customers accede that the majority of their interactions are routine and ordinary. Certainly there are merchants who greet their customers rudely, as well as rude customers who slam money down on the counter and refuse to make eye contact. However, most agree that daily commercial life is just business as usual.[20] In fact, throughout my months of participant and nonparticipant observation, most striking were the normalcy and civility in the day-to-day routine of mercantile life in black neighborhoods.

What is important to note, however, is that the routine does not come without effort; it is the product of work on the part of the merchants and their employees, who realize that heading off altercations with their customers is their primary goal in running a successful operation. Whether that work entails acquiescing to customers' charges that stains were left on their dry cleaning, taking something back that has been used or damaged, or simply holding their tongue, merchants understand that to keep the peace, they need to bend the rules and comply with customers' demands. That the vast majority of merchant-customer interactions are conflict free demonstrates that the interactions in themselves are not the source of the hostility that leads to boycotts, firebombings, and riots, a point I will elaborate on in Chapter 7.

Nonetheless, within the merchant-customer relationship, there is a considerable amount of variation. The retail niche, the merchant's experience and fictive kinship, the customers' age, and the merchants' gender are variables that affect merchant-customer relations. With time, merchants come to recognize that the residents of inner-city neighborhoods are not all welfare queens, drug addicts, or criminals. Experience teaches Jewish and Korean storeowners that these urban neighborhoods are organized, structured, and in fact quite normal. Likewise, with repeated contact, the customers come to realize that merchants are individuals, not the rigid and monolithic racial and ethnic stereotypes the media purport them to be. African American merchants hold a distinct advantage in this regard, as their race allows them to evoke a sense of fictive kinship with their clientele. Finally, gender is an important interactional resource for merchants in poor black neighborhoods. Female retailers adopt roles that require specialized emotional labor, and women also act as maternal brokers, effectively handling the day-to-day routine and soothing rising tensions.

Nevertheless, Korean and Jewish storeowners realize that, regardless of how long they have been in business or how well they may get along with members of the community, as racially distinct minorities in predominantly black neighborhoods, their race can inflect merchant-customer interactions in diverse and conflict-ridden ways. Race can indeed become the source of protest motivations that lead to boycotts and other, more violent forms of overt conflict. The following chapter explores how seemingly trivial economic disputes become racialized and ethnicized and describes the useful strategies that nonblack storeowners adopt to minimize tension and keep it from erupting into conflict.

CHAPTER 5

How Race Polarizes Interactions: Cultural Brokers and the Meaning of Black

I'm white, and I deal with the black customers. Sometimes you have problems, but 99 percent of the time you never have problems because we always try to deal with the customer. We always have the philosophy that they're right. But always, you're going to have problems that we're not able to solve, but you see that if it gets to a racial point, or if the customer feels that it's racial, then you give him to somebody of his own race, and he cannot say that anymore.
 —Greek salesman in a Jewish-owned furniture store

It just shows that it's totally backwards. It's reverse racism is what it is. And anytime there's an argument about anything, it always comes down to, "You damn Orientals are taking over all the businesses in the neighborhood!" or "You Koreans are doing it!" . . . This isn't all the time, but every once in a while you get a customer who's totally unreasonable, and if things don't go their way, they pull that old card out of their pocket, the race card, and throw it down.
 —Korean merchant in West Philadelphia

Although the daily commercial life in black communities may be characterized by routine and civility, merchants must sometimes deal with the resentments of race and class that are present in low-income black communities like New York's Harlem and West Philadelphia. Seemingly trivial arguments—for instance, over exchanges without receipts or exchanges of used or damaged merchandise—can quickly become racialized when the merchants are Jewish, Korean, or, for that matter, from any nonblack racial group. Race can infuse merchant-customer relations in diverse ways and can polarize the simplest interactions.

For examining the tricky area of merchant-customer conflict, Robert K. Merton's concept of "in-group virtues" and "out-group vices" is particularly useful.[1] Merton demonstrates that similar patterns of behavior by what he calls in-group and out-group members are differently perceived and evaluated. Seemingly trivial economic disputes between Jewish and Korean merchants and their black customers can become loaded with symbolism, with both parties responding not only to the objective features of the situation but also to the meaning the situation has for them. Recognizing that arguments can easily become racialized, some nonblack business owners have responded by hiring black employees as cultural brokers to defuse mounting tensions, obviate conflict, and socially embed their businesses in black neighborhoods. However, hiring black employees does not necessarily mean employing African Americans. America's new urban immigrants are affecting hiring practices in the inner-city retail niche in unforeseen ways.

In-Group Virtues and Out-Group Vices

Throughout my research, I examined the extent to which Jewish, Korean, and black storeowners behave differently toward their black customers and the extent to which similar patterns of behavior are defined and differently perceived by their customers.[2] The Haitian manager of a large, chain, inner-city sportswear store in East Harlem explained why the owners of his store—who happen to be Jewish—always have a black store manager instead of a white manager in this Harlem location by describing the following scenario. If a customer comes in, he said, and wants to return a pair of sneakers that he bought, and for whatever reason the black manager does not take them back, the customer might get upset but that is the end of it. But if it is the white storeowner who does not take the sneakers back, then the customer might immediately assume that it is because the owner is white that he will not take them back. Similarly, if the storeowner is Korean and refuses, the customer might assume that it is because he is Korean.

The same behavior by black, Jewish, and Korean storeowners can be differently perceived and evaluated by the black customer because he sees Jewish and Korean merchants as part of the out-group, or as outsiders, and the black merchant as part of the in-group, or as an insider.[3] As Merton explains, "The very same behavior undergoes a complete change of evaluation in its transition from the in-group [black merchants] to the out-group [Jewish and Korean merchants]."[4] What is not a racial argument to begin with can take on a racial tone or become racially coded when the storeowner is racially or ethnically different from the customer. A Puerto Rican employee of a Jewish-owned electronic store in West Harlem observes,

> It only comes up when you don't give them [customers] proper service or they think they're getting ripped off . . . If someone wants to bring something back after four or five months because it doesn't work anymore and they don't have their receipt, we don't replace it. Then they'll say something stupid, something racial.

Recalling a former black employee at the same store, he explains how customers didn't "say anything racial to him because he was black. They [black customers] tend to separate us. It's harder for us to calm down someone who . . . [is not] of the same race or color."

Similarly, a Jewish merchant in a furniture store in East Harlem complains that when he brings to court delinquent customers to whom he has extended credit, "They say to me, 'You're doing this because I'm black.' And I say to them, 'I don't care if you're yellow, white, green, purple or whatever. I'm taking you to court because you haven't paid your bill.'" Even long-time Jewish storeowners admit they have been the recipients of racial and ethnic slurs from angry customers, who have said everything from "damn whitey," "Jew bastard," and "cheap Jew," to "We can Jew him down." Jewish veterans claim that regardless of how long they have been in the community, some irate customers will resort to sly remarks about their race, ethnicity, or religion when they are dissatisfied with the store's policies. For instance, a second-generation Jewish storeowner on Jamaica Avenue relays, "I've had incidents in the past where I've heard some racial mumblings coming from their ignorant breaths, but I live with it. Like a black guy says, 'You white motherfucker,' or something like that, but I don't let it bother me." Although their practices may not be any worse than those of other retailers, Jewish merchants' dominating commercial presence—in the past and the present—leads black customers to define their complaints against them in racial or ethnic terms. When the businessowners are Jewish, customers' gripes are apt to find expression in anti-Semitic or antiwhite stereotypes.[5]

Although Jewish businessowners complain about the slurs leveled against them by angry customers, as racially and ethnically distinct newcomers to America's urban scene, Korean immigrant merchants are even more vulnerable. All of the Korean merchants interviewed say that at some point while doing business (particularly at the beginning), monetary arguments have quickly taken on racial overtones. For example, the Korean owner of a furniture store in West Philadelphia explains that when customers become irate, "the argument always goes down to race." Accusations such as, "You damn Orientals are coming into our neighborhoods taking over every fucking store!" are not uncommon in poor communities when merchants and customers come to an impasse over exchanges or refunds of merchandise. In one particular case, when the Korean storeowner refused to take back the floor model furniture that he had recently sold to a woman at a discount, she immediately said to her mother, "He's just a chink and a gook." Incensed by the racial epithet, the Korean merchant retorted, "Now wait a minute, what would happen if I called you a nigger? What would happen then? You're sitting here calling me these names, what if I did that to you?" Infuriated, the woman threatened to start picketing outside the store but ultimately did not follow through. The Korean storeowner, commenting about the matter, decries what he calls a system of "reverse racism" where blacks now exploit the "race card."

> And it's a shame that they got to stoop to that level just to get what they want. I mean if they were to talk to me reasonable, without yelling and ranting and raving, we probably would have got things worked out more to their liking. But you can't come in here and yell at somebody and expect to get what you want.

Even long-time Jewish and Korean veterans of Harlem and West Philadelphia—who know most of their customers—fully realize that their nonblack status can easily make them targets for hostile customers, boycotters, and rioters. For example, after the firebombing of Freddy's, the Jewish-owned clothing store in West Harlem, protestors immediately moved to boycott a long-established Jewish-owned store on the same avenue, yelling, "Kill the Jew bastards" and "This block is for blacks only, no whites and Jews allowed."[6] Similarly, a Korean grocer on Jamaica Avenue, whose business has served the Queens community for twelve years, experienced a six-month-long boycott, with protestors shouting such taunts as, "Go back to Korea!" Other Jewish and Korean businessowners on the same block readily recall receiving racial and ethnic slurs ranging from "damn whitey" and "cheap Jew" to "chink" and "gook" at the time of the Jamaica Avenue boycott. The fact that a Korean merchant has been in business for more than a decade and a Jewish merchant is a second-generation storeowner who has been in business for more than forty years can hold little relevance when tensions run high and discourse becomes racialized or ethnicized.

How Race Polarizes Interactions

When simple economic arguments become loaded with symbolism, customers and merchants begin to respond primarily to the *meaning* that the argument has for them. Eric Yamamoto's discussion of stock stories elucidates how race polarizes simple interactions, transforming economic arguments into racialized conflict. Stock stories are "a conglomeration of group members' selective historical recollections, partial information of events and socioeconomic conditions, and speculations about the future . . . The narratives create social identities for group members. They also influence the dynamics of interracial relations by providing the lens through which group members see and understand other groups."[7] Stock stories are used to justify a group's perceptions of and interactions with others. For example, when African American customers are denied a refund by a Jewish or Korean merchant, they may adopt the stock story of an exploitative outsider affronting and taking advantage of a black customer and the black community at large. The merchant's refusal reinforces the stock story and, furthermore, becomes symbolic of the power, class, and status distinctions between two racially and ethnically distinct groups. Correlatively, when black customers become angry and yell at merchants because they are denied a refund, or when they have defaulted on their payments, Jewish and Korean storeowners may indulge in stock stories about blacks—that they are violent, ignorant, uneducated, and not to be trusted. In each scenario, merchants and customers draw on stock stories to interpret behavior and, consequently, racially code what are essentially economic arguments.

Because race is the most apparent distinction between people, an

economic dispute between a merchant and a customer can easily become a racialized dispute between a black and a Korean or a black and
a Jew. Here, class matters. Whereas Jewish and Korean merchants must
sometimes deal with the resentments of race and class that are present
in low-income neighborhoods fraught with poverty, and extreme inequality, their counterparts in middle-income neighborhoods such as
Mount Airy are generally shielded from this type of bitterness and animosity. An African American customer in West Philadelphia explains
the complexities of the merchant-customer relationship and offers
insights about the tension and frustration resulting from life in the inner city.

> Well there is a certain amount of sensitivity here because black folks,
> living the way we do, we have a certain amount of cynicism, so when we
> go into these stores, we're like angry, cursing them out and everything,
> and they're like, "You come in my store and you're cursing at me! You
> get out my store!" And a lot of people around here, they're stealing,
> they're strung out on something, don't know no better, trying to be
> cool. It's a whole myriad of things. That's why when I walk into a store,
> they're watching me. I haven't stole a thing in my life, too scared. I'm
> not going to say I never had a thought, but I'm just too scared, and I'm
> not going to do it. And there's a certain amount of despair, which is
> why they don't care if they get caught.

By contrast, in middle-class black neighborhoods—where residents
are far more likely to be financially secure—arguments between merchants and customers rarely escalate into racially or ethnically charged
altercations. An African American customer expresses this clearly:
"When you're in an environment where you're struggling to just try to
feed your family and then you have to deal with outside influences,
sometimes things can overheat. Whereas if you're in an environment
where you're feeding your family and taking care of your bills, little
problems won't bother you as much."

Moreover, when there exist ready-made anti-Semitic, anti-Asian, and
anti-immigrant frameworks in the larger society, customers can easily
situate their negative personal experiences with Jewish and Korean
merchants. In other words, the presence of anti-Semitism and anti-immigrant sentiment make being Jewish and being Korean (or Asian
more generally) a salient characteristic of being a bad merchant.[8] Cor-

relatively, the ready-made frameworks for blacks in our society make it all too easy for nonblack merchants to situate their negative encounters with black customers.

As merchants and customers adopt these frameworks, social processes begin to override individual, psychological processes. Social psychologists have long noted that people interact not only as individuals on an interpersonal level, but also as members of their groups standing in defined relationships to members of other groups.[9] While a person may have experienced dozens, hundreds, or even thousands of positive encounters with individuals from an out-group, one negative experience can stir stock stories that have little to do with the situation at hand. When tensions run high, numerous positive interpersonal experiences are easily abandoned in favor of negative out-group stereotypes.

Schema theory helps us to understand this pattern. A schema is "a cognitive structure through which interpretations of the world are made."[10] Schema theory posits that individuals perceive out-groups as less variable than in-groups and, moreover, that individuals remember behavior that confirms a group stereotype.[11] For example, when a customer recalls an instance of being followed around a store or having trouble returning an article of clothing or a pair of sneakers, it reinforces the stereotype that out-group merchants are untrusting and stingy. Likewise, when a customer wants to return a dress that has already been worn, it reinforces for the merchant the stock story that poor black customers are sly, untrustworthy, and will try "to get over on you" whenever they can. When the merchant is Jewish or Korean and the customer is black, these behaviors may be seen as particularly fitting since they become just another example of the relevant schema.

By contrast, black customers perceive black merchants as part of the in-group, thereby shielding them from this type of resentment. Their "blackness" gives them a "coethnic advantage" over their Jewish and Korean counterparts in business. For instance, when asked whether her merchant-customer disputes ever take on racial overtones, the African American owner of a furniture store in West Philadelphia laughed and replied, "They don't say that to me. Well they can't because I'm black and they're black!" Because both are black, when customers become irate toward black merchants, arguments do not become racialized or ethnicized in the same way that they do with Jewish or Korean merchants. However, black merchants must deal with another form of racialization—in-group racialization—that has different origins and meanings, but has severe consequences nonetheless.

Blacks as Cultural Brokers

To minimize arguments with their customers, both Jewish and Korean merchants have found a viable alternative: hiring black employees and managers to act as "cultural brokers" between them and their predominantly black clientele. Black employees serve this function in a variety of ways: as language bridges, as cultural bridges, as symbols that the merchants are "giving something back to the community," and, most important, as conflict resolvers. The logic of the market and culture obliges color-coded hiring. For many Jewish and Korean merchants in the inner-city, race has become a bona fide occupational qualification (BFOQ) in hiring.[12] However, many businessowners prefer hiring blacks for reasons that have nothing to do with Title VII of the 1964 Civil Rights Act or government pressure for affirmative action, but rather because of their perceived utility as cultural brokers in dealing with a predominantly black customer base.

Language Bridges

For first-generation immigrant merchants—who often do not have a good command of the English language—hiring black employees is particularly instrumental, since the employees bridge the language barrier between them and their native-born clientele. Correlatively, black customers in immigrant-owned shops appreciate finding black employees with whom they can communicate. Without language brokers, black customers can easily become frustrated when they have difficulty conveying their needs to foreign-born storeowners, as an African American customer from West Harlem illustrates.

> These people are running the register, and they can't speak the language. I asked the [Korean] lady for 600 Polaroid film, and she's like, "600?" I'm like, "Right there." You know, I don't mean to be ignorant, but I was like, "It's right there, right there! The blue one!" She didn't know what blue was, but she could count the money!

Even more bothersome for this customer is that although immigrant storeowners may not comprehend English well enough to fully serve their customers, they have no problems counting and taking their money, reinforcing the stereotype of the money-grubbing ghetto merchant. Another customer from Philadelphia admits that the language barrier is one chief source of frustration associated with shopping in "foreign" stores. Not only does she have difficulty explaining what she would like, but she also finds it impossible to understand the merchants. In turn, she senses that the shopkeepers assume that it is *she* who is stupid.

> I want to be waited on by someone who understands what it is I'm looking for. Sometimes there's a communication problem when you go into foreign stores, so I tend to not go into them, because you're getting frustrated because you can't get them to understand what it is you want. And they're getting frustrated because they don't understand, and they think you're stupid. So I really don't frequent them a lot.

Language brokering is also reflected in the increasing number of Latino employees in East Harlem and Jamaica, Queens, both of which have sizeable proportions of Latino customers. The growth of the Spanish-speaking population leads storeowners to hire bilingual employees to serve as language brokers for their clientele, as a Jewish gift shop owner in Queens explains.

> I have black and Spanish employees because we have a lot of Spanish people coming into the store, and they don't speak English.[13] And they want somebody who can speak Spanish. They spend a lot of money in the stores, just like anybody else, and most of them are brand new immigrants to the country. I mean, if I had Oriental people, I'd hire an Oriental. You have to go by the customers. It's like me having a store in a black neighborhood and having only white cake tops, you know? You can't sell that way. You have to go by your customers' needs and what they are.

The practice of race matching is not unique to inner-city retailers, as Harry Holzer and Keith Ihlanfeldt's work on employers' hiring preferences illustrates. They find that the racial composition of a firm's customer base has a sizable effect on who gets hired, particularly in businesses that involve customer contact. The hiring of blacks and Hispanics rises dramatically with the percentages of customers who are members of each group. More specifically, Holzer and Ihlanfeldt find that "the percentages of new hires who are black or Hispanic each rise from about 10 percent to 60 percent as we move from customers who are predominantly white to those who are mostly black or Hispanic, respectively."[14]

The use of black employees as language brokers is a practice not only among Korean immigrant entrepreneurs but also among American-born Jewish merchants, who affirm that black employees have a certain way of "talking" and "dealing" with fellow blacks. Although Jewish merchants are fluent in English, they benefit from hiring black employees because they claim that blacks have distinct interactional styles, tastes, and modes of communication—often using street slang or the black English vernacular.[15] The use of language brokers by native-born Jewish retailers reveals how different the black, inner-city speech patterns and cultural styles have become from those of middle-class whites. A Jewish retailer in Mount Airy frankly states,

> It does help when you have an African American employee in an African American neighborhood. It creates a good atmosphere, rather than, let's say, an all Jewish or all white, Anglo-Saxon staff in a neighborhood that is opposite of you, or all Koreans for that matter. It makes good communications, and he can talk to the customers in many ways I cannot relate to, just by him being a man of the neighborhood. And that helps a lot in many ways.

Black employees are generally better at dealing with coethnics and have an ease with their customers that nonblacks may develop only with time. As an African American manager of a Jewish-owned clothing store in Queens acknowledges, "Sometimes you have to develop a way of talking to people. You have to know who you're talking to. And with most of our trade coming here, 95 percent black, if you don't have the right way of talking, you're in trouble." While I was interviewing the African American manager, three black customers (one male and two females) interrupted us to purchase a red T-shirt. Following is the taped conversation that ensued between the African American manager and the male customer, who attempted to bargain for a discount on behalf of his friend:

Customer: Don't charge her tax, she's broke.

Manager: Why not?

Customer: She's broke.

Manager: No she's not. Nobody's broke. You're never broke. And besides I can see why you have so much money. I can see all the money written all over your faces. That's the money sign you have on your faces there. It's only $9.73. We'll wait 'til you're broke. We'll wait 'til you're broke and then we'll make a deal. We'll wait 'til an emergency. It's $9.73 today, and next week we'll talk about it.

Customer: Only $9.73. Next week we'll work on our bargain. Okay, see you next week.

The three young customers left the store without even a grumble. In this interaction, the manger refuses to give the customers a tax break or a discount, yet he handles the interaction with aplomb, in a manner in which he does not offend the customers by declining their request. In effect, he uses flattery to convey that his customers appear to have money and therefore should not need a discount.

This interaction stands in sharp contrast to one that I witnessed between a black male customer and the Korean storeowner while I was working as a cashier in a sneaker store. The customer intended to purchase four pairs of sneakers, each ranging in price from $100 to $140. As the salesman placed the sneakers on the counter for me to ring up, the customer asked him, "How much do I get off for buying all these shoes?" The salesman turned to the female Korean storeowner, who replied, "We don't do that here." The customer then fired back, "I'm buying four pairs of shoes, and you won't work with me? Who can I talk to here?" The storeowner repeated more firmly, "Nobody does that here." The customer walked to the register and slammed a wad of bills on the counter, which the storeowner helped me count. After counting the money and bagging up the sneakers, I handed the customer the four bags, and said, "Thanks. Have a nice day." Without looking in my direction, the customer grabbed the bags and walked out of the store.

Although the Korean merchant and the African American manager both denied their customers a discount, the way in which they said no powerfully affected their interactions. In the first interaction, with the African American manager, the customer left without any signs of dissatisfaction, whereas in the second, the male customer avoided eye contact and abruptly left the store after the transaction came to a close. Merchants and managers can say no to customers in many ways, but as these interactions illustrate, most immigrant shopowners do not possess the sophisticated interpersonal skills required to deal artfully with such customer requests.

Cultural Bridges

Black employees also serve as cultural bridges, because they have the culturally specific knowledge needed to sell to a black clientele. They are more familiar with ethnic products, such as food, wigs, and skin- and hair-care products, thus bridging the cultural gap between the nonblack owners and their black clientele. Black employees are also better at selling apparel, sneakers, and jewelry to coethnics, since they have a keener sense of the fashion trends in today's urban black market. "Black employees are better for the customers. They're better for language and thinking. They know what the customers want," states the Korean owner of a jewelry store. A Korean woman who sells inner-city sportswear in West Harlem says that her black employees know how to sell to her black customers: "Black people say each other, 'Oh you look good. This look good.' They know everything, they know." Even her American-born son, who helps out on the weekends, recognizes that race matching provides benefits that go beyond language brokering. "African American employees respond better to the customers, talk to them better, and they're better salesmen."

Furthermore, black customers seek out black employees, conveying that there is a "cultural connection" and that "black employees understand what I'm looking for better." Evoking a sense of fictive kinship with black employees, a young female shopper from Queens simply explains, "My sister or my brother can relate to me better than a Korean or a Jewish person. A sister, if it's a girl, she'll really talk to me and tell me what looks good." Black employees increase the comfort level for customers who prefer dealing with "their own" while shopping, as a Jewish merchant in West Harlem notices: "If you have African Americans working in the stores, the customers feel more comfortable. If all of my employees were white, then people probably wouldn't want to shop here." The customers affirm this sentiment. An African American male shopper in West Philadelphia tries to elaborate why he prefers dealing with coethnics: "I usually feel more comfortable asking help from the black attendants because I feel more comfortable with black people. That's not saying much, but that about sums it up. I feel more comfortable, more relaxed. I like being around my own." The importance of creating a comfortable shopping environment for black customers should be underscored. Black-dominant social spaces—and black communities more generally—are refuges from the daily strain of navigating in predominantly white and racially heterogeneous social settings.

Cultural brokers are not new. When Jewish merchants predominated in neighborhoods like Harlem and West Philadelphia decades ago, they too employed many blacks in order to cater to their ethnic market. An African American merchant who specializes in gospel music explains that in the 1950s and '60s, Jewish merchants often entered black ethnic niches—such as gospel and rhythm and blues music (then labeled as "race" music)—because they could rely on black employees to assist their customers. He explains, "Well, Jewish people had black employees. They had a lot. Sometimes you walked into the store, and you might not even see the Jewish person at all. He might be home some place, and the manager would be there, running the place, taking care of the business."

Giving Back to the Community

Apart from their roles as language and cultural bridges, black employees are also visible symbols that merchants are giving something back to the community from which they profit. Jewish, Korean, and black merchants agree that because they earn their living from the community, they feel that it is important to hire from within—virtually reciting the rhetoric of past and present black nationalist leaders such as Marcus Garvey; Ira Reid; Adam Clayton Powell, Jr.; and Al Sharpton. In fact, when Jewish and Korean merchants do not employ blacks, especially in the larger businesses, merchants feel pressure from black nationalist leaders and even from some local residents to hire black employees. For example, a Jewish storeowner on Jamaica Avenue in Queens senses a subtle form of disapproval when his black employees take the day off, leaving only his cousin and himself to run the store.

The argument in these neighborhoods is, if you don't have blacks employed for you, they object to that. They feel as though you come in
and you take money out of the community, but you don't give anything
back. I've had times where it was just Eric [my cousin] and myself here,
and people would come in and they would look, and I know what
they're looking at.

For some residents, the number of black employees in a business is an
indicator of the extent to which Jewish and Korean merchants "give
back" to the community in which they make their living. An African
American shopper in West Harlem states that it would just be "out-
landish" for nonblack businessowners who set up shop in black communities not to hire from within: "A lot of times you see black people
working in these stores. I think that is because it would be just outland-
ish for someone, if you're not from the community, to just not have
anybody representing the community. You need to give back something."

The ideology of giving back to the community stems from the black
nationalist philosophy of the "double-duty dollar"—recycling profits
back into the neighborhood, thereby uplifting and advancing the community at large. First proposed in 1941 by Carlos Cook, the founder of
the African Nationalist Pioneers, the ideology of giving back to the
community is strongly embraced by African Americans even to this
day. The customers we interviewed firmly believe that because Jewish
and Korean merchants do not live in their community, the dollars they
make leave with them at night. The politics of the double-duty dollar
rests on the belief that black businessowners will live in the community
in which they serve, thereby recycling the revenue back into their
neighborhood. With the infusion of recycled capital, the double-duty
dollar will ultimately lift the community out of its depressed economic
condition and advance blacks as a group. However, only two of the
black storeowners in my sample actually live in the low-income community in which they do business; most black businessowners are no
different from their Jewish and Korean counterparts, who reside in
more affluent suburbs outside of the inner city. Therefore, the ideology behind the double-duty dollar—which residents support in theory—is an antiquated and romantic notion that is no longer viable
today. However, hiring black employees is a simple and, more impor-

tant, visible symbol of giving something back to the community and a means of socially embedding nonblack-owned businesses in black neighborhoods.[16]

De-Racializing Tension

Aside from their function as language bridges, cultural bridges, and symbols of giving back, most critically black employees serve as arbitrators who can defuse and de-racialize anger.[17] To capture his relationship with his Korean employer, an African American man in East Harlem asked me, "Did you see the movie [*The Bodyguard*] with Whitney Houston and Kevin Costner? That's me. I'm her bodyguard, her protection, her interpreter." Similarly, sitting near the door of a Jewish-owned pawn shop in West Philadelphia is a large African American man named J.D., who weighs more than 300 pounds. His black cowboy hat covers his forehead, and his dark, tinted sunglasses mask his eyes so that one cannot discern who he is watching. The pawn shop owner feels that J.D.'s menacing presence alone not only protects him from racialized tension but also deters robberies. Black customers agree that black employees often protect nonblack merchants from rising tensions or conflicts, often labeling blacks as the "front person" or "strong man."

While working as a bag checker in a clothing store on 125th Street in West Harlem, I observed the defusing process in action as a Korean merchant explained his reliance on black employees to smooth out incidents. He said to me, "If you have black management, no problem, but if you have a Korean manager or whatever, you can get into trouble." On the heels of this logical explanation, a black customer tried to exchange the dirty pants he was wearing for a new pair. The Korean storeowner handed him off to the black manager, who told the man, "I'm not disputing that you bought the pants here, sir, but we wouldn't have sold them to you like that. Look at all our pants here, none of them look like that. That's your hand that made them like that. Here, look at my pocket. If I'm reaching in there all the time and my hand is dirty, then they're going to get dirty. It's your hand." The storeowner, visibly nervous when the man refused the manager's explanation, said, "Call the police." But the manager reassured him, "We don't need to call the police. He's just drunk. When he comes around tomorrow, he'll come back and apologize." The storeowner then turned to me and said, "If that was a Korean manager, there would have been a little bit of commotion."

As new immigrants who do not have a firm grasp of the English language or its nuances, Korean merchants agree that black employees are notably better at understanding grievances and calming irate, unreasonable, drunk, or high customers. Black employees also serve as protectors who sometimes physically wedge themselves between their employers and angry customers. For instance, when a Korean storeowner refused to give a woman a refund for an already-worn dress, the customer became belligerent, raising her voice at the merchant. A black female employee immediately walked from the back of the store and stood between the furious customer and her employer to defuse the tension. She later explained why she chose to position herself physically between the two parties: "When customers get into fights with Mrs. Lee, I'll get in the middle. If they start fighting with Mrs. Lee, I don't like that. I don't like it when they're nasty to her like that."

Jewish merchants have also adopted the strategy of using black employees to negotiate racialized disputes with their customers. As the Greek salesman in a Jewish-owned furniture store on Jamaica Avenue says, the "racial element" can be made to disappear simply by handing the customer off to a black salesperson: "If it gets to a racial point, or if the customer feels that it's racial, then you give him to somebody of his own race, and he cannot say that anymore." Black employees negotiate with customers, often preventing economic arguments from escalating into racially charged anger.

The 1992 Los Angeles riot proved to be a turning point for Korean merchants in South Central L.A.; their number of black hires nearly doubled after the massive uprising.[18] Looking back historically, Jewish merchants reacted similarly after riots swept the nation's major cities in the 1960s; they too began hiring more black sales associates and managers to alleviate tensions.[19] Black residents were quick to note the change in the hiring patterns following the nationally televised L.A. riot and the boycotts of the Korean-owned fruit and vegetable markets in Brooklyn. One customer said that Koreans now hire blacks because they fear another uprising.

The community had some problems with a particular store in Brooklyn, and Al Sharpton did a lot of demonstrating in front of the store, and since then, they started hiring blacks. Before, they would never hire our people, and since they had that problem, they hire them. The ones that have blacks in them, they afraid something gonna happen, so what they do, they hire our people.

From the perspective of black managers and sales associates, brokering and mediating heated arguments between the customers and their nonblack employers is just part of the job. And even when customers accuse the managers and workers of "taking the other side" and acting like "Uncle Toms," black employees firmly hold their ground, recognizing that their job is not worth succumbing to peer pressure. At same time, however, some black employees may choose to turn a blind eye to small-time shoplifters, which can leave Jewish and Korean merchants unable to fully trust their workers. But regardless of whether nonblack merchants completely trust their workers, they understand that their black employees serve a critical function that is well worth the price of petty theft. And fully cognizant that their presence defuses rising tensions, black employees realize all too well that there would be far more racial animosity between the black customers and the nonblack storeowners were they not there to handle customer gripes. A black manager of a clothing store in Harlem candidly maintains,

> When I'm here, 99 percent of the time, everything comes through that door [exchanges or returns], I gotta look at it. And I have gotten some things that are worn, chopped off. It's an absolute fact that if I weren't the manager, they would have more problems with exchanges. It's a fact because the customers always think, "Whitey's trying to get over them." They use that expression. So they will get hostile very fast. The owners would have to change their way of talking very much or either take back a lot of stuff they don't want to take back just to keep the peace because there really would be a hostile situation. All you have to do is see it once.

Black customers can easily interpret the refusal to exchange merchandise within a racialized framework, with the refusal representing the power relation between whites and blacks. Statements such as "Whitey's trying to get over on me" and "You damn Orientals are coming into our neighborhoods taking over every store" are symbolic expressions of how black customers construct race, opportunity, and exploitation. Implicit is the sense that blacks resent the racial and ethnic hierarchy in which they find themselves, once again, at the bottom. Jewish and Korean merchants are acutely aware that black employees bridge the racial, class, and status gaps, and most important, defuse and neutralize arguments. The black employees' in-group status often protects merchants from exploding tempers, largely keeping day-to-day tensions at a controlled level.

The Racial and Ethnic Meaning of "Black"

To simply describe these employees as "black," however, obscures the way the term carries both ethnic and racial meanings. With regard to the retailers' hiring practices, this is where the New York City and Philadelphia comparison is most illuminating. The black hiring in New York City reveals a preference for Caribbean and West African blacks over African Americans. In contrast, the blacks who work for Jewish and Korean businessowners in Philadelphia are largely African American. What may be construed as a preference for such ethnic groups as West Indians and Africans reveals a preference for immigrants. Table 5.1 illustrates that in New York City, foreign-born blacks are significantly more likely to be hired than the native-born in these retail businesses, accounting for 69 percent of the black hires in Jewish-owned stores and 76 percent of the black employees in Korean-owned stores. Even the black-owned stores in New York City had a slightly higher proportion of foreign-born hires, reflecting black immigrant managers' preferences for coethnics. Table 5.2 shows that in Philadelphia, merchants hire African Americans. In New York City, where one-quarter of the black population is foreign-born, Jewish and Korean merchants and black immigrant managers alike overwhelmingly choose to hire black immigrants over African Americans. By sharp contrast, in Philadelphia, where only 3 percent of blacks are born outside of the United States, virtually all of the black hires are African American.

By illustration, a Jewish storeowner in West Harlem who underscored the need for hiring "African Americans" has three black employees, a West African, a Haitian, and a Colombian. New York City retailers generally agree that black immigrants, regardless of ethnic background, are more willing than African Americans to put in the

Table 5.1 Percentage of foreign-born and native-born black employees in New York

	Jewish merchants	Korean merchants	Black merchants
Foreign-born (%)	69	76	55
Native-born (%)	31	24	45
Total N	45	43	22

Table 5.2 Percentage of foreign-born and native-born black employees in Philadelphia

Black employees	Jewish merchants	Korean merchants	Black merchants
Foreign-born (%)	0	7	0
Native-born (%)	100	93	100
Total N	9	14	15

long hours and the physically exhausting labor required in retail. However, small retailers in inner cities are not the first to disclose their preference for immigrants. Studies of employers' hiring preferences in the hotel, restaurant, fast-food, and manufacturing industries, coupled with the high employment rates of immigrant groups, reveal that in industries across the spectrum, employers overwhelmingly choose black immigrants over African Americans.[20]

Most merchants—especially those who are foreign-born and especially those who have "made it"—do not understand why native-born Americans do not take advantage of the business opportunities before them. Immigrants—whether Korean, Jewish, or black—are extremely critical of the American-born, particularly African Americans in low-income neighborhoods, whom they believe lack the drive to take advantage of the opportunities open to all and use past oppression as a crutch. An immigrant from Spain—who worked his way up from janitor to sales manager in charge of hiring for a large Jewish-owned furniture store on Jamaica Avenue—speaks candidly about his disdain for the work ethic among native-born Americans, defending his preference for immigrants and scoffing at race-based affirmative action policies in hiring.

> It has a lot to do with the culture. See, I also come from outside. The reason why I became the vice president of the previous company is because of my background. Hard work. It's like your background. *We were taught that nothing is going to be given to us from this world.*[21] You got to be respectful of your elders and the company that you work for, and you have to be dedicated and prove to yourself that you're better than the rest. And don't look at your limitations but your potential, and don't come up with excuses.
>
> Unfortunately in America because of the social and political upheaval in the '60s, early '70s, everything changed and everybody thought that we had to give our kids everything for free. People that are born here don't have the drive. They don't have the values and the principles that are going to make them successful because this is unfortunately a society that's a welfare society. They give you a job because you're a minority. They're going to give you a job because you are Asian American, because you're black, because you speak Spanish, and that is the wrong way to assess the work force. You give the job, in my book, to the one who deserves it the most, even if they're pink, as long as they show proficiency in what they do.
>
> Unfortunately, society is trying to come up with excuses to promote people without capabilities, without knowledge, based on color, based on appearance, based on limitations. They're not trying to get the most capable people; those are the ones you help, if you give them a chance. But they're not doing it.
>
> You, me, and people who come from outside because our way of living is so hard, we were taught that we have to work hard for what we want. Don't wait for handouts. That's a big difference. It's very simple. Everybody knows it, but only a few want to admit it because it's not politically correct.

Similarly, a storeowner in Queens shares his view that affirmative action is "a bunch of baloney" and should not sway the hiring process:

> That's why I'm not a believer in affirmative action, because affirmative action is not based on your qualifications, it's based on whether you're a man, whether you're a woman, whether you're black, whether you're

white, whether you're yellow. That doesn't qualify for me. If you were here, and there's a polka-dotted person, and that person had more knowledge about my business than you do, I'd hire them, not because they're polka-dotted, but because they have knowledge. That's the way jobs were based on, not on anything else. And that's why I think affirmative action is a bunch of baloney, it really is.

Small business owners believe that they should be able to hire those who are most qualified for the position, but the most important qualifications seem to be a willingness to work long hours for little pay, with few, if any, benefits and no chance of job mobility. Retailers largely prefer immigrants over the native-born because they feel that native-born Americans are socialized to expect decent working conditions, no less than the minimum wage, and certain benefits that many small retail businesses do not offer. Compared with the native-born, immigrants appear to be more docile workers who are far less likely to complain about a low (often below minimum) hourly wage, a six-day work week, and a lack of health or material benefits. Their tractability places them ahead of native-born Americans in the labor queue. Retailers assert that a sense of entitlement epitomizes much of the difference between African Americans and immigrants.[22]

For instance, a second-generation Jewish merchant in West Harlem who has between forty and fifty employees frankly states that African Americans are less willing to work in retail than black immigrants. His preference for immigrants over native-born Americans is evident from the majority of foreign-born employees in his workforce. He explains,

Native African Americans tend not to like to work in a retail store. It's not *our* choice, it's *their* choice. They feel that they're at a different level for the most part, so you don't get them applying as much. The retail level is an entry-level position, it's a little bit above minimum wage, but it's not a great wage. Somebody comes in and the color of their skin is black but their heritage is not American, they're willing more to start at a lower pay and hopefully get a little bit ahead. You don't have to stay here your entire life, but it's a nice place to start.

Korean and Jewish storeowners are not the only ones to demonstrate a preference for immigrants; black immigrants in New York City neighborhoods also favor the foreign-born when hiring. For example, a black storeowner in West Harlem, who is American-born but whose parents are of Caribbean descent and who identifies herself as West Indian, has three employees, all of whom are immigrants: one from St. Martin, one from Trinidad, and another from Africa. She—like her Jewish and Korean counterparts—expresses the same preference for the foreign-born and disdain for African Americans.

Accounting for differences in work ethics, employers often place the blame on the generous crutch of the welfare system. For example, when asked whether he notices a difference between West Indian and African American employees, a Korean storeowner in West Harlem readily comments,

> There's a big difference. The worst employees that you can hire are those employees that have lived especially in the city all their lives, people from Harlem. My best workers are college students that live outside of Harlem, and people that are from the West Indies. And from what I can tell is, especially those people from Harlem, the entire welfare system, it created a generation where they have no work ethic. They won't come to work on time, and when they're here, they're here to waste time away, not do any work. I mean a paper can fall right in front of your face, and they'll just walk by without picking it up. If they see clothes all in shambles, they won't fix it unless they're told to do so. And when they're told to do so, it takes them a long time to do what they're supposed to do. It's like a different work ethic.

Reinforcing his preference for West Indians over African Americans, he conveys his opinion of the West Indian work ethic,

> People from the West Indies, I mean you can see the hunger in their eyes. They want to work! They want to make more money. They want to work harder, but people on welfare, there is no incentive for them to work harder.

Merchants and managers not only favor the foreign-born but also express a bias against inner-city fashion and culture, ascribing negative values to these class and ethnic markers, and using them as a proxy to measure work ethic. Inner-city–style clothing, the use of non-standard English, the manner in which applicants walk and carry themselves, and certain fashion accessories, such as large gold jewelry, signal to employers that these applicants have a poor work ethic, a bad attitude, and a propensity toward absenteeism.[23] A West Indian manager of a Jewish-owned store in West Harlem reveals the way he scrutinizes an applicant's personal style when interviewing: "I look at their dress. I don't like them to be too flashy. I don't like it when they have the gold teeth or big earrings or if they wear their pants down low like this (putting his hands below his hips). That looks delinquent to me." Merchants and managers discriminate against applicants whose styles of dress or demeanor connote an inner-city culture, which they perceive as threatening and indicative of delinquency and a poor work ethic.[24]

Moreover, West Indian and African employees generally share their employers' views. For instance, a Trinidadian employee in a Korean-owned clothing store in West Harlem articulates that, unlike African Americans, he does not have the luxury of the welfare safety net; consequently, he works harder.

> I think West Indians generally work harder than Americans. I'm not saying that to put Americans down, but I find that in my opinion that I observe that most West Indians, when they come to America, they work very hard for their money. It's just the maturity of West Indians, they work very hard for their money. We show up on time. We do what we're supposed to do without having the manager tell us what to do.

When asked to give a concrete example of what he means by "work harder," he offers the following example:

> I just observe Robert [the manager]. I just observe his behavior, how he goes about folding his stuff, knowing what items to put on the racks, knowing what the sizes are that are needed on the racks, where the merchandise is located in the basement, so I can bring it out without following his direct orders. I just go automatically and locate it in the basement, bring it up, and put it on the racks. I won't like to say the names, but some people, Robert has to beg them to make sure that they're doing stuff.

When asked why there are no African American employees in the large Jewish-owned clothing store in which he works, an African security guard replies frankly, "They don't want to work for $4.25. They think it's an insult to work for only $4.25. They go on welfare, and they don't want to work." Immigrants make it clear that, compared with the limited opportunities for employment and economic mobility in their country of origin, even low-paying, low-status retail jobs are attractive options; they gauge their position using a dual frame of reference.[25] Comparing their willingness to work with what they perceive as lacking in African Americans, black immigrants endorse retailers' hiring practices.

Because hiring in retail businesses is most frequently done by word of mouth or through employee referrals, it is also important to note that networks are a crucial means of securing employment, especially for the least educated.[26] As employment networks become embedded in immigrant communities, African Americans who apply for retail jobs find themselves increasingly excluded, even in their own neighborhood.[27] So even in an all "black" labor market, African Americans lose out because employers prefer hiring foreign-born blacks over the native-born.

From an African American perspective, it is not that immigrants work harder; they are just more willing to work for less, and thus they undermine what African Americans achieved with the civil rights movement. An African American merchant explains his disdain for immigrants, particularly black immigrants:

> Someone that comes from the West Indies has not lived through the '60s as a black man who lived here. So he has to understand the racial thing like going to segregated bathrooms and stuff. So for someone to come after the fact, after things have changed, and make these comments is insulting to a black person. Yeah, that's why you have these divisions, these racial divisions among them, because how can you say that? You haven't lived here.

Explaining why he would never work for less than the minimum wage, he indignantly maintains,

> I shouldn't have to work for less than minimum wage when I know what we struggled for. You might come here and take that dollar, but I'm not supposed to. It's not a sign of laziness, it's about understanding the history why. It's not that they're desperate. I think sometimes it's a lack of not really knowing what goes on and how those people [whites] have treated you.

An African American beauty salon owner in Harlem complains that the Korean owners of the fruit and vegetable store adjacent to her business hire very few African Americans and instead prefer hiring Latinos, who work for less than the minimum wage because they are unauthorized and therefore have few employment options. She asserts that if merchants were to pay a decent wage, many African Americans would be willing to work in immigrant-owned retail businesses.

> They hire Mexicans for minimum wage, less than minimum wage, and they don't hire any blacks. I asked them why they don't hire any blacks, and they said it's because they don't want to work. These people want to work, but they won't work for nothing. If they told me they wanted to hire someone and I made an announcement in my church, there would be lots of people interested. Now they have one black guy sitting outside watching the store, looking in (a security guard). That's an insult. That's insulting.

Very seldom was this point mentioned among Jewish, Korean, and black immigrant storeowners and managers. Few merchants felt that, as native-born Americans, African Americans should expect more than newly arrived immigrants with respect to wages, working conditions, or opportunities for mobility. Instead, the majority pointed to what they perceive as cultural and behavioral differences between the native- and foreign-born. Interestingly, only one Korean merchant argued that, as native-born Americans, African Americans should be paid a decent wage if storeowners expect them to work in these retail shops. She attributes the relatively low percentage of African American employees in these neighborhoods to the merchants' unwillingness to pay them fairly.

> You go into a Korean store, you see not many black people work. But Korean people, they try not to pay right way. They keep long hours and they try to give them hundred something [dollars]. That's not right. So a decent black guy, they want to work for Korean, and when they get a check, they don't want to work. I pay that guy [the manager] over $500 a week plus bonus. You have to pay right. If you want right guy, you have to pay right. And Korean people, mostly they hire Spanish; they got cheap labor. They not residents, they illegal, so they can give $100, $150, it don't matter. If you looking for nice black worker, you got to

pay decent. Korean people have to realize why they cannot hire blacks. Because black is lazy? No, not that. Because they don't pay right.

Because this study solely examines employers' attitudes, it cannot address the question of whether American-born blacks want retail jobs. The number of American-born blacks working as cultural brokers in Philadelphia stores, however, does suggest that they do. Furthermore, Katherine Newman's research on the low-wage labor market in Harlem reveals the fierce competition for minimum-wage fast-food jobs, with both American- and foreign-born blacks vying for these positions.[28] However, because fast-food managers prefer hiring immigrants over native-born Americans, African Americans are more likely to be rejected for these positions. This suggests that the problem may not be that American-born blacks have a reservation wage; rather, the problem lies in employers' hiring preferences for immigrants. Since many African American residents of inner cities are poor and have limited employment opportunities available to them, it is easy for employers to compare them to newly arrived immigrants and question why they may not be willing to take these retail jobs, even if they pay very little and offer no chance of advancement. But what the New York employers fail to recognize is that other retailers, in Philadelphia, for example, who do not have a choice between foreign- and native-born blacks willingly hire African Americans to work in their stores—and, more important, African Americans are willing to take these retail jobs, suggesting that they are wrong about African Americans' desire to work.

The shop floor has become a site where Jewish, Korean, and black storeowners, along with their black customers, construct and negotiate race, ethnicity, and opportunity. As nonblack merchants doing business in predominantly black neighborhoods, Jews and Koreans are fully aware that race can infuse merchant-customer interactions in conflict-ridden ways. Their out-group status can easily make them targets of racially charged altercations, boycotts, and violence. Because they are visible racial and ethnic outsiders, Jewish and Korean merchants hire black employees to serve as cultural brokers who bridge the linguistic, cultural, racial, and class gaps between them and their predominantly black clientele. When customers are poor and black and have dealt with oppression and discrimination in other realms, the particularities of merchant-customer arguments can easily be interpreted within a racialized framework, where racial meanings become embedded in the interactions. Cultural brokers mediate, defuse, and de-racialize arguments, preserving the day-to-day business routine in the community. However, although cultural brokers may neutralize individual-level tensions between nonblack merchants and customers, black employees cannot preclude the emergence of protest motivations that lead to intergroup conflict, as I will illuminate in Chapter 7.

"Black" is a flexible category—connoting race, ethnicity, and nativity—and immigration from the Caribbean, Africa, and Latin America is redefining what "black" means in this country. In the city that leads the country in the percentage of foreign-born black residents, New York's merchants overwhelmingly hire black immigrants over African Americans. From the customers' perspective, African American customers are pleased to find black employees in a shop at all, regardless of their ethnicity or nativity. Race is constructed and negotiated dialectically—that is, according to who the "other" is. If the "other" happens to be nonblack merchants, such as Jews and Koreans, then West Indians, Africans, and black Latinos are black to the customers. However, as we will see in Chapter 7, when African Americans jockey for position vis-à-vis West Indians in the ethnic hierarchy, the category of black becomes far more narrowly defined.

African American customers take note that employers favor black immigrants over them in the hiring queue, and their cause for concern is not without merit. Retailers' hiring practices have a significance that extends far beyond the inner city, mirroring national trends. In the United States, nearly 45 million people work in small businesses; 27 million are paid employees. The retail trade accounts for 21 percent of small business workers, second only behind the service industry, and perhaps more important, retailing accounts for 40 percent of Americans' first jobs.[29] Therefore, the retail sector is a vital source of early job experience for all Americans, particularly youths.

In northeastern cities like New York and Philadelphia, where manufacturing jobs have declined in the past thirty years, service-sector and retailing jobs are an increasingly important source of employment.[30] If employers disfavor native-born blacks over other groups, *including* black immigrants, this has significant consequences for the employment opportunity structures for African Americans.[31] And because hiring in these retail businesses is often done through existing employee networks, African Americans are increasingly excluded, even in their own neighborhoods.[32] Thus we can see that race-based hiring in black neighborhoods does not necessarily mean that African Americans will win out.

CHAPTER 6

The Coethnic Disadvantage
of Serving Your Own

> Blacks don't buy from each other. They complain about the Koreans, the Jews, and the Arabs, but if a black opens a store in the middle, they go to the same people they complain about. They won't go to the black.
>
> —African American customer in West Harlem

> With the blacks, they get their prices and they try to get more than what it's really worth. But then when you go into the Korean store and the Jew store, they have a reasonable price for you, and not only is it reasonable, they make the price so that they can get you to come back. And that keeps their business going. But in the black store, with the prices being so high, they kind of turn you away, and the business will turn down. After a while they'll close down, and they wonder why.
>
> —African American customer in Mount Airy

One of the deepest sources of contention within the black community is black business ownership. On one level, blacks object to the presence of out-group merchants such as Jews, Koreans, and other immigrant newcomers. However, as much as black residents may complain about the commercial domination of nonblacks, they continue to patronize them, sometimes even at the expense of African American merchants. Furthermore, while black customers may perceive African American retailers as in-group members, they remain the most critical of them. In numerous ways, African American merchants have historically experienced, and continue to experience, coethnic disadvantages in serving their own.

African American businessowners complain that their customers fail to patronize them as frequently as they do nonblack businesses and hold them to an impossibly high standard. Alleging that black customers prefer to do business with other racial and ethnic groups, African American merchants complain that their customers consciously or subconsciously believe black-owned businesses have lower-quality goods, higher prices, and worse service. Black customers complain that the storeowners close their businesses early, deliberately charge higher prices, and offer inferior merchandise and service. Perhaps most striking is that, despite this fractious relationship, most of the black customers we interviewed said they would like to see the majority of the stores in their community owned and operated by coethnics. This contradiction reflects the paradox between the realism of black business ownership and the symbolism of black control over black communities.

Battling the Negative Stereotypes of Black-Owned Businesses

The charge that black customers refuse to patronize their own—as contentious as it may seem—is not new. Over half a century ago, in their study of an African American community in Chicago, St. Claire Drake and Horace Cayton noted that one of the chief complaints of black businessowners was that their own people refused to patronize their stores. In 1946 an African American businessowner candidly revealed, "Negroes . . . feel as if they must buy from a white man or that a white man's commodities are better than those of a Negro."[1] A quote from a shoemaker in Drake and Cayton's book illustrates the extent to which black customers were skeptical of doing business with fellow ethnics: "The Negro has no faith in the colored business. He thinks I can't fix his *good* pair of shoes. He don't know that the Jew down the street brings his work for me to do."[2]

Today African American merchants admit that they must still battle the negative stereotype that black-owned businesses are not on a par with their Jewish and Korean counterparts. For instance, an African American retailer in West Harlem reluctantly explained that older blacks in particular are the most critical of black-owned businesses and continue to find excuses to shop elsewhere: "Basically, the older people especially, I guess they've always felt that if you had a store—if a black man had a store—your merchandise wasn't as good, or it's just the way that it seemed, or that your prices were too high. There always was some excuse as to why they couldn't shop with you." An African

American fruit and vegetable vendor in West Philadelphia who competes with a thriving Korean vendor across the street from him admits, "Black people have a problem dealing with other black people. Black people would rather buy from a Korean than a black person because the Korean has lighter skin." As evidence, he points to the steady stream of black customers who wait patiently in line to purchase their fruit and vegetables from the Korean vendor while his place remains empty. When a female customer crossed the street to say hello to the vendor after purchasing some fruit from his competitor, he jokingly chided her, "Now why you don't buy that from me?" As she bit into her juicy mango, she retorted, "They got fresh mangoes over there." The vendor answered, "I got fresh mangoes too," to which the customer responded, "Theirs are fresher." When she left, the African American vendor repeated, "See? Blacks don't like dealing with other blacks."

Not only do customers assume that the merchandise in black-owned businesses is lacking in quality, but African American merchants also add that coethnics often assume that black-owned stores will inevitably go under. Customers have little confidence that black-owned businesses will be around for the long-term. So strong is this perception that an African American coffee shop owner on Jamaica Avenue explains that some of her customers greet her with surprise each time they see her behind the counter.

> Somehow they feel that black businesses are lacking. If other ethnic groups are a ten, then black businesses are an eight, and that it's temporary. I have people that come here and they say, "Wow! You're still here!" And I say, "Why? Who goes in business just to go out of business?"

In addition, she admits with a touch of frustration that her customers "expect more" from black businessowners, insisting on a higher standard of service—a benchmark that seems to be reserved exclusively for coethnics. "They expect perfection from us. I haven't figured out why that is, but they don't expect perfection from other groups."

The historical similarities that Drake and Cayton observed decades ago are quite astonishing. They too noted that black merchants complained that their customers expected more from them than from white businessowners. "There is a general tendency to feel that Negroes 'expect more' from a colored merchant than from a white, that they are 'touchy' and constantly make comparisons with the type of service offered by whites."[3] Quoting an African American merchant, Drake and Cayton noted that blacks judge coethnics more severely than Jewish merchants for failing to carry the merchandise they would like to purchase.

> We, as a group, are much more lenient with other groups than with our own. If we go into a Jewish store and ask for something and the Jew doesn't have it, we either buy something else in its place or go on without a murmur. Our own people could stock everything we want, but we fuss and carry on and say: "You see, that's the reason we can't patronize our own; they never have anything we want." If they'd just buy from us, we'd stock all the things they want.[4]

Today, black customers continue to compare the merchandise provided, or, more accurately, not provided, in black- versus nonblack-owned stores.

Customers also complain that African American storeowners do not keep the long hours of their Korean immigrant counterparts, as an African American teenager in West Philadelphia observes:

> When you go to a black store, and you ask for a pizza steak sandwich, and they usually don't have it. So if they don't have the supplies, then I go to the Koreans, and they always seem to have the supplies. Plus black stores, sometimes they put a sign there, they're gone for lunch, or even they close early.

The male customer explains that his negative experiences with the owner of this particular black carry-out restaurant have led him to avoid patronizing coethnics altogether. Little seems to have changed in the latter half of the twentieth century, as black customers today are still the most critical of black merchants. African American business-owners recognize that, as a group, their customers hold a higher standard for coethnics yet fail to patronize them as readily as they do other merchants, contributing to the cycle of black business disadvantage.

This is the paradox: although black customers may complain about the presence of Jewish and Korean storeowners in their neighborhood, they continue to patronize them even at the expense of African American merchants. For instance, a Harlem resident sadly admits,

Blacks don't buy from each other. They complain about the Koreans, the Jews, and the Arabs, but if a black opens a store in the middle, they go to the same people they complain about. They won't go to the black. If they go to him, they won't shell out any money. If they come here, they either got a $20 or a $10 bill, but they come to you to get change. Or somebody say, "I owe you 75 cents, I only got $2.75." They always do that! But they'll go right back to a Korean or an Arab store and buy a 50-cent soda with the 75 cents they got back from you. They do it in my brother's cleaners. He complains about that all the time.

The poignant criticism that blacks do not patronize their own resounded throughout the interviews with both African American merchants and black customers. While African American merchants point the finger at their coethnic customers, the customers claim that the merchants are to blame for their lack of patronage. However, merchants and customers alike emphasize that their failure to "stick together like other groups" is one of the paramount obstacles to achieving African American entrepreneurial success and economic mobility.

In-Group Racialization

Although nonblack businessowners are more susceptible to racialized altercations with their black customers, black merchants are not entirely immune to them. This seems ironic, because both merchants and customers are black, race should hold no place in an argument, yet black customers also racially code economic disputes with black merchants. The racial coding between blacks, however, has a different meaning than the racialized discourse between black customers and nonblack merchants. Whereas the racialization process between black customers and Jewish or Korean businessowners stems from the ethnic and racial distinctiveness of out-groups, combined with their overarching presence in black communities, the racialization of black merchants is rooted in the notion that black-owned businesses are inferior to nonblack-owned businesses. At times, dissatisfied consumers in low-income communities attack coethnic merchants with acerbic remarks such as, "That's why I don't like doing business with black folks," immediately conjuring up images of black business inferiority.

By illustration, the African American owner of a furniture store in

West Harlem explains that when the inexpensive furniture that he has sold falls apart, angry customers complain that they should have bought their furniture from a Jewish or white retailer.

> The first thing they say is they should have went to the Jew, they should have went to the white man. It's very famous, "I should have went to the white man." I think, I wish you had went to the white man, give him this problem, you know, because I don't need this. When they say they should have went to the white man, that's racial.

The criticism here is twofold: first, customers are insinuating that the merchandise sold in black-owned stores is never reliable, and second, they are adopting the ideology of nonblack—and more specifically, white—superiority. When customers retort, "I should have gone to the white man," or "That's why I don't like doing business with black folks," rather than rejecting the individual black merchant with whom they are dissatisfied, they reject black businessowners as a group, consequently treating them as an undifferentiated mass. Like the process of out-group racialization, schema theory reminds us that individuals remember incidents or behavior that confirms a group stereotype.[5] When black customers have a negative experience with a black merchant, the experience affirms the widely held notion of black business inferiority.

Black customers can use or, more accurately, misuse race in poor black neighborhoods when merchants and customers have a conflict. The idea of black business inadequacy and inferiority is rooted largely in the inability of some black-owned businesses to compete with their immigrant counterparts. So enduring is the belief that white-owned businesses are superior to black-owned businesses that one African American storeowner claims that if he hired a Jewish man to act as the owner, his sales would soar: "If I had a Jewish guy walk around my store and just stay here to look like he's the boss, my business would triple. And all he has to do is hang around and talk to the customers, and my business would triple."

For several decades, African Americans have seen ethnic groups such as Jews and Koreans dominate the retail business in black communities, and as a consequence blacks have become accustomed to dealing with outsiders. The black customers with whom we spoke were candid about their skepticism of black merchants and their reluctance to do business with their own, sentiments the merchants clearly perceived. For example, a Jewish pawnshop owner in West Philadelphia notices that his black customers often prefer that *he* write the tickets for the items they wish to pawn instead of his black employees. He voices this almost apologetically: "I hate to say this, but a lot of blacks don't trust other blacks. I've noticed that when they come in here, they say, 'I want him,' and they point to me, and I say to them, 'I trust him [pointing to his black employee]. Is it all right if he writes the ticket?'" The perception that blacks are not proficient in business matters negatively affects the level of trust that black customers accord coethnic merchants.

Despite the example of the pawnshop, most of the black customers we interviewed said they prefer to be helped by black salespeople when shopping in Jewish- or Korean-owned retail stores. But what is especially curious about in-group racialization is that these same customers are wary of shopping in stores owned by blacks. Therefore the issue is not in-group prejudice with respect to customer service. Rather, the problem lies in the customers' subscribing to the negative stereotypes associated with black business ownership.

However, most African American merchants are not able to compete on a level playing field with their nonblack counterparts.[6] As I discussed in Chapter 3, African American businessowners often do not have the economic capital—or access to it—to compete successfully with Jewish and Korean merchants. Because African American merchants are unable to buy stock in large quantities, or to pool their resources to place collective orders, they do not get their merchandise as cheaply from suppliers as other merchants do. And without the added benefit of "coethnic vertical integration"—suppliers who are of the same ethnic background as retailers and may give discounts and credit based on shared ethnicity—African American businessowners often find themselves at a severe competitive disadvantage.[7]

The higher prices black merchants have to pay their suppliers are reflected in a higher retail markup, and in the end, customers must bear the burden of higher prices. What is not readily apparent to the customers is that black merchants must often charge higher prices not because they want to, but because they *need to* in order to make the same profit margin as other merchants and survive in business. An African American owner of a lingerie store in West Harlem explains why the retail prices may be higher in black-owned stores compared with other shops.

> If someone's not happy with something, they should just ask questions and find out why the prices are higher. Maybe your rent is higher. Maybe there's a reason why you have to raise your prices up. Maybe other people get a better bargain than you do, so when you buy, maybe you have to pay more.

The notion that African American merchants deliberately charge higher prices pervades the discourse not only among customers but also among black employees who work in Jewish- and Korean-owned stores. For example, an African American manager of a Korean-owned inner-city sportswear store in West Philadelphia presumes that African Americans charge more for the same items compared with Korean storeowners because they want to make a lot of money in a short period of time. She notes,

> When we get into a business, the prices go sky high for the same item. It's because we want the money to come fast. I worked for a Korean, and he always told me, if he paid $10 for it, he puts no more than $7 [markup] on it. If he pays $20 on it, he puts no more than $9 on it. And that way, you don't lose. Anything that you paid, if you get a penny over, you made a profit, you know? And that's the way business should be run. A lot of people don't see that, because I have seen it not only in this business, but in a supermarket, furniture stores, and I know that they don't pay half of what the prices that they [African American merchants] put on the thing!

Yet structural barriers such as higher prices from wholesalers are not visible to the consumer or the employee, who only notice the higher retail prices and therefore assume that black merchants deliberately charge higher prices to make a larger profit.

Such invisible structural barriers to business have very real consequences for black storeowners. Many of the black customers we interviewed readily confessed that they avoid patronizing black-owned businesses altogether because they notice a sizable price difference for the same merchandise. For example, a female customer in Philadelphia says that the price difference between white- and black-owned businesses is "outrageous" and leads her to shop in white-owned stores.

She asserts that "getting the best deal," not racial solidarity, is paramount when choosing where to shop.

> I've been into a black-owned shoe store, and the prices are so outrageous, and you know that they're outrageous, because I've been in shoe stores with my Mom, and she goes from store to store to see which one has the best prices. And the comparison between a white store as opposed to a black store, the prices are so different, and for the same shoe! It's just outrageous! And if you can find it cheaper, why pay the expensive price to get the same thing? I'm not going to shop there just because you're black. I look for the best deals, whatever saves me money.

Black customers, like all customers, prefer shopping where they can get the highest quality merchandise for the lowest price. When faced with a decision between racial loyalty and getting the best deal, most often it boils down to a simple formula that's strictly business.

But it is not just higher prices that place African Americans at a competitive disadvantage. African American merchants face another problem with their customers that is uniquely their own. When dealing with coethnics, black shoppers often feel at liberty to ask for lower prices, using fictive kinship as their bargaining chip. Customers may request discounts from African American retailers, asking them to "give a brother a play" or "give a sister a play." An African American shop owner in Queens explains,

> I have people come in here and ask for a discount based on the fact that they are black. I mean they just come right out and say that, "Give a brother a play," or "Give a sister a play." [Interviewer: A play?] A play meaning a break, a discount, a little more, make allowances. Why? I treat all my customers the same.

Unlike Jewish or Korean merchants, African American merchants are in an ambiguous position as businessowners in black communities. As businessowners, they must make a return on their investment, but as African American businessowners, they are also expected to interact with their customers beyond the economic exchange. This tension is not new. In their study of black retailers in Boston, Chicago, and Washington, D.C., following the riots of 1967 and 1968, Howard Aldrich and Albert Reiss found that 53 percent of African American businessowners reported making loans or giving money to customers.[8] This is because African American storeowners must continually prove that they are *African American* merchants and not just merchants.

African Americans' Ambivalence toward Immigrants

Measuring their success against first- and second-generation immigrant groups such as Koreans and Jews, the black customers we interviewed concur that if only blacks were to work harder as a group, delay gratification, stick together, and trust one another enough to pool their resources, they too, could open businesses and succeed like other groups. There is a great deal of ambivalence not only in the way blacks feel about African American businessowners but also in their feelings about immigrant ethnic groups. On the one hand, African Americans resent the fact that immigrants appear to have access to resources that they are denied, giving the foreign-born unfair advantages in self-employment. On the other, African Americans admire Jews' and Koreans' grit in their quest for mobility and their willingness to help fellow ethnics in need.

The underlying ambivalence and resentment that some African Americans express toward immigrants has to do with what sociologist Robert K. Merton labels in-group virtues and out-group vices. Merton insightfully notes that "ethnic outgroups are damned if they do embrace the values of white Protestant society and damned if they don't."[9] In a vivid example of in-group virtues and out-group vices, Merton explains how Abraham Lincoln's virtues of industriousness, perseverance, and eagerness receive a completely different evaluation when they are shifted from the in-group Abe Lincoln to the out-group Abe Cohen (Jewish) or Abe Kurokawa (Japanese). While the in-group Abe Lincoln is perceived as hard-working, persistent, and eager to realize his full capacity, the out-group members Abe Cohen and Abe Kurokawa are disliked, he says, for "their sweatshop mentality, their ruthless undercutting of American standards, and their unfair competitive practices."[10] While seizing opportunity is cause for praise among in-group members, overt ambition among out-groups is often cause for contempt and censure. Merton further illustrates the way in which in-group virtues undergo a dramatic change to out-group vices:

Was Abe Lincoln eager to learn the accumulated wisdom of the ages by unending study? The trouble with the Jew is that he's a greasy grind, with his head always in a book, while decent people are going to a show or a ball game. Was the resolute Lincoln unwilling to limit his standards to those of his provincial community? That is what we should expect of a man of vision. And if the out-groupers criticize the vulnerable areas in our society, then send 'em back where they came from.[11]

Merton elucidates that in-group members are quick to resent any personal achievement not warranted by social position. "The moral virtues remain virtues only so long as they are jealously confined to the proper in-group. The right activity by the wrong people becomes a thing of contempt, not of honor."[12] Comments by African American residents directed at Korean immigrant storeowners such as "I never see them outside," "They never socialize," and "They just run that business from morning to night" reflect in-group reasons for disdaining out-group immigrants who appear overly ambitious and ruthlessly competitive. Thus the in-group virtues of hard work and commitment become out-group vices. (While Merton perceptively explains the transformation of in-group virtues into out-group vices, he consequently assigns all out-groups a functionally equivalent role. As I will demonstrate in the next chapter, the black customers we interviewed resent Jews and Koreans for different reasons.)

The negative stereotypes of out-group merchants (such as Jewish merchants are shrewd and Korean merchants run their business from morning to night) do not affect customer patronage, however. While these stereotypes may negatively influence the way in which black customers perceive Jews and Koreans as people, they do not preclude blacks from patronizing them. In fact, the out-group vices ascribed to them work to positively influence the way that black customers perceive Jews and Koreans as businessowners. By subscribing to the belief that Jews and Koreans are ruthlessly competitive, black customers reinforce the stereotype that these groups make very capable businessowners, if not decent people.

The African American residents we interviewed express a great deal of ambivalence about immigrants. Rather than conveying pure disdain for the foreign born, many African Americans readily reveal behind closed doors that, were they themselves only more willing to follow in their footsteps, stick together, and not rely on outsiders for help, they could be just as successful in business. Subscribing to the American ideology of individualism, the black customers we interviewed felt that they too could pull themselves up by their bootstraps, work together, and realize the "American dream" of success. For instance, an African American customer on Jamaica Avenue in Queens points out that blacks as a group "have to stop being lazy" and "help each other" to move ahead.

> If black people were to unite and stick together and reinvest our money, we could own a lot of businesses also. We have to stop being lazy and relying on every other race to come into our neighborhood and do something for us. See, Jews are willing to help each other as opposed to blacks. We're not willing to help each other because we're like, "I got mine, you need to get yours." But with Jews, they're like, he's Jewish, I'll help him out.

Similarly, an African American merchant in West Philadelphia remorsefully articulates that of the many black ethnic and religious groups, African Americans are the least likely to work together, "The Muslims and Jamaicans are tight. The blacks are the least together. Historically there hasn't been anything to bring blacks together."

It is not only the African American customers we interviewed who sense that Koreans and Jews "help each other out" and "look out for each other" much more so than blacks; the African American merchants also agree with this assessment. For instance, an African American storeowner in Mount Airy likens blacks to "crabs in a basket," who pull each other down as individuals try to climb up and out. She regretfully admits how true this metaphor has seemed since she opened her business:

> It's like this mentality that I'm afraid to let you get a little more than me. Somebody used an analogy that blacks are like crabs in a basket. When one's trying to crawl up to come out, there's one down there in the basket trying to pull him back down. Now I've heard it, and since I've been in business I've been hearing that so much. But if we all work together, we can all get out. I think we're afraid you're going to get a lit-

tle more than me. There's enough room out here for all of us. If you help me, I can help you.

So strong is her belief in the "crabs in the basket" mentality that she refuses to drive her new Mercedes Benz to work. In lieu of driving her Mercedes, she takes her old Buick to her store to project the image that she is still struggling. When asked why it is important to project such an image, she explains that she drives her Buick to obviate envy or resentment on the part of her black customers. She says her customers' envy could lead them to refuse to patronize her business, providing them with yet another excuse to take their business to the Jewish merchant on the next block. Black merchants understand that succeeding in business can be a double-edged sword, provoking resentment that could lead coethnics to shop elsewhere.

At the Nexus of Culture and Structure

Although the majority of the African Americans in our sample strongly believe that both Jews and Koreans receive special loans and benefits to open their businesses, they also feel that these groups work hard and stick together to achieve success. African American customers may adhere to the belief that African American storeowners are not accorded the same loans and benefits as other ethnic groups, but they are also quick to point to cultural explanations that lead them to fault blacks as a group for their low rate of entrepreneurship. By adopting the negative stereotypes that "blacks aren't good businessmen" or "blacks don't want to work together," African Americans ignore the larger historical and structural barriers that have impeded and continue to impede African American self-employment.

A century ago, in his classic work *The Philadelphia Negro,* W. E. B. Du Bois recognized that one of the paramount barriers to African American self-employment was the lack of tradition for mutual cooperation. Du Bois noted, "Negroes are unused to cooperation with their own people and the process of learning is long and tedious . . . they are just beginning to realize that within their own group there is a vast field for development in economic activity."[13] Historically, African Americans have been unable to develop the traditions of lending and mutual exchange that other ethnic groups have—the consequences of which still affect small business development to this day.

For example, an African American bookstore owner on Jamaica Avenue explains that, while other ethnic groups rely extensively on mutual financial support from their family and coethnic friends, he was unable to exercise this option. Critical of his family, whom he describes as "conservative" with their lending practices, he explains how difficult it has been to borrow money from them.

> One of my sisters was very cooperative. She would lend me some money. But other members of my family were very, I hate to use the word conservative, but you know, "How am I going to get my money back? I don't want to do this," and all that. My brother was like that, and a lot of guys are like that . . . Other groups borrow from each other because they can do it. And the reason they can do it is because other groups understand the importance of that.

He relays that while blacks are reluctant to lend to each other, they are less reticent when it comes to investing their money outside the community. The African American storeowner asserts that blacks have been "poisoned against each other," making mutual cooperation extremely difficult.

> We've been poisoned against each other. That is not good. I'll give you an example. You take somebody outside of the community, outside of the black community, to come in with a program, a scheme, an MTM, multilevel marketing. And they can come in and say, "Hey, I'm going to show you guys how to make money." You give them that whole pyramid scheme bit, and you're going to make X number of dollars. And if they work for the city, they will go and borrow three, four, or five thousand dollars from their pension or from their credit union and they will put it into that multilevel marketing program, thinking that there's some kind of a pot at the end of the rainbow.

Becoming increasingly aggravated, he remarks that blacks hold greater trust in businesses conceived and operated by whites over blacks.

> Then you go to them and say, "Listen, I'm starting this business, it's going to be in the community. I need about $500 or $1,000 short-term."

Then they'll say, "I don't know." It's this thing that if somebody white tells you, it's okay, but you have no credibility with someone black, whether it's your family or not.

Likewise, when asked whether she would turn to her family if she needed money for her business, another African American merchant replied, "No, not my style, because I've learned from experience, both in the business world and my private life, that family should be a last resort. I try to keep my business, business, and my personal, personal." Similarly, an African American business owner in Mount Airy adds that, as a group, African Americans lack the access to resources and the networks that other groups rely on in business, making her feel "behind the ball" compared with her Jewish and Korean counterparts.

> We as a group don't know where to go. I really think Jewish people, even Orientals like the Koreans, I think everybody have their own thing, their own network. And unfortunately, I think that blacks, we're just behind the ball. We're like years behind in trying to get where maybe the Jewish and the Koreans are. So we're trying to run up and catch up, but we don't know a whole lot of information. So we're getting back what's thrown back.

However, what African Americans fail to understand is that the criticism that blacks do not work together is in large part a function of their native-born American status rather than a feature that is particular to African Americans as an ethnic group. Immigrants work together and help each other out more easily than African Americans *and* native-born Americans of all types because the foreign born are not yet acculturated into the long-standing tradition of middle-class individualism in American society. The notion that one must depend on and extend help to others in order to succeed stands in stark contrast to models that posit an atomistic person piloting his or her way with only human capital as the controlling feature. The tradition of individualism in America is so strong and pervasive that even when white, middle-class families face the prospect of downward mobility, turning to kin for financial assistance creates tension on all sides. In her study of downwardly mobile middle-class whites, Katherine Newman states that "nothing queers family relationships faster . . . family can feel obligated to help, but resentful. Confusion and embarrassment can intensify over whether material help is a loan, a gift, or a right—self-abasement or a statement of love and sharing."[14] Thus, like African Americans, middle-class white Americans are also reluctant to offer financial assistance to each other.

Moreover, the African American merchants we interviewed do not have resource-rich networks, making it impossible for them to borrow the large sums of money that are often needed to keep a business afloat during slow periods, as I discussed in Chapter 2. By contrast, Jewish and Korean storeowners have admitted to borrowing tens of thousands of dollars from family or fellow ethnics for business purposes such as buying stock, helping with rent during a slow season, or pulling them through an unforeseen emergency. Because African Americans lack the economic capital that Korean and Jewish storeowners have at their disposal, they have no chance of employing social capital.[15]

And perhaps just as significant in circumscribing the growth of African American entrepreneurship is the fact that blacks historically have been limited to opening businesses within the confines of their own community. Unlike other racial and ethnic groups who have been free to open businesses in communities outside of their own, African American entrepreneurs were forced by segregation laws to remain within black communities. Blacks operated under an "economic detour" and were prohibited from setting up shop elsewhere.[16] Kenneth Clark describes this inequity: "Although the white community has tried to keep the Negro confined in ghetto pockets, the white businessman has not stayed out of the ghetto. A ghetto, too, offers opportunities for profit, and in a competitive society profit is to be made where it can."[17] Even today, the black-owned store operating beyond the boundaries of a black neighborhood is a rarity. As apparent as these structural barriers may be for social scientists, too often they remain invisible to black customers and merchants alike, leading them to adopt cultural explanations for the relatively low rate of African American entrepreneurship and the competitive advantages of nonblack-owned businesses.

The Symbolic Significance behind Black Business Ownership

As I have discussed, there exists a critical paradox about the significance of black business ownership in black neighborhoods. While blacks can be extremely critical of their own, most of the black customers we interviewed assert that they would like to see *more* black-owned businesses in their communities; nearly three-quarters of the black customers we interviewed want to see more black-owned businesses in their neighborhood. Seventy percent of the black customers claimed that they would like to see the vast majority (at least three-quarters) of the stores in their community owned by fellow ethnics. The demand for more black-owned businesses in black communities has historical roots. In his account of black ghetto life in the 1940s, Kenneth Clark quotes an African American woman who expressed both her disdain of Jewish commercial domination as well as her desire to see more black-owned stores in Harlem. She remarked, "Another thing I am sick and tired of, I am sick and tired of all these Jew business places in Harlem. Why don't more colored business places open? This is our part of town. They don't live here but they got all the businesses and everything."[18]

Yet, as I have demonstrated, not only do black merchants in these communities complain that there is a lack of sufficient patronage to sustain them, but also black customers have numerous complaints about black retailers. The customers' distrust of black merchants and their tendency to shop in Jewish- or Korean-owned stores is often the result of simple economic choices and decades of conditioning. Historically, Jewish and now Korean merchants have enjoyed the best business locations and have lured customers by extending credit and lowering prices, while black merchants have remained comparatively disadvantaged. Rather than bidding for patronage based on reputation, African American merchants have had to appeal to their customers' sense of racial loyalty.[19] As early as the 1930s, with the formation of the All Negro Businessmen's Association, African American businessowners sought black consumer patronage through their role as "race-protector." The association's president defended his policy by declaring,

> This situation boils down to the law of nature known as the struggle of the survival of the fittest. And our slogans, our program, are a weapon in that struggle . . . The Jews' weapons are reputation, business contacts, control of the best business districts, and a good training in business. The Negro doesn't have those weapons and if he's going to sur-

vive and get ahead, then he's got to insist that his people patronize his store, and not the Jew's. After all, the Jew can open up a store outside of the Black Belt, but can the Negro?[20]

Appealing to racial solidarity extends to this day. Black nationalists attempt to invoke a sense of racial allegiance by promoting events like Black Tuesday—a day when black customers are asked to exclusively patronize black-owned businesses. However, customers rarely follow the calling. An African American merchant in West Philadelphia explains the philosophy behind Black Tuesday and illustrates why it fails to work:

> "Black Tuesday" or "Buy Black Day" is a day to generate revenue in the ghetto. The idea is to buy only from blacks for economic reasons. It's to give revenue into the inner city. But it could be plastered all over the newspapers and on the radio in the morning, and then it'll just fly over people's heads. They'll just forget about it. You know why that is? They'll come out here, and they'll see other people shopping in other stores that aren't black, and they'll say to themselves, "Well they're not doing it. Why should I do it?" They think that one person isn't going to make a difference. It's like voting. They don't think their vote counts.

Here again, we find the paradox attached to black business ownership. Black customers may complain about higher prices and inferior service in black-owned stores, and they may even ignore occasions such as Black Tuesday. Even so, they say they would like to see the vast majority of the stores in their community owned by blacks, firmly clinging to the ideology—not the reality—behind black business ownership.

Also apparent is the crucial distinction between individual-level processes and group-level ideologies. Although black customers may complain about black storeowners, and some may overwhelmingly prefer shopping in nonblack-owned businesses, blacks want to see *more* black-owned stores in their community because of what these businesses symbolize. Black business ownership holds a significance that extends far beyond economic exchange or the dollars that these businesses generate. Who owns the stores in black neighborhoods is a visible indicator of who controls black communities and is also a powerful gauge of America's racial and ethnic hierarchy. The overarching presence of

Jewish- and Korean-owned businesses in black neighborhoods is a symbol of black economic subordination to these groups. It reflects the objective position of blacks, Jews, and Koreans, and clashes with the subjective image of where these groups believe they ought to stand vis-à-vis each other. As Herbert Blumer noted long ago, the disjuncture between *what is* and *what ought to be* can trigger protest motivations that lead to intergroup conflict, as I will demonstrate in the following chapter.[21]

Entrepreneurship in black urban communities is a real and symbolic construction of opportunity and mobility. It is a point of contention where blacks, Jews, and Koreans make claims and jockey for position. Even in middle-income black neighborhoods where the residents are economically secure, some still object to the majority presence of out-group merchants in their community, claiming, "It's time for us to take back our neighborhoods." The boycott of the Korean-owned fruit and vegetable market on Jamaica Avenue in Queens illustrated that storeowners in middle-income black neighborhoods are not immune to conflict. Although blacks may patronize Jewish- and Korean-owned stores over black-owned businesses, the black customers we interviewed—poor and middle-class alike—object to the symbolism of out-group entrepreneurs in their community.[22]

Who owns the stores in black communities is a deep source of contention for black residents, holding far more significance than what these businesses generate in revenue. The black customers we interviewed expressed a great deal of ambivalence toward Jewish and Korean merchants, but they conveyed even more ambivalence toward coethnic businessowners. On one level, black customers object to the presence of out-group merchants because their presence represents outsider control of their community and the black economy more broadly. However, their objection to out-group Jewish and Korean merchants does not preclude black customers from patronizing them. When presented with the choice between racial loyalty and getting the best deal, the black customers in the sample overwhelmingly choose to shop where they can get the most for their money, consequently opting to patronize Jewish- and Korean-owned stores over their black-owned counterparts. Yet it is not simply a question of who offers the best prices or the greatest selection of merchandise that matters to the customers. Through the years, black shoppers have become accustomed to dealing with nonblack merchants, regardless of the objections they may have to them. Black shoppers are not accustomed to patronizing their own, making them even more critical of black businessowners as a whole.

Although black customers may patronize Jewish and Korean storeowners, they also criticize them for working too hard, failing to socialize, and doing little more than running their business from morning to night. The in-group virtues of hard work and ambition are perceived as out-group vices, reinterpreted as demonstrating a sweatshop mentality, ruthless competitiveness, and an undercutting of fair American labor practices. Yet it is understood that it is precisely these vices that work in the favor of Jews and Koreans as businessowners. And blacks' ambivalence goes one step further. As much as they may criticize out-group merchants, behind closed doors the black residents we interviewed say they admire Jews and Koreans for their willingness to make sacrifices, work hard, and stick together to help out their own. Black consumers charge that if blacks were only willing to do the same, they could be just as successful in business.

The tendency to criticize one's own ethnic group is certainly not unique to African Americans, nor is the willingness to accept cultural stereotypes, such as "blacks don't work together" or "blacks aren't good businessmen."[23] Yet adopting these stereotypes divorces one from the real structural forces that produce certain business outcomes. African American merchants do not pool their resources because there are fewer of them in business to begin with. This explains why they do not and cannot work together. Black merchants charge higher prices because nonblack suppliers often charge them higher prices, not because they wish to make their customers pay more. However, such structural barriers to business are often invisible to the consumer, who is simply looking for the best buy regardless of who is doing the selling.

Clearly there is a great deal of ambivalence behind the meaning of business ownership in black neighborhoods, reflecting the disjuncture between the reality of black business ownership and the symbolism of black control over black communities. The reality leads black customers to patronize Jewish- and Korean-owned stores on a day-to-day basis, but the symbolism leads them to support black-owned businesses in theory. As we shall see in the following chapter, the symbolism behind black business ownership and group position is the ideological tool that can transform prosaic routine into racial conflict.

CHAPTER 7

From Civility to Conflict: Individualism, Opportunity, and Group Position

Blacks are always the low man on the totem pole, always have been, since I was a kid, and I'm fifty years old, until now. Nothing changes. Like I tell you, there's no black-owned businesses up here. Everybody that comes here, every nationality is always put before us. If you were to go on the subway stations, I would guarantee you, every newsstand you see is Indian owned and all the medallion cabs too. You got your Korean restaurants, your Indian newsstands, your Greek or whatever frank stands. What do you have that's black, except maybe something on 125th Street?
—African American resident of West Harlem

I tell [black customers], "I love you guys some part, but some part I don't like it because whenever something comes out, you try to put it under racial. Racial got nothing to do with it. You guys been damn lazy, and government give you some money to open up store. You open it up and you make money and you start buying Cadillac and diamond, and jewelry almost choke your neck, because they got so many jewelry. And you don't pay rent and don't pay the light bill, so you start falling off, and you start blame somebody."
—Korean merchant in West Harlem

Civility is maintained from day to day because merchants and their employees actively work to preserve it. Jewish and Korean merchants hire black employees, place women at the front end of the business, and accede to customers' demands in order to keep the business routine in place. That the vast majority of merchant-customer interactions are conflict free may not come as a surprise to ethnomethodologists, who recognize that there is a self-generating order in everyday life.[1] However, while ethnomethodology focuses on the accountability of social order, it pays far less attention to the breakdown of order. Against the backdrop of everyday routine, how can we explain the protest motivations that lead to large-scale conflicts such as the firebombing of Freddy's clothing store in Harlem or the boycotts of Korean- and Jewish-owned businesses throughout the nation?

While everyday life may be civil, race can inflect merchant-customer relations in diverse ways, sometimes polarizing the simplest interactions and, in extreme cases, becoming the source of protest motivations that lead to intergroup conflict. Groups constantly jockey for position in America's racially and ethnically stratified society. Imported into interethnic relationships are beliefs and ideologies about individualism, opportunity structure, and group position, and it is precisely when subordinate groups challenge their position in the ethnic hierarchy that protest motivations surface.[2] Jewish and Korean merchants recognize that positive merchant-customer relations on an interpersonal level do not preclude the possibility of protest motivations and intergroup conflict. As nonblack businessowners serving a predominantly black clientele, they understand that their nonblack status can make them targets of racially charged altercations, boycotts, and even violence.

In this chapter I look at merchant-customer relations within a structural context to demonstrate how structural forces can produce certain modes of interaction.[3] Extreme inequality coupled with the presence of upwardly mobile immigrant newcomers create a potential for conflict that is more likely to emerge in lower-class neighborhoods versus middle-class neighborhoods and in high-immigration cities such as New York rather than low-immigration ones like Philadelphia. However, rather than stating that structural conditions allow few options beyond conflict, or that merchants and customers freely choose their behavior without constraints, I wish to provide an integrative framework for understanding both civility and conflict.

Previous research on merchant-customer conflict has highlighted structural explanations, reducing black-Korean and black-Jewish conflict to class differences and competition between groups.[4] Conflict theories based on competition and class differences neglect to explain how routine is maintained each day and thus overpredict the level of conflict that we are likely to find in poor black neighborhoods. Furthermore, competition theorists assume that the underlying cause of conflict is intergroup competition, yet Jews, Koreans, and African Americans do not directly compete with one another, as I have noted. In addition, because one would expect that competition should emerge among businessowners, therefore conflict should appear among the merchants, not between the merchants and the black residents. Adding a nuance to the competition line of argument, Susan Olzak and her colleagues posit that racial conflict occurs where segregation has been initially high and has later declined, leaving greater opportunity for competition and conflict.[5] Yet my findings reveal that conflict in the form of boycotts, firebombings, and riots is *less* likely to emerge in middle-class black neighborhoods where segregation, poverty, and inequality are less extreme.

Other research relies on the middleman-minority framework, positing that conflict is inherent in the merchant-customer relationship because merchants are caught in a conflictual role between the elites and the masses. The middleman-minority theory consequently assigns Jewish and Korean merchants functionally equivalent roles.[6] However, despite their similar roles as out-group merchants in poor black neighborhoods, Jewish and Korean merchants are *not* functional equivalents. The black customers we interviewed resent Jews and Koreans for different reasons.

Merchant-customer relations are far more complex than the middleman-minority or competition models posit. The causal mechanisms behind conflict motivations are dissimilar at the individual and collective levels. Whereas factors such as retail niche, familiarity, gender, and cultural brokers shape merchant-customer interactions at the individual level, at the collective level, groups battle over the tenets of individualism, opportunity, and group position. By examining how merchants and customers interact in the store and how they view one another as members of racial and ethnic groups, we can find an explanation and a synthesis of both civil relations and racial conflict.

Individualism and Equality of Opportunity

American ideology embraces the values embodied in the Protestant ethic, such as individualism and self-reliance—emphasizing the belief that hard work, perseverance, individual achievement, and upward mobility are inherently linked.[7] As Seymour Martin Lipset affirms in his elegantly argued work *American Exceptionalism,* much of Americans' attitudes and behavior may be explained by the cultural emphasis on achievement. For example, three-fourths of Americans agree that "in America, if you work hard, you can be anything you want."[8] Therefore, when individuals and groups succeed, the ideology behind the American dream attributes their upward mobility to individual effort, hard work, and grit. Correlatively, when individuals and groups fail, the American dream attributes their failure to a lack of effort, hard work, and commitment. By illustration, political scientists Herbert McClosky and John Zaller note that nearly half of Americans agree with the statement, "It is entirely the fault of the man himself if he cannot succeed."[9] Furthermore, 88 percent of Americans assert that ambition is very important "for getting ahead in life."[10] The belief that individualism and ambition are paramount in getting ahead makes the American dream a powerful ideological tool for explaining both success and failure.

A crucial feature of the American dream and the ideology of equality of opportunity is the idea that groups should not violate the traditional American value of individualism and self-reliance in their quest for mobility. For instance, Paul Sniderman and his colleagues find that white and black Americans strongly adhere to the ethic of self-reliance, asserting that both new immigrants and blacks should take responsibility for working their way up on their own.[11] Consequently, when individuals feel that certain groups violate these values, those groups often face resentment and prejudice in one form or another. Political scientists Donald Kinder and David Sears explain, for example, that the persistence of white anti-black prejudice is based on the perception that whites believe blacks violate the principle of individualism when they are given preferential treatment in the form of government set-asides and affirmative action.[12] In fact, 60 percent of whites agreed with the statement, "If blacks would try harder, they would be just as well off as whites."[13] However, we should note that it is not only white Americans who cling to the ideology behind individualism and the American dream; Americans of all hues have come to adopt these beliefs.[14] While 60 percent of whites believe that, by trying harder, blacks could be just as well off as whites, 60 percent of blacks feel the same.[15] In fact, blacks so firmly believe in the American dream that they are nearly as convinced of its reality as whites.[16]

Embedded in the American dream of success is the notion that while the playing field may not be level, the opportunity to get ahead is there, so "it's all about who wants it more," as an African American customer from Mount Airy succinctly put it. Those who strive the most and work the hardest reap the rewards—it is that simple. Entrepreneurship is one of the most visible symbols of the American dream and one of the most concrete forms of evidence that the dream works. Regardless of how recently arrived, no matter how humble one's origins, and regardless of race or ethnicity, if an individual works hard, he or she can open a business. Immigrants and native-born citizens alike subscribe to this dominant belief, even disadvantaged minorities. For instance, an African American man from East Harlem says that blacks may want to own a business but are unwilling to work as hard for it as Koreans and Jews.

> The desire is not as strong with blacks as it is with Koreans and Jews. I don't particularly know why, but it just seems to be that way. I just feel like they have more of an initiative to get things done. It's just all within themselves. I mean, it seems as though the blacks, they want the business, and they want the money coming, but they don't want to go through the hassle—they don't want to go through the work of going through the process of getting everything started. It's a lack of effort.

That he mentions characteristics such as "desire," "initiative," "effort," and "work" points to his credence in cultural attributes as an explanation for Jewish and Korean entrepreneurial success, especially compared with that of African Americans. The belief that cultural differences explain, at least in part, the low rate of African American entrepreneurship is embedded in the normative belief in the open opportunity structure—that the path to mobility is open to all individuals and groups who are willing to work hard, make sacrifices, stick together, and move ahead. Reiterating his belief that the willingness to overcome obstacles is paramount in getting ahead, the East Harlem resident concludes,

> Someone else can't be responsible for you to make you get to the top. Part of you has to say, "Look, no matter what the odds, no matter who happens to be in the power structure, I got to make it by hard work and faith." That's really it.

It may come as a surprise that a low-income resident of East Harlem has so firm a grip on the ideology behind the American dream. However, as Jennifer Hochschild's work reveals, poor blacks are even more likely to cling to the American dream than their middle-class counterparts.[17] Middle-class blacks recognize that their lives are far more problematic than those of middle-class whites, making it evident that society has a long way to go before equality of opportunity is fully achieved. By contrast, poor blacks look to middle-class coethnics who have "made it" to reinforce their faith in the American dream. In addition, affluent blacks hold less tenaciously to the beliefs behind the American dream, not because they fear for their own social or economic position but because they realize that less affluent coethnics will continue to fare poorly, demonstrating that individual self-interest does not always structure one's beliefs. African Americans have a strong sense of "collective identity," or what Michael Dawson describes as a "perceived link between one's own fate and that of the race."[18] For instance, in a nationwide survey of African Americans, 65 percent were found to have a "common fate" racial identity—that is, they believe that what happens generally to black people in this country will have something to do with what happens in their own life.[19]

It is important to note, however, there are exceptions to the strong belief in American individualism and the ethic of self-reliance. As John Skrentny illustrates in his persuasively argued work *The Ironies of Affirmative Action*, Americans may embrace the ideals of individualism and may even object to preferential treatment for some groups, but they do not object to all forms of special treatment.[20] The question of who is deserving and who should legitimately receive preferential treatment varies depending on the group in question. For example, Americans do not object to preferential treatment for veterans or those who have disabilities, but they firmly draw the line when it comes to blacks. Skrentny rightly points out that the ideology behind individualism, meritocracy, and the question of who is "deserving" is context specific.

Belief in the American Creed

In mainstream, middle-class America, whites feel that blacks violate the tenets of individualism, but in black urban America, it is not African Americans but the foreign-born who take the heat. One of the chief sources of contention between African Americans and immigrants is the assumption that the U.S. government helps the foreign-born adapt to their new host country with financial resources—in the form of welfare, small business loans, and tax breaks—giving immigrants an upper hand in their quest for mobility.

The controversy behind government-supported immigrant aid stems from two principle concerns at the heart of the American creed. First, African Americans object to the notion that immigrants violate the deeply ingrained link between individualism and upward mobility. No group should receive preferential treatment in their quest for mobility. African Americans' views in this regard are not unique. In a survey of white and black Americans, 79 percent of whites and 70 percent of blacks claimed that new immigrants ought to take responsibility for working their way up without any special favors.[21] Second, and more critically, blacks object to the notion that the government appears to help *all* groups—regardless of how recently arrived and regardless of how "un-American" they may seem—before helping African Americans, who have been here for centuries. Korean immigrants' heavy accents and inability to speak English fluently appear to matter little as they seem to climb effortlessly up the mobility ladder. For instance, an African American Queens resident says in disbelief, "They come here, and not to put them down, but they don't even speak the language. They don't speak English, and you're wondering, how come they're already owning these businesses?" Koreans are able to advance rapidly, and once again African Americans find themselves left behind, as illustrated by an African American resident of East Harlem who asks, "Well, how come we don't get the same opportunity that Third World people get?" Implicit in these questions rest the underlying queries, Who helped these immigrant groups out, and why has help not come our way?[22]

Convinced that the U.S. government and U.S. banks provide loans for the foreign-born to start businesses but not for native-born blacks, the African Americans we interviewed point to the preference for aiding immigrants as one of the chief reasons for the low rate of African American entrepreneurship and African American economic progress more generally. A West Harlem resident articulates this sentiment:

> I feel like somebody's responsible for giving them the money, or they wouldn't all be coming here to start a business. It has to be the banks here in the United States, or they wouldn't even be coming here. You know, this is a place to get a loan, so the Koreans come here. You don't

see as many black-owned businesses because the banks are not giving the blacks the loans like they give Koreans.

Moreover, there is a grave sense of injustice, a sense that every immigrant ethnic group—not just Jews and Koreans—receives benefits before African Americans, as a Mount Airy resident elaborates:

> I think Koreans and Jews and every other ethnicity besides blacks get more loans than we do, through the government, the banks, or whatever the case may be. I feel as though a lot of foreign people, not only Koreans, but other people who just come into the country, get loans easier than blacks that's already citizens here. I think other ethnic groups are allowed to advance or develop better than blacks.

When probed further and asked whether she feels that African Americans receive any special loans or benefits, she quickly retorts, "Of course not! This is America. The special thing that blacks get is the negative things that keep piling on us to make sure that moving forward is a difficult task for us. That's the kind of special treatment that African Americans get in America."

In fact, more than 60 percent of the blacks in our sample believe that Jewish and Korean merchants receive special loans, benefits, or tax breaks to help them open their businesses. In stark contrast, only 10 percent believe that blacks receive such benefits. By far, the majority of the blacks in the sample (90 percent) feel that black business-owners are denied such privileges, making it seem impossible for African Americans to compete effectively with immigrant newcomers.[23] The belief that all immigrant entrepreneurs receive special government and bank loans that are unavailable to African Americans is a common stock story.[24] However, critical investigation of stock stories reveals that they are often based on misinformation. None of the Jewish or Korean storeowners in our sample had received bank or government agency loans to help them start their business, but it is through this stock story's lens that the African American residents we interviewed perceive immigrant storeowners. In fact, the African American merchants were far more likely to have benefited from such resources; 20 percent of the African American entrepreneurs in the sample started their business using a bank or government agency loan. Perception and reality are clearly not one and the same. Nevertheless,

African Americans' misperception that Jews, Koreans, and other immigrant groups receive special benefits to help them open their businesses has very real consequences, as we shall see.

The African Americans' belief that immigrants receive special government loans stems in part from their belief that the U.S. government wants "to do blacks in." Their distrust of the government is not without cause, given the unique deprivations that blacks have suffered and the history of black-white relations in this country. However, the extent to which blacks feel that the government conspires against them as a group is quite startling. For instance, Paul Sniderman discovered that nearly half the blacks in his survey agreed with the statement that "the FBI and CIA make sure that there is a steady supply of guns and drugs in the inner city."[25] Moreover, 28 percent of blacks agreed with the statement that "white doctors created the AIDS virus in a laboratory and released it into black neighborhoods." Given blacks' keen distrust of the U.S. government and their belief in conspiratorial thinking, it should come as little surprise that African Americans strongly adhere to the belief that the government favors newly arrived immigrants over them.

West Indians' Perception of "Immigrant Superiority"

It is precisely on the point of special loans and benefits that the African American and West Indian perspectives diverge sharply. Whereas African Americans feel that Koreans and other immigrants receive unfair benefits that help them open their businesses, West Indians believe otherwise, pointing to the "immigrant mentality" of "hard work and sacrifice." For example, when asked whether he feels that Koreans receive special loans or benefits, a young Jamaican American who resides in Harlem says, "Honestly, I think it's they work hard and make sacrifices. They make sacrifices that I think a lot of people aren't willing to make." When asked to elaborate on what he means by "sacrifices," he vividly recalls an example from his youth:

> This is stereotyping, but, like, all the Korean kids I knew, Asian kids I knew when I was growing up, like, all the black kids and the white kids, we always had to have fly designer gear, whatever. The Korean kids, it's like, they were always dressed, not shabbily, but they were never up to

par as everyone else. And it didn't make a difference to them. It didn't make a difference to them that they weren't up to par with everyone else, as long as in school they did well. And it wasn't so much their attitude, but it was their parents instilling it.

West Indians' immigrant status becomes strikingly prominent in questions of immigrant loans, immigrant mobility, and "immigrant superiority" over native-born Americans—particularly their sense of superiority over African Americans. Although West Indians firmly subscribe to the belief in immigrant superiority, they are caught between their racial ascription as black and their status as immigrants, their blackness pulling them to assimilate as African Americans and their foreign-born status keeping them apart. The racialization process of black immigrants is so powerful that West Indians and Africans must constantly fight to assert their ethnic and immigrant status in order to distinguish themselves from African Americans. As the growing body of literature on West Indian immigration and identity clearly shows, the black ascription is not easily rebuffed.[26] For instance, a West Indian resident of Harlem powerfully says of his identity, "When the day is done, you're just a black man in America with no power, no say."

When their identity is challenged and tested, the West Indians in the sample admit, they feel a closer affinity to African Americans than to other newly arrived immigrants—such as Koreans, Asian Indians, or Middle Easterners—who set up shop in black communities. Although their situation as immigrants produces similarities between them and other newcomers, in the merchant-customer context in black urban America, West Indians' ethnicity and immigrant identity often take a backseat to their status as blacks in America's racial hierarchy.

Who Makes Up the Rules to the Mobility Game?

Some immigrant groups, such as Koreans, not only are new to this country but also look and sound obviously foreign. As a Jamaica Avenue resident candidly admits, "Just looking at Koreans physically, I just see them as foreigners." Perhaps most puzzling and disconcerting for the black residents we interviewed is that Korean immigrants achieve economic success without having to acculturate—without having to speak English fluently and without having to learn the dominant social behaviors and norms—thus decoupling the conventional model of acculturation and economic mobility. Racially and ethnically new and distinct "foreigners" seem to move ahead without having to first become "American," leading some African Americans to question the rules of the mobility game. Whereas in the traditional model, economic mobility required acculturation, today's immigrants are proving otherwise, causing many raised eyebrows among African American residents of Harlem and West Philadelphia. For instance, an African American resident of West Philadelphia complains that Koreans do not seem to want to become "American," yet they get ahead nevertheless.

> To me, it seems like they don't want to accept any culture, other than their own. They rather just stay to themselves. They want the American money, but they don't want the American ways of the American people. I never see them outside. They don't socialize. They just run that business from morning to night. You never, never see them outside the workplace.

To many, Koreans seem to reject American culture altogether, forsaking acculturation and socialization and working for the sole purpose of economic gain. "All they do is work, work, work!" says an African American resident of West Harlem. The African American residents we interviewed said they feel that Koreans would like to take a piece of the American pie in terms of profit but want no part of American life—and certainly no part of African American life. In addition, they seem to give nothing in return for what they take from black neighborhoods.

Further, the African Americans in our sample believe that, in a "Jewish-run society," Jews are largely responsible for providing the business loans to Koreans and intentionally denying African Americans similar opportunities. For example, a West Philadelphia resident complains,

> Koreans are getting loans from the banks that Jews own, and I believe that the Jews and the Koreans work together to do African Americans in. And I feel that if it's so easy to come to our country and get these loans and get these grants and get all these different types of things, then why isn't it easy for our people to do this? Because we have been

discouraged and we have been stepped on, and it's just a continuous pattern. And it will never stop.

Immigrants' mobility and relative success leads African American residents in both low- and middle-income communities to wonder exactly who is American, who is most deserving, and who makes the rules to the mobility game.

In black communities, the categories of race, ethnicity, opportunity, and Americanism are constructed and negotiated on different terms than in academic discourse. It is in these neighborhoods that minority groups struggle to secure their position in the system of ethnic stratification. By traditional indicators, Koreans are un-American, yet they appear to be afforded better opportunities than native-born blacks, leading African Americans to believe that they are once again being shoved aside while newer ethnic groups are allowed to move ahead. The resentment that African Americans feel toward out-group merchants has more to do with the notion that Koreans—and other "less deserving" ethnic groups—seem to be handed opportunities before they are. The African American residents we interviewed feel strongly that the foreign-born of all types are moving ahead of them, presumably with governmental aid, and seemingly at their own expense.

As Jews have moved up and out of black neighborhoods and new immigrants, such as Koreans, Middle Easterners, and Asian Indians, have moved in, African Americans have watched a succession of newer groups realizing the American dream of success.[27] The image of immigrants (and nonblacks more generally) coming into black communities, buying the businesses, and leaving with the profits at night, is a provocative one for most African Americans. The prominence of nonblack-owned businesses is a symbol of nonblacks' position in the racial hierarchy.

"Jews Hold a Whole Lot of Power"

African Americans realize that Jews are not immigrants, and their resentment of Jewish merchants takes on a different form. In addition to embracing anti-Jewish stereotypes of clannishness and shrewdness, the blacks in our sample believe that America is a "Jewish-run society," with Jews controlling all of America's leading institutions. From their perspective, Jews "hold a whole lot of check, a whole lot of pull, and a whole lot of power." Hence, the resentment that blacks feel toward Jews is a unique variety, illustrating that the middleman minority framework—which assigns all minority merchants the same role and attributes resentment to the same source—is too simplistic a model for explaining the intergroup resentment, tension, and conflict that exist.[28]

However, blacks are not anti-Semitic simply because they are anti-white, as James Baldwin pronounced in his prominent essay more than thirty years ago.[29] In fact, more than 60 percent of the black customers we interviewed feel that Jews are not white but instead "something in between," "their own separate category," or simply "a minority." The debate about whether Jews are white seems to be divided sharply along intergenerational lines. Older blacks—those who have witnessed blatant anti-Semitism—recognize that historically Jews have been treated differently from other white ethnic groups, whereas younger blacks see no difference between the categories "white" and "Jewish." For example, an elderly African American resident of Queens elaborates, "I'm from the South, and as I was growing up as a child, the whites didn't accept them [Jews]. They used to always be sitting around in the black area because they couldn't go in white areas." A middle-aged African American from Harlem further elaborates that, regardless of whether blacks see Jews as white, Jews realize that they are distinct from the dominant white majority: "A Jewish person knows that he or she is not white. They know that they're their own separate category, and they get treated as such." The findings mirror those of scholars who addressed African Americans' perception of Jews in the 1960s. Gary Marx, for example, wrote that African Americans perceive Jews as a "minority group who have also suffered at the hands of the dominant group," and Roi Ottley added, "In the minds of most Negroes, the Jews are a separate and distinct unit from the white community."[30]

African Americans realize that, like other minority racial and ethnic groups, Jews have experienced hostility, prejudice, and overt discrimination, and this leads some to see very little difference between Jews and other minority groups. For instance, a black resident of East Harlem posits, "Other races—I'm talking about Italians, Germans, Irish, or whatever—they see them [Jews] like they see us blacks. The only difference with Jews and blacks is that they have money." By sharp contrast, younger blacks do not recognize a difference between Jewishness and whiteness, "lumping Jewish people and white people together." Perhaps the most poignant example of the intergenerational difference is the question an eighteen-year-old African American posed: "I don't know how you tell the difference between a white person and a Jewish person. How can you tell unless a Jew tells you they're a Jew? How can you tell? They're white to me."

But even their shared status as minorities—who have suffered from both prejudice and overt hostility—does not make today's blacks feel empathetic toward Jews or vice versa. According to blacks, Jews are far too rich and powerful to feel an affinity toward them. For instance, when asked whether she believes that blacks and Jews share a common bond as minorities, a middle-aged African American pointedly reveals that there is no special relationship between the two groups. She says that the tragedies of the Holocaust cannot begin to compare with the legacy of slavery and centuries of racial subordination. "When my brothers and my sisters go to war, they're put on the front line. They forget about the KKK, and the slaying, and the white cops that are out there shooting up my brothers and my sisters. They forget all about that, so screw the Holocaust!" The sentiment that African Americans and Jews have not suffered equally in the United States was crystallized in 1967 in a statement by the black intellectual Harold Cruse, who remarked, "The average Negro is not going to buy the propaganda that Negroes and Jews are brother sufferers in the same boat."[31] Likewise, today's Jewish storeowners do not recognize a special bond between the two groups. In fact, one Jewish merchant laughed at the idea, questioning, "Why? Because we were both slaves or something like that? I've heard that said before, but I don't really feel it."

Racial Formation and Group Position in Urban America

Identity and racial formation are not one-sided internal processes but rather part of a "dialectical process involving internal and external opinions and processes, as well as the individual's self-identification and outsiders' ethnic designations—i.e., what *you* think your ethnicity is, versus what *they* think your ethnicity is."[32] Jews may see themselves as white, but older African Americans certainly do not see them that way. Koreans may believe that they are American and therefore have the right to open a business wherever they choose, but African Americans regard them as foreigners who take opportunities away from them. And African Americans may see themselves as hard working but suffering from discrimination, while often Jews and Koreans perceive them as lacking the drive to take advantage of opportunities open to all, using past oppression as a crutch.

A Jewish storeowner in East Harlem rebuked poor blacks: "One hundred years ago the Jews were the minorities, like the blacks and Puerto Ricans today. But instead of going on welfare and crying about it, we slaved away and studied to make a better life." Similarly, a Korean merchant on Harlem's 125th Street who has very favorable relations with her customers and recognizes most of them by name, candidly states, "I love these people, but some of them, basically, they try to put everything into the racial excuse. You know, 'We don't get any benefits, we don't get this . . . We don't get anything.' They try to blame."

Embedded in these statements are beliefs about race, opportunity, self-reliance, and group position. If you want to get ahead, all you need to do is get an education, work hard, and pull yourself up by your bootstraps. As foreign-born newcomers, Korean immigrants firmly subscribe to the ideology of self-reliance and individual mobility. West Indian immigrants could not agree more on this count.[33] As newly arrived Americans, Koreans and West Indians feel that they have no choice but to work harder than those born here, but African Americans feel that both Koreans and West Indians just "want to be white" and intentionally distance themselves as much as possible from blacks.[34]

In urban America, racial, ethnic, and identity formation are interactive processes negotiated on different terms than in mainstream white America. Much of recent scholarship on race, ethnicity, and identity concerns how native-born whites define other groups, but in the inner cities, the social actors are all minorities and the claims distinct. For instance, middle-class white Americans care little or not at all about small business ownership in black neighborhoods. Middle-class white neighborhoods are segregated from the inner city, and therefore who owns the businesses there is of little consequence to most whites' daily lives. But for blacks, Jews, and Koreans, entrepreneurship is a real and symbolic construction of opportunity, mobility, and group position. The ethnic groups battle over where each should stand on the ladder to mobility.[35]

Immigration has become a key variable that shapes and constructs race, ethnicity, and opportunity in diverse ways. In New York City, where one out of every four New Yorkers was born outside the United States, African Americans more strongly object to the presence of immigrant-owned businesses—and immigrants more generally—than do their counterparts in Philadelphia. African Americans from New York more readily adopt the discourse that immigrants compete with native-born Americans, drain the nation of its resources, and give nothing back in return. By contrast, in Philadelphia, where the native-born presence greatly overshadows the foreign-born, the immigrant presence is far less contentious for African Americans. Questions such as Who is American? and Who is deserving? are not as highly charged.

However, it is crucial to note that it is not immigration per se that is contentious; rather, it is the belief that immigrants receive special loans and benefits that are denied to native-born Americans, and that this gives them unfair advantages in their quest for mobility. The belief that the foreign-born are given privileges over African Americans is more prevalent among blacks in New York compared with Philadelphia. Eighty percent of the blacks in New York believe that Koreans are handed special loans and privileges to help them open their businesses, and 76 percent believe the same thing about Jews. By contrast, in Philadelphia the figures drop to 67 percent and 43 percent, respectively. Increases in immigration raise the perception that the foreign-born take away opportunities from native-born Americans.[36]

Boycotts of Jewish- and Korean-Owned Businesses

Although social order is maintained from day to day, race, opportunity, and the struggle for group position can easily inflect merchant-customer relations and become sources of protest. In other words, civility may characterize the daily lives of both merchants and customers, but the normalcy of everyday interactions does not preclude the emergence of protest. The fact that boycotts, firebombings, and riots take place in black neighborhoods that are normally characterized by routine demonstrates the precarious balance between civility and conflict.

New York and Philadelphia provide a useful comparison on this note. Although the everyday relations between merchants and customers are similar in both cities, intergroup conflicts between blacks and Jews and blacks and Koreans are far more common in New York City.

For instance, New York experienced nearly four times as many black race riots as Philadelphia in the latter half of the twentieth century. From 1960 to 1993, New York experienced twenty-two black race riots whereas Philadelphia experienced only six, which might demonstrate that increases in immigration and racial and ethnic inequality may initiate the outbreak of collective action.[37]

Against the backdrop of everyday routine, how can we explain overt incidences of conflict such as the firebombing of a Jewish-owned store or boycotts of Korean-owned businesses? Herein lies the paradox: although most merchants and customers may have positive relations on an individual level, racial and ethnic conflict persist on a collective level because groups must vie for position in America's racially and ethnically stratified society. Imported into interethnic relationships are beliefs and ideologies about opportunity structure and group position.[38] It is precisely when subordinate groups develop a new conception of themselves and challenge their position in the ethnic hierarchy that everyday routine breaks down and conflict arises.[39]

Black communities such as Harlem and West Philadelphia are some of the few places that symbolize black culture, pride, and perhaps most important, autonomy. "The dream of autonomy resonates powerfully for people who have never felt fully at ease in America yet can never feel fully apart from it," as Philip Kasinitz and Bruce Haynes insightfully observe in their study of the firebombing of Freddy's in West Harlem.[40] African Americans recognize that they are American in terms of nationality, but they stipulate that regardless of their American citizenship, they feel they are not accorded the same privileges and status as other racial and ethnic groups in America.[41] They may cling to the American dream and believe that with hard work and motivation they can get ahead, but the African Americans in our sample critically state that they do not compete on a level playing field, that other ethnic groups seem to be given preference over them.

For example, when asked whether he feels that blacks are American, an African American customer retorts, "Do I think blacks are Americans? Black people are really not accepted basically. They don't have the rights that Americans should have, you know, so in that respect, we're not completely Americans." This feeling that blacks are not really American with respect to rights and privileges resounds throughout our interviews with black customers. Most agree that in our predominantly nonblack society, blacks are not offered the same treatment and opportunities as other groups and therefore have to work twice as hard for the same rewards. An African American resident of East Harlem boldly states that, regardless of one's achievements, "to everyone else, you're still what you first were, a nigger."

Black communities offer a refuge, a respite from feeling not completely American. There, blacks are the numerical majority, and black culture is pervasive and celebrated. Images of Martin Luther King, Jr., Malcolm X, Adam Clayton Powell, and black autonomy prominently grace storefronts, billboards, street signs, and bookstands. Traditional African kenta cloth and headscarves adorn many black residents, blending in effortlessly with the urban ethnic sportswear worn by today's youth. Black neighborhoods are pieces of America over which blacks feel that they have—or, at the very least, should have—authority and control. Hence, black business ownership is a source of much contention, because it symbolizes black control over black communities.

When blacks choose to boycott a Korean-owned fruit and vegetable market or to picket a Jewish-owned business, their cause transcends the individual Korean or Jewish retailer. The boycotting of an individual business becomes emblematic of the larger issue of black control over black communities. Nonblack businessowners understand this point very well. For example, a Korean owner of a soul food restaurant who has been in Harlem for more than a decade and is a mainstay in the community realizes that she can easily become the target of racially charged anger. Even this veteran—who has numerous regulars who eat in her establishment every day—understands that as a Korean merchant on 125th Street in New York's Harlem, she is always at risk of conflict, regardless of how many people in the community support her. Her nonblackness—and her Koreanness even more specifically— can easily make her a target for dissatisfied customers. She says,

> We always feel like a boycott could happen no matter how you famous on 125th Street, no matter how much they like you, no matter how you good to this community. Always one bum or one knucklehead hates you. He can bring you a ton of problem. So far, people support me, but some people against me too.

When asked whether this insecurity stems from the simple fact that she is not black, she immediately replies,

That's right. And they can put me as Korean merchant coming here to make money out of this community. So I got a thousand of them full of respect, it don't mean anything. Something happen, a thousand people I don't know them, they can against me, coming here for protesting, hollering, shut down business. It could happen, you know. Some person get mad at me, so I argue, and he start picket outside. Maybe some other people say, "You crazy, why you do that to this store?" But few people going to do that.

And a lot of those protesters, they don't know me, they could stay there shouting and give me a lot of trouble because it always could happen no matter how much you are good to this community or something like that. And that kind of crazy thing can happen, and nobody can stop it. Nobody can move those protesters out in front of my door. They got a right to stand there and shouting. And the ones who shouting, I don't know them, and they don't know me. They just want to be here. They angry because I'm Korean. But they not get mad at me, they get mad some place else.

The Korean merchant understands that regardless of how many customers support her, and regardless of how many years she been a part of Harlem's business scene, her race and ethnicity mark her as an outsider.

The firebombing of Freddy's, the Jewish-owned clothing store in Harlem, in December of 1995 underscored the precariousness of the nonblack merchant's position. When Fred Harari, the previous owner of Freddy's, decided to expand his business, he in effect terminated the lease of his African American subtenant, Sikhulu Shange. Shange appealed to both Harari and the African American church that owned the property, but neither would change their mind. Shange then went to the African American leaders in the Harlem community, who organized a boycott of Freddy's clothing store to protest Harari's decision. When the protestors began to shout remarks like "Kill the Jew bastards," Harari decided it was time to file for a restraining order. But by the time the order was granted, it was too late. Roland Smith, an African American resident of Harlem, had entered Freddy's with a .38 caliber gun and a can of paint thinner, shot and wounded four employees, and set the store ablaze, trapping and killing seven of the store's nonblack employees before killing himself.[42] Immediately following this tragic event, protestors moved to boycott a veteran Jewish store-owner on the same block—even though this businessowner had served West Harlem's community for more than forty years. The protestors shouted racial and ethnic taunts such as, "This block for blacks only! No whites and Jews allowed!"

When we asked about the incident at Freddy's, most of the Harlem merchants and customers agreed that although it was Harari's right as a businessowner to terminate the sublease with Shange, it was not the "morally right" thing to do. For instance, a Jewish sneaker store owner in Harlem remarked, "You just don't kick a black man out of Harlem," mirroring an African American customer who rhetorically asked, "How can you move blacks out of Harlem when that's all we have?" An East Harlem resident and former customer of Freddy's com-mented, "Well, I think when a black man has been in business for a long length of time, and he's in danger of losing his business, emo-tions are going to run high." The fact that protestors immediately moved to boycott another Jewish-owned store on the same block im-mediately following the firebombing of Freddy's illustrates the way in which race and ethnicity can mark insiders and outsiders. That this storeowner is completely unrelated to Harari was of no consequence to the protesters. Both are Jewish, and at the time that was enough. Protestors can easily adopt the roles of political, racial, and ethnic identity entrepreneurs, who use blackness to justify their cause and, correlatively, nonblackness to determine who does not belong in the community.[43]

The well-known 1990 boycott of a Korean-owned fruit and vegetable market in the Flatbush section of Brooklyn offers another case of marking outsiders from insiders. The momentum of the Flatbush boy-cott quickly moved into other neighborhoods throughout New York City. The boycotts garnered both local and national media attention, giving black nationalist leaders a forum in which to propagate the broader issue of black control over black communities.[44] In one of the other shops that was boycotted, a Korean-owned fruit and vegetable market on Jamaica Avenue in Queens, the merchant who was targeted had served Jamaica Avenue for twelve years. Nevertheless she experi-enced a six-month-long boycott, with protestors shouting such taunts as "Go back to Korea!" The fact that this Korean merchant had been in business for more than a decade, and that the Jewish merchant who was boycotted after Freddy's was a second-generation storeowner who had been in Harlem for more than forty years, held little relevance when tensions ran high and discourse became racialized or ethnicized.

It should be made clear that the views of protestors do not necessarily reflect the views of all black residents. For instance, the Korean merchant in Queens noted that her regular customers had bravely crossed the picket line in order to help sustain her business, choosing to side with her over the black boycotters and illustrating the heterogeneity among black residents. Her Jewish neighbor next door confirmed that, indeed, many residents of Jamaica Avenue's community had supported the market over the boycotters' cause.

> There were many customers that really didn't care [about the boycott]. They wanted to go in for their head of lettuce or loaf of bread. They would go in, and people would be yelling and screaming at them, and a woman screamed back, "Listen, you don't tell me where to shop or where I buy my food!" This is one black versus another. They were fed up because this was inconvenient for them.

Each time customers had crossed the picket line to buy from the Korean grocery store, boycotters had responded with a loud, hostile roar.

The point here is twofold. First, boycotters do not represent the opinions of the community more broadly.[45] And second, boycotters and residents may not have problems with the individual merchant per se, but they do find problematic the image of "parasitic" out-group businessowners, whom they perceive as taking away resources and opportunities from the black community at large. Chants such as "Whose streets? Our streets," "What time is it? Black nation time," and "Too black, too strong" underscore that the boycotters' cause far transcends the individual Korean or Jewish merchant. At stake are black control of black neighborhoods and black autonomy.[46]

In middle-class black neighborhoods, protest motivations concerning black autonomy rarely emerge. Middle-income neighborhoods such as Philadelphia's Mount Airy have not been the sites of overt conflict, demonstrating the importance of class in shaping intergroup relations. Yet class differences alone do not explain all of the variation in intergroup conflict, as the boycott in the middle-class black neighborhood of Jamaica, Queens, reveals. Higher numbers of immigrants, as in Queens, can raise the perception that newcomers are given advantages in their quest for mobility and consequently take away opportunities from African Americans. While the cultural hierarchy intrudes only occasionally in middle-class black neighborhoods, the occurrence of boycotts and other protests illustrates how easily the business routine can unravel, demonstrating the fine balance between civil relations and racial conflict.

Tension is mediated on an everyday level because merchants and their employees work hard to maintain the normal routine. However, Jewish and Korean merchants fully realize that their nonblack status in predominantly black neighborhoods can easily make them visible targets for angry customers, residents, and political entrepreneurs.[47] While customary civility may characterize everyday life in poor black communities, for both merchants and customers, that normalcy does not preclude the possibility of interethnic conflict. Boycotts, protests, and even violence and riots can erupt in these neighborhoods. Moreover, the fact that long-time merchants in black neighborhoods have been targets of boycotts demonstrates how easily race can inflect merchant-customer relations and become a source of conflict and protest. Inner-city poverty and inequality, coupled with the visible presence of socially mobile newcomers, provide fertile ground for the growth of protest motivations and intergroup conflict.

Group position theory helps us understand the importance of groups' subjective beliefs about where they ought to stand vis-à-vis others. It is precisely when groups contest their position in the ethnic hierarchy that social order breaks down. Although black customers may get along with local Jewish or Korean merchants on an individual, interpersonal basis, on a collective level, they object to the presence of out-group merchants in their communities because of what they symbolize. Nonblack-owned businesses are a symbol of black economic subordination to other groups. Jews and Koreans appear to receive benefits and opportunities denied to African Americans, which further inhibits African American economic progress.

It is important to embed merchant-customer relations within a structural framework. By incorporating two levels of race and ethnic relations—how merchants and customers interact in the store and how they interact as members of their racial and ethnic groups—we get a fuller understanding of the social processes that explain both civility and conflict, how they influence each other, and how they coexist.

CHAPTER 8

Shopping While Black: Symbolic Racism or the Same Old Racism?

I go into stores, especially downtown in the larger stores, and you're followed because they think you're going to pick something up. It's a fact. They will follow you. And it's just because when you walk into the store, the color of your skin determines how they will treat you.

—African American woman

It's almost impossible to understand what a black male goes through in our society. It is impossible. They cannot understand it.

—African American man

A great deal of scholarly research on merchant-customer relations in black neighborhoods focuses on the attitudes of inner-city merchants and the economic role of out-group businessowners such as Jews and Koreans, highlighting the negative treatment that black customers receive in their communities.[1] However, none of the previous studies has included the views of the customers themselves. Drawing on our seventy-five in-depth interviews of black customers in five predominantly black neighborhoods in New York City and Philadelphia, this chapter focuses on what black customers have to say about their shopping experiences, not only in their own communities but also in predominantly white neighborhoods.

Journalistic and scholarly accounts have highlighted the tension between Jewish and Korean storeowners and their customers in low-income black communities, focusing on the negative treatment that black residents receive in their own neighborhoods. However, my research indicates that black customers are treated far *worse* when they shop in white neighborhoods. To explain, they point to what they say is the age-old problem of racism. Expecting poor treatment, the black customers we interviewed explain that when shopping in white neighborhoods they regularly employ strategies to deal with encounters with whites. In addition, because middle-class blacks are more likely to move in white social worlds that few blacks regularly frequent, they are consequently *more* likely to encounter interracial prejudice and discrimination than less affluent blacks.

Even though black customers may be treated worse when they shop in white neighborhoods, in recent years black collective action has not been directed at larger white establishments. Rather, as political scientists Paul Sniderman and Thomas Piazza have noted, "Civil rights groups came to boycott not well-established businesses of white segregationists but tiny grocery stores run by Korean immigrants."[2] Why have black boycotters targeted local Mom and Pop immigrant-owned shops rather than larger, well-established corporations?

Racism in Everyday Life

Recent research on race and ethnic relations posits that blacks today face a new kind of racism—what David Sears and Donald Kinder refer to as "symbolic racism." Gone is the old-fashioned racism of Jim Crow laws and red-neck bigots. Researchers suggest that today's racism is far more nuanced and subtle, involving "the expression in terms of abstract ideological symbols and symbolic behaviors of the feeling that blacks are violating cherished values and making illegitimate demands on the racial status quo."[3] True, whites today are less likely to agree with blatantly negative stereotypes that blacks are stupid, violent, or lazy, compared with whites several decades ago. But does this necessarily mean that racism has changed in a definite and fundamental way?[4] Do black customers today face a new kind of racism when they shop in white neighborhoods, or is it simply the same old racism?[5]

Philomena Essed's comparative study of racism in the United States and the Netherlands introduces the concept of "everyday racism" to capture the covert expressions of racism in everyday situations. Everyday racism is a process that "is routinely created and reinforced through everyday practices . . . [and] connects structural forces of racism with routine situations in everyday life. It links ideological dimensions of racism with daily attitudes and interprets the reproduction of racism in terms of the experience of it in everyday life."[6] Everyday racism reflects the underlying power dimensions between groups, and it is rarely questioned because it is seen as a familiar part of everyday practices. Not surprisingly, Essed finds that one of the most prominent spheres in which blacks experience everyday racism is while shopping, because it involves frequent contact with whites. Sociologist Joe Feagin adds that shopping is not a relaxing activity for blacks, regardless of their wealth or status, because they must constantly deal with "the recurring strain of having to craft strategies for a broad range of discriminatory situations."[7]

While past research has documented the inferior treatment that blacks often receive while shopping in white neighborhoods and the poor treatment that blacks sometimes receive in black neighborhoods, no studies have compared black customers' shopping experiences in both black and white neighborhoods. The black customers we interviewed maintain that they receive *better* treatment from the storeowners in their communities than in predominantly white neighborhoods. They report that regardless of age, class, or gender, they are more frequently followed, ignored, treated rudely, or skipped over while they shop in department stores or small shops located in predominantly white neighborhoods. In fact, the black customers in the sample are nearly four times *more* likely to routinely have negative experiences while shopping in white compared to black neighborhoods. Whereas 9 percent of the black customers we interviewed report consistently negative treatment in their own community, 35 percent report consistently negative treatment when they shop in white neighborhoods. And whereas 56 percent report routinely positive experiences with the businessowners in their neighborhood, only 35 percent report that they routinely receive positive treatment when shopping in white neighborhoods. From a comparative perspective, blacks are treated far worse when they travel outside of their community to meet their consumer needs.

Based on their experiences shopping in white neighborhoods, blacks adopt myriad strategies to rebuff poor treatment. Some avoid shopping in white-owned businesses altogether, while others consciously dress to convey middle-class status, hoping that their appearance will inform white sales clerks and businessowners that they can afford to shop in their store. However, as we shall see, what clothing and accessories blacks wear can be irrelevant when white storeowners and sales associates recognize blackness on sight, and little else.

Shopping in White Neighborhoods

Most commonly, the blacks we interviewed complain that they are constantly followed when they shop. Although young blacks are often tailed in stores in their own community, once they become familiar with the merchants they are less likely to be followed while they browse. By comparison, black shoppers note that white business-owners and sales clerks in predominantly white neighborhoods routinely follow them, regardless of the shoppers' age or social status. For example, a nineteen-year-old Haitian American college student explains the difference between shopping along West Harlem's main business thoroughfare and in New York's Greenwich Village.

> Okay, like when I'm shopping on 125th Street, it's like, they just ask you [in a friendly tone], "Can I help you?" and it's like "No, it's okay, I'm just looking," or whatever. They're very courteous, very nice, they smile a lot. I went to the Village the day before yesterday, and this woman, she was white, and she said [in a serious, unfriendly tone], "Can I help you?" I was just like, "No, I'm just looking." She was like, "Okay, fine." So I go upstairs, and she comes and follows me, and she's like fixing up the clothes. And I said out loud [to my friend], "She knows that she's not even trying to fix these clothes. She just wants to make sure that I'm not trying to steal her ugly clothes."

The student explained that she is followed far more frequently when she shops outside of black neighborhoods than when she shops in her own community. When probed further and asked to what extent her age rather than her race may cause sales associates to follow her in stores, she quickly retorted, "Not even! It's just the color factor. It's insulting, because they're not following any of the white customers." She then elaborated that even when she shops with her mother, white sales associates in department stores continue to tail them.

> I was in the underwear department, and they followed me! And I was with my mother! And my mother was just like, "I'm not going to steal your bras lady. Come on, there's no need for you to follow me."

You can tell because they're not doing anything. They're like standing there. And they try to watch you from the periphery. It's like, they're not being sneaky.

African American businessowners reveal that they too have experienced this type of treatment when they are on the other side of the counter, recognizing that white storeowners target black customers because they immediately assume that blacks come to shoplift rather than buy. Some black customers choose to ignore these slights, while others openly challenge them. An African American woman from Mount Airy who became increasingly frustrated with a sales associate who followed her from one section of a department store to the next finally turned to her and bluntly stated, "Look, I may be black, but I have a credit card [from this store] with a $10,000 limit, so please stop following me around." Black customers recount numerous stories like this, adding that sales associates rarely, if ever, follow white customers, making it evident that race alone is used as a marker to screen customers. The blacks we interviewed say that the actions of the sales associates make it clear that they place white and black customers into two distinct categories—those who belong and those who do not.

Aside from being followed, black customers complain that sales associates erroneously accuse them of theft. They painfully recount the hurt, anger, and embarrassment of being singled out and accused of stealing merchandise for no apparent or justifiable reason. For instance, a forty-two-year-old African American woman tells how the employees of a department store located in a predominantly white section of Brooklyn stopped her on her way out because they suspected that she had stolen something from the store:

> I was in this department store, and once I was shopping around, and these people who worked in the store came up to me, and they said, "Someone saw you put something in your purse." And I was outraged! I couldn't believe that! And I just took out my purse, and I just dumped everything out on the counter, which you know, I didn't really have to do that. But then I just walked out, and I didn't go back to shop there.

Her staunch refusal to patronize that particular department store is a common response—one that I refer to as avoidance. Black shoppers assert that race continues to be a marker for storeowners and employees who are not accustomed to seeing black customers in predominantly white neighborhoods. This unfamiliarity leads them to question black customers' intentions and their presence more generally.

This cumulative personal experience with racism is at the very least hurtful and takes a heavy psychological toll on blacks, who must constantly remain alert in order to navigate difficult and offensive predicaments.[8] The African American woman who was accused of theft explains her reaction and sadly states that hurtful experiences such as these can lead blacks to be "paranoid" about entering white neighborhoods:

> You have to have been a victim of those things to really understand. You get very paranoid about certain things and going to certain places because you know it's a very hurtful thing to be accused of something you didn't do and know that you can't be comfortable shopping.

The black shoppers we interviewed explain that these recurring experiences elicit a range of responses from disbelief to anger to outrage to paranoia. For instance, a West Indian minister says that he often becomes paranoid about sales associates scrutinizing him while he shops in department stores.

> When I walk in a store, I feel that sometimes I walk back out paranoid. I walk in the store with money in my pocket, with the purpose and the intention of simply to buy something. I go in there to shop. But you go look in there, and they stop and think, "There's another blacky there." That kind of thing. There's cameras all over the store, and you still have people walking behind you to see what you're doing. And this is a fact, you become paranoid, you know, because you ask yourself, "Why is this person looking at me?"

Not only do the blacks in the sample claim to consistently receive poor treatment, but they also regretfully explain that white customers obviously receive preferential treatment. Observing the way white sales clerks treat white customers provides blacks with a fair barometer for how they feel they should and would like to be treated. For instance, they say that sales associates greet and approach white customers more promptly than they do black customers, sometimes even skipping over blacks in order to help whites who were clearly behind them in line. This type of preferential treatment may stem from assumptions that sales associates may make about black customers—that they cannot af-

ford to purchase the high-ticket items found in upscale department
stores or boutiques or, alternatively, that white customers will buy
more, thereby ensuring a higher commission. Or the negative treatment may simply reflect white sales associates' antiblack sentiments
more generally. Regardless of the source, the consequences for black
customers remain the same. Joe Feagin and Melvin Sikes find in their
study of middle-class African Americans that "whites with images of
black criminality engage in excessive surveillance, and . . . Black shoppers at all income levels report being ignored when in need of service."[9] The blacks we interviewed feel that sales associates use race to
classify customers and determine which shoppers are a better bet.

Businessowners and sales associates often practice statistical discrimination—the practice of using group membership as a proxy in the
absence of clear information about individuals—and, consequently,
negatively color black customers' shopping experiences.[10] Although
statistical discrimination has for the most part been used to explain
employers' hiring preferences and practices, it is also a useful tool for
understanding white sales clerks' behavior toward black customers in
white neighborhoods. Classical economic theory posits that the market will eventually tease out all forms of discrimination, since discriminating on any grounds is unprofitable, thereby ultimately producing a
color-blind market.[11] However, based on these vivid accounts, it appears that the taste for discrimination has not disappeared. The discriminatory and aloof treatment that black consumers receive when
they shop in predominantly white neighborhoods reflects the ideological dimensions of racism constructed in everyday practices. Shopkeepers' actions vividly illustrate that racism in white neighborhoods
has not changed in a definite and fundamental way. While segregation
laws have long been declared unconstitutional, black customers explain that they are still treated poorly when they venture into white
neighborhoods. While blacks may be free to shop wherever they
please, this does not necessarily ensure that they will be treated fairly
when they do so.

Legitimation and Wearing Your Class

To help them deal with the frustration of these negative encounters,
black customers have developed various responses to rebuff, or at least
minimize, the poor treatment they often receive when they shop in

white-owned and operated businesses. One common response is "legit-imation." Blacks, especially middle-class blacks, are often tempted to prove that they can afford to purchase the merchandise sold in the stores, to legitimate their class status to others. For instance, an African American man in Mount Airy explains how the haughty attitude of the sales associates in an upscale boutique nearly provoked him to pur-chase an article of clothing that he did not particularly want, just to prove to the sales associates that he could afford to buy it.

> I walked in, and they looked at us like, "Oh you can't really afford any-thing in here." And just to prove a point to them, I did look at some-thing, and what I was going to do was buy it, and then my wife was like, "You need to come up out of here. We'll go to another store." I wanted to show them that I can buy something out of there, but then I was like, they don't need my business if they're going to treat me like that.

Another means blacks have of dealing with the negative treatment is to consciously "wear their class" while shopping, using markers such as style of dress, expensive accessories, conservative hairstyle, and white middle-class speech and mannerisms to convey that they can afford to shop in the stores. Such visible class and status indicators communi-cate that the black shoppers "belong" just like everyone else. In *The Rage of the Privileged Class,* Ellis Cose notes that middle-class blacks use the tactic of dressing up or carrying expensive accessories to counter racial assumptions that sales associates often make.[12] While whites may be able to enter upscale shops and department stores wearing a T-shirt, jeans, baseball cap, and sneakers without feeling uncomfortable, when black customers are dressed in this fashion, they are routinely followed, treated rudely, or ignored by sales associates who assume that they are poor or threatening. An African American man from Mount Airy explains how sales associates treat him differently when he dresses well compared with when he dresses more casually. When he dresses up, he says he finds that sales associates are noticeably more friendly, courteous, and helpful. When black customers dress casually, however, salespeople will go so far as to ask them to wait outside of the store if they do not intend to purchase anything.

> I think it's all based on how I'm dressed. If you're going in dressed like you really don't have any money or whatever, you might not get too

much sales help. But if you walk in there and you present yourself nice, hair is combed and stuff like that, they pretty much treat you nice.

He says he noticed the stark difference in treatment one day when he went shopping with a black female friend who wore a baseball cap and no makeup:

> And the reason why I noticed the difference was because we were traveling with a friend, and she had her son with her, and she just came out like, "I'm just coming out here to get one thing, and then I'm going home." We wound up shopping, and she looked kind of like, she had a baseball cap on, and no makeup, and she was just out there having a nice time. But her appearance wasn't too great. And when we went into some stores, it was like, "Well what do you want? If you're not buying anything, then please wait outside the store," and stuff like that.

Middle-class blacks use dress as a means of visually communicating their class status. To be treated as well as middle-class whites, middle-class blacks assert that they must consciously convey their class position, yet even then there is no guarantee that they will be treated well. Black shoppers are acutely aware that their status is precarious in the eyes of outsiders, who primarily see their race and make judgments based on race alone.

In predominantly white settings, race often becomes *more* significant than class, because the label "black" is laden with negative connotations, often translating into "poor" and even "dangerous."[13] Ellis Cose refers to this as the "permanent vulnerability of one's status," because middle-class status for blacks is "provisional." Too often, race undermines class and status.[14] Many middle-class blacks do not enjoy the privileges that should go hand in hand with a good education, a high-paying job, and the economic resources that allow them to shop according to their class and status positions.[15]

Because middle-class blacks are far more likely to move in a predominantly white or racially integrated social world, they are more likely to experience racial discrimination than their less affluent counterparts. Jennifer Hochschild thoughtfully elaborates that middle-class blacks may be "structurally most freed from the constraints of race," yet they find themselves "often obsessed by it."[16] By contrast, poor blacks live in a far more segregated world and are therefore much less likely to come into day-to-day contact with whites. They experience less racial discrimination on a daily basis because they have less opportunity to experience it. Race matters in the everyday lives of middle-class blacks in a way that it does not for poor blacks precisely because their class position opens opportunities for daily interracial contact.

The West Indians we interviewed are in a situation similar to middle-class blacks. In a white social milieu, they say ethnicity, like class, takes a backseat to race. In white dominant social spaces such as department stores, black ethnicity matters little or not at all. Like the middle-class African Americans in the sample, the West Indian customers strongly assert that white sales associates and businessowners in white neighborhoods recognize only blackness on sight, rather than ethnicity, nativity, accent, or class.[17] Immigrating from countries that recognize vast differences among the West Indian population in terms of social status, ethnicity, and skin color, many first-generation West Indians are shocked to find that most white Americans simply see them as black Americans and treat them accordingly. Mary Waters's extensive research on West Indian immigrants vividly describes how black immigrants are not prepared to deal with the degree of "interpersonal racism" that they encounter in their everyday experiences with whites.[18] Race permeates the daily lives of black immigrants in both subtle and not so subtle ways. Waters explains that these "daily hassles" and "indignities" make black immigrants all too aware of America's "overarching concern with race in every encounter."[19] According to the black customers we interviewed, while Jewish and Korean merchants in black neighborhoods soon become attuned to the vast heterogeneity in black communities, white sales associates in mostly white neighborhoods are far less discerning and adopt the negative stereotypes that are associated with race. In short, the black customers feel that white sales clerks statistically discriminate against black customers as a group, making them feel unwelcome when they shop.

Avoidance

Low-income shoppers who reside in poor neighborhoods are less likely to shop outside of their community, since many cannot afford to pay the transportation costs or do not have a car to travel beyond the confines of their neighborhood on a regular basis. While public transportation in New York City and Philadelphia is far-reaching and easily accessible, the low-income blacks we interviewed rely mainly on local neighborhood stores to meet their consumer needs. They explain that shopping outside of their community is often not worth the extra time, the hassle of commuting, or even the price of two subway tokens. Unlike the poor, middle-class blacks are considerably more mobile and also can afford to shop in department stores and businesses that cater to a more affluent clientele. Yet because of the negative experiences they routinely have while shopping, some middle-class blacks choose to avoid these settings altogether. One African American woman who worked in an office on Manhattan's Upper East Side explains why she refuses to patronize the boutiques in that predominantly white, affluent neighborhood:

> I used to work on the Upper East Side, and I didn't really shop at any of the stores because I didn't want to be followed, and that's a problem. That's definitely a problem. I have the money, and I demand respect, but my way of demanding respect is just to avoid going to those stores.

Others take avoidance a step further, refusing to follow the dominant norms just to be accepted by whites. For instance, an African American man who lives in a middle-class suburb in Queens contends that he refuses to adopt middle-class white mannerisms, behavior, speech patterns, and styles of dress for the sake of others. Moreover, he is critical of coethnics who willingly do so, declaring, "We as black people make such an effort to please the greater society, the society in control, just because we want to be accepted and want them to say, 'This one is civilized. This one is okay.'" He avoids frequenting stores in neighborhoods that make him feel like an outsider or a criminal. Avoiding certain department stores, shops, and even neighborhoods is more than a tactic to avoid discrimination. For blacks, it is an act of quiet retaliation and sometimes a staunch refusal to enter social spaces where they are not treated fairly.

The avoidance tactic is not reserved only for shopping. Some middle-class blacks explain that the negative treatment they receive in nonblack neighborhoods is one principal reason they prefer living in black communities. For example, an African American businessowner in Queens explains that he refuses to live in a predominantly white neighborhood where he feels that he would have to fight discrimination and racism on a daily basis. He says a close friend of his who lives near Lincoln Center (an affluent neighborhood in midtown Manhattan) feels like an outsider because his neighbors fear his presence, even hesitating to ride in the same elevator with him in his very own apartment building.

> I would *never* live where my friend lives, because if I had to live somewhere where I'm just sleeping, and I can't even be part of the community, what good is it? He gets in the elevator, and people hesitate to get on the elevator with him. I mean, he lives in the building!

He describes visiting his friend at his apartment, explaining that white women are fearful and uncomfortable when he steps into the elevator with them, immediately putting on a "plastic smile" in order to "disarm" him.

> When I go to visit him and get into the elevator, the women especially, they all act like they're airline stewardesses or something, they have this plastic smile on. They give you this plastic smile as if like, "Oh I know how to disarm this so-called whatever he is. I'll smile at him; this way he won't do anything to me." That seems to be the tactic you know? It's not only Lincoln Center, it's also other areas of the city.

Complete avoidance of white neighborhoods or white milieus is virtually impossible for members of the black middle-class, since their class position often requires that they travel in racially integrated settings—not only while shopping but also for work, school, or even leisure activities.[20] Middle-class blacks say that when they encounter white strangers in public spaces, many whites assume that they—and all blacks—are lower class and dangerous and respond accordingly, with fear or threats.[21] Unlike whites, who rarely if ever face these awkward, insulting, embarrassing, and hurtful situations, the blacks we interviewed explain that they must constantly remain aware, to cautiously moderate their behavior and employ strategies to deal with these racially prejudiced encounters. Blacks have a strong sense of collective identity, both because they choose to identify with other blacks and because they cannot escape their racial identity.[22]

The Salience of Race and Group Position

Race remains salient in the daily lives of blacks, poor and middle-class alike, who must regularly employ strategies to deal with an array of discriminatory encounters. However, because middle-class blacks are more likely to move in white social worlds and enter settings that few blacks regularly frequent, they are consequently *more* likely than less affluent blacks to encounter racial prejudice and discrimination. Shopping in predominantly white neighborhoods is just one context in which the blacks we interviewed must deal with negative encounters with whites. Given the poor treatment that blacks receive while shopping, has race declined in significance for the black middle-class, as William Julius Wilson pronounced so strongly more than two decades ago?[23] While the race-class debate remains hotly contested among sociologists, growing research on the black middle class illustrates that race significantly affects one's life chances, even for affluent blacks, who, unlike affluent whites, do not have the privilege of escaping their racial identity.[24]

When black shoppers enter predominantly white businesses, they often sense that white storeowners, sales associates, and customers feel that they are encroaching on "their space." The poor treatment that black customers receive, coupled with the preferential treatment of whites, signal to blacks that they are not welcome—or at the very least, less welcome—in white-dominated social spaces. So while de jure segregation no longer exists, black customers feel that it has merely been replaced by de facto segregation. For blacks, racism does not seem to have changed in a definite and fundamental way.

If black customers are treated far worse in predominantly white neighborhoods compared with their own, why do we see less evidence of overt intergroup conflict in the form of boycotts in white communities? As Paul Sniderman and Thomas Piazza ask, why are there boycotts of "tiny grocery stores run by Korean immigrants" but not "well-established businesses of white segregationists?"[25] Why is it that black customers are more likely to accept the poor treatment they receive in white neighborhoods, while they vociferously decry to poor treatment from the storeowners in their own communities and object in general to the presence of nonblack-owned businesses?

Here, we turn to the work of social psychologists Henri Tajfel and John Turner for some guidance.[26] Tajfel and Turner noted long ago that groups do not compare themselves to every possible out-group. Instead, they are far more likely to compare themselves with groups that are closer to them with regard to physical proximity, situational salience, or status. Blacks and whites do not live in close residential proximity—quite the opposite, in fact, as Douglas Massey and Nancy Denton have empirically demonstrated in their convincingly argued work *American Apartheid*.[27] In many racial and class spheres, blacks and whites occupy opposite poles, and as a historically subordinated group, American blacks today are far less likely to challenge white-dominated structures and institutions. Immigrant entrepreneurs in black communities are not part of white society, and, furthermore, they set up shop in black neighborhoods. Not only are immigrants closer to blacks in physical proximity, but they are also closer to them in status and situational salience. Their proximity—in every sense of the word—makes protest more likely to be directed toward the Jewish and Korean businesspeople in black communities, rather than toward white businesses in white neighborhoods.

Furthermore, the resources—both economic and social—required to attack white institutions such as large department stores are far greater than those needed to boycott the Korean-owned fruit and vegetable market on the corner or the local Jewish-owned clothing store. Boycotting small retail shops in one's community is fairly simple, especially because political entrepreneurs can easily garner community-level support. It would be a far more complex and difficult task in a white social space, where a largely white population would perceive black boycotters far less sympathetically. Therefore, although black customers may object to the treatment that they receive in the businesses located in white neighborhoods, they realize all too well that the negative treatment is rooted in a long and complex historical legacy. White-dominated institutions are often too formidable to take on, since blacks would be up against the numerical, racial, and status majority, and their charges would likely fall on deaf ears.

Blacks have a far better chance to challenge and secure their group position in their own communities. Poor treatment in one's own community should not be and is not tolerated. In black neighborhoods, blacks are clearly the numerical majority and black culture is revered. The black customers we interviewed strongly believe that in their community, they should not have to legitimate their status by "wearing their class" as they do in white neighborhoods. Nor should they have to adopt nonblack styles, mannerisms, and behavior to be accepted by the Jewish, Korean, Asian Indian, and Middle Eastern merchants in their neighborhood. Relinquishing control in the white social world may be anticipated (or at the very least not unexpected), but relinquishing control in the black community is to be confronted and challenged.

A great deal of research on race and ethnic relations in inner-city neighborhoods focuses on interethnic conflict and the prejudicial attitudes of businessowners, highlighting the negative treatment that black customers receive in their own communities. However, none of the previous studies has included the views of the customers themselves. My research focuses on black customers' shopping experiences, comparing their encounters in black and white neighborhoods. Black shoppers attest that they are treated far *worse* in predominantly white neighborhoods than in their own communities. In fact, I found that black shoppers are three and a half times more likely to consistently experience negative treatment when they shop outside of their communities than when they shop within them. They are more likely to be routinely followed, ignored, or skipped over by clerks in stores located in white neighborhoods. Therefore, when we speak of black-Jewish or black-Korean relations, it is important to understand these customer-merchant relationships within the larger framework. From a comparative perspective, we can see that focusing on the binary minority-minority relationship shifts our attention away from the poorer treatment that black shoppers receive in predominantly white neighborhoods.

Middle-class blacks often respond to this negative treatment by wearing signs of their class status, but even obvious class markers such as expensive clothing and accessories do not guarantee that whites will treat blacks fairly while they shop. Race continues to be the most salient factor in the daily lives of black consumers, who must carefully adjust their behavior while shopping and regularly employ strategies to deal with an array of offensive encounters. These encounters call into question whether the racism of today is fundamentally different from the racism of old. The subtle and not-so-subtle acts of discrimination reported by black shoppers illustrate that, in the end, it is still the same old racism.

Middle-class blacks who shop and travel outside of their community confront the stigma of race and the negative stereotypes of the under-class on a regular basis. As Raymond Franklin writes, "The overrepresentation of blacks in the lower class casts shadows that stigmatize working- and middle-class blacks for reasons of race alone."[28] It should also be noted that the constant slights, and the outright preferential treatment that white shoppers receive, have deleterious consequences not only for black shoppers but also for white merchants, who lose the business of a significant portion of America's population.

Many of the young black men we interviewed admitted to having been searched and questioned unnecessarily by police officers just because they happened to be hanging out on an apartment stoop or street corner, or simply because they were at the wrong place at the wrong time. Police also stop black drivers for no apparent reason. Black men and women maintain that white women often clutch their purse as they pass by. Others, particularly men, say they make an effort not to run at full speed in public, because people tend to assume that a running black man has just committed a crime. These experiences transcend class and affect low- and middle-class blacks alike.

Race continues to shape the daily lives of blacks in ways that whites and other nonblacks may not understand, since they do not experience what one black middle-class customer calls "silent discrimination" on a daily basis. As an African American transit authority worker asserts with a mix of frustration, sadness, and resignation, "It is almost impossible for a white person to understand what a black male goes through in our society. It is impossible. They cannot understand it."

CHAPTER 9

Conclusion: Forging a Culture of Reciprocity and Respect

This book addresses two main questions. What are merchant-customer relations like in black communities? And what do merchant-customer relations tell us about race and ethnic relations more generally among blacks, Jews, and Koreans in urban America? The 1992 Los Angeles riot, the 1995 firebombing of Freddy's clothing store in Harlem, and the 1990–1991 boycotts of Korean-owned grocery stores helped to reinforce the public's belief that racial conflict and violence are facts of life in urban America. The media's framing of these events depicted inner cities as communities fraught with racial tension, with African Americans pitted against Koreans, Jews, and other immigrant newcomers. Black-Korean and black-Jewish conflict—as these conflicts were glibly labeled—were quickly reified by the media and public alike. Snapshots of conflict, however, offer an incomplete portrait of the complex realities that underlie them.

While media images have focused on outbreaks of conflict, previous scholarly research has examined the structural context in which interethnic conflict emerges. To explain interracial conflict, sociologists have directed our attention to structural conditions such as chronic unemployment, persistent poverty, and interethnic competition. These conditions, researchers have argued, provide a context ripe for boycotts, violence, and riots. However, what this line of reasoning fails to resolve is that boycotts, firebombings, and riots are anomalous events in the inner city, while structural conditions such as poverty, unemployment, and inequality are ever present. By focusing strictly on structural conditions, past research has overpredicted the level of conflict we are likely to find between merchants and customers in poor black neighborhoods.

The main argument I make in this book is that there is an important, previously untold story—that of the routine nature of daily life between merchants and customers that businessowners and their employees work hard to maintain each day. While media images highlight racial warfare, I find that most merchant-customer interactions are positive and civil. Using routine as a heuristic model, I examine the ways in which civility and routine are negotiated and maintained each day. Using an ethnomethodological lens, I discover that civility prevails in everyday life because merchants and their employees actively work to preserve it. Jewish and Korean merchants hire black employees, place women at the front-end of the business, and give in to customers' demands to keep the business routine in place. By making these investments, merchants actively work to minimize altercations with customers and racially charged anger. Furthermore, the fact that the vast majority of merchant-customer interactions are free of conflict demonstrates that merchant-customer interactions in themselves are not the source of hostility that leads to boycotts, violence, and riots.

I should mention one caveat before continuing. By emphasizing everyday routine and social order, I do not propose that conflict is unimportant or less important in the study of merchant-customer relations, or in race and ethnic relations more generally. Interethnic conflict is obviously an important topic in its own right. Conflict has had historical significance for minorities in the United States, particularly racial and ethnic minorities, who have made unprecedented gains through protest and conflict in our society—the civil rights movement being a perfect exemplar. Clearly, protest and conflict have played significant roles in advancing the status of racial and ethnic minorities in our society, especially African Americans. Hence, conflict has been and continues to be pivotal in shaping the nature of race and ethnic relations in this country.

Conflict is viewed by some scholars as a part of the everyday social order, and by others as a breakdown of that order. In this book, I have taken the latter perspective, because conflict emerges so infrequently and fails to characterize the everyday life in the black neighborhoods that I have studied. Interethnic relations are composed of both social order and conflict, as I have demonstrated, but to overemphasize the level of tension or conflict would be to paint an inaccurate portrait of the daily life in black urban communities.

Having spent a great deal of time in neighborhoods like Harlem and West Philadelphia, I have witnessed far more prosaic and even humanizing encounters than conflicts between merchants and customers. For example, one Korean owner of a clothing store in Harlem is known by her black employees and even some of her customers as *Umma* (Korean for Mom), which accurately describes her maternal nature. She takes care of a man who was formerly homeless, buying him lunch every day and giving him clothes as well as paying him for performing small daily tasks. She even went so far as to locate his sister so that he would have a place to live and could get the proper medication for his diabetes. Encounters like this, often overlooked by the media in favor headlines that portray racial warfare, also make up the fabric of commercial life in black communities. Amid the warmth of some relationships and the antagonism of others, most merchants and customers agree that it is just business as usual, forging a commercial culture of reciprocity and respect.

However, civility does not come without effort. It is the product of hard work and investments on the part of the merchants and their employees, who realize that thwarting altercations with their customers is of primary importance in running a successful business. That work may entail acquiescing to customers' demands, perhaps by taking something back that has been used or damaged; storeowners quickly learn to bend their rules in order to preserve the everyday routine. The role of cultural and maternal brokers should also be underscored. Black employees in nonblack-owned businesses can act as cultural brokers who mediate, defuse, and, most important, de-racialize tensions between merchants and customers. Black employees also signal to customers that storeowners are giving something back to the community from which they profit, thereby socially embedding nonblack-owned businesses in the neighborhood. Female merchants fulfill a similar function as maternal brokers who serve as an "interactional resource" when dealing with customers. Often, female merchants perform the emotional labor in the stores, defusing rising tensions and bringing a more humanizing dimension to commercial encounters. Cultural and maternal brokers work to ensure that the day-to-day routine runs as smoothly as possible. Constructing ordinariness is an important goal, especially when the failure to do so can have dramatic consequences.

Racialization and Stereotyping Out-Groups

While the vast majority of merchant-customer interactions are civil, from time to time merchants and customers do get into arguments. Most arguments arise from small economic disputes, such as when a customer wants to return an item without a receipt or bring something back that has been used or damaged. When this happens, a merchant's denial of a customer's request for a refund or exchange can easily be translated into a racialized framework. A Korean merchant's refusal to give a cash refund for a defective beeper or an already-worn dress, for example, or a Jewish merchant's decision to repossess furniture that has not been paid off in full, can be seen as symbolic of cheap, exploitative out-group businessowners who take advantage of the black customer and the black community at large. The irate customer who is denied the cash refund or has his wages garnisheed because he failed to keep up his monthly payments for furniture that he purchased on credit may react not to the objective features of the situation but instead to what the situation represents. Correlatively, when black customers get angry and yell at merchants because they do not see eye to eye, or when customers default on their payments, Jewish and Korean storeowners may quickly engage in stereotypes about blacks—that they are ignorant, uneducated, and irresponsible. In each scenario, merchants and customers alike may reinterpret and racially code what are essentially economic arguments. Race can polarize the simplest interactions and become mobilized in conflict-ridden ways.

Sociologist Herbert Gans wrote about black-Jewish relations in the 1960s that "when Negroes express their anger in anti-Semitic terms, it is only because many of the whites who affect their lives are Jewish; if the ghetto storeowners, landlords and teachers were Chinese, Negro hostility would surely be anti-Chinese."[1] And as the work of Robert K. Merton reminds us, when merchants and customers engage in stereotyping, they often react not to the objective features of the situation but instead, and at times primarily, to what the situation represents.[2] So while merchants and customers may get along with one other on an individual basis, their routinely positive encounters do not preclude the possibility of negative out-group stereotyping and racially charged conflict.

Racial and ethnic stereotypes are readily available, and when tempers flare, stereotypes can quickly be evoked and adopted. Although an individual may have experienced hundreds or even thousands of positive encounters with individuals from out-groups, one negative experience can easily conjure up negative stereotypes that have little to do with the situation at hand. The presence of anti-Semitic, anti-Asian, and anti-immigrant sentiments in the larger society provide meaningful and ready-made frameworks into which blacks can place their negative personal experiences with Jewish and Korean merchants. At the same time, the presence of anti-black sentiment provides stereotypes with which Jewish and Korean merchants can label their negative experiences with black customers. Furthermore, when tensions run high, something powerful blocks the generalization of positive feelings about individuals to the out-group as a whole. In other words, although blacks, Jews, and Koreans may regularly engage in positive interpersonal encounters, individual interactions do not necessarily translate into positively changed views of out-groups as a whole, as the contact hypothesis would have us believe.

Jewish and Korean merchants in black neighborhoods recognize this all too well. One Korean fast food restaurant owner who has been in Harlem for thirteen years and is a mainstay in the community understands that she can easily become the target of racially charged anger at any point. Even this veteran of the street—who has many regular customers who eat in her establishment every day and who charges her elderly customers only half price—knows that as a Korean merchant on 125th Street, she is always at risk of conflict, regardless of how many people in the community support her. Her nonblackness— and her Koreanness, even more specifically—could easily make her a target for dissatisfied customers, who could decide to picket outside her store and protest to move Koreans out of Harlem.

Similarly, a second-generation Jewish businessowner in Harlem who has long hired people from the community and has watched with pleasure as former employees have opened businesses of their own realizes that he is not immune to boycotts, a lesson he learned after Roland Smith firebombed Freddy's clothing store several years ago. Undeterred by the violence of the incident and the deaths of the seven nonblack employees of Freddy's, overzealous supporters of Smith's cause immediately turned their attention to this businessowner, whose store is just a few blocks away. Picketers outside his store shouted "Kill the Jew bastards" and other violent, anti-Semitic slogans to demonstrate their dissatisfaction with Jewish-owned businesses in Harlem. This commercial veteran had no connection to Fred Harari, the owner of Freddy's, other than the fact that both are Jewish. However, in the heat of the moment, race, ethnicity, and religion were apparently enough of a commonality, and out-group stereotyping and racially charged anger spilled over from one Jewish retailer to the next. Longtime Jewish and Korean merchants in low-income communities—who know and get along with their customers—fully comprehend that their nonblack status is a clear marker that leaves them open to hostile customers and boycotters.

From Civil Relations to Racial Conflict

I have argued that past research and the media accounts of merchant-customer relations in urban communities have been biased toward conflict and controversy and do not reflect the full range of commercial life in black communities.[3] Conflict may be good raw material for newspaper headlines and television leads, but there is a wide gap between the true nature of merchant-customer relations and their public image. The prevailing image of racial warfare is inconsistent with most merchant-customer interactions, which are far from hostile and antagonistic. Instead, most merchant-customer interactions are characterized by civility, routine, and the simple philosophy of business as usual.

That said, while the day-to-day interactions between merchants and customers may be civil and ordinary, small events can trigger anger, with race polarizing the simplest interactions. Race can inflect merchant-customer relations in diverse ways, and in extreme cases race can become the source of motivations for protest that lead to boycotts and violence. Conflict, and the threat of conflict, can arise in spite of positive merchant-customer relations and in spite of the merchants' investments to maintain civility, because issues of race, opportunity, and the struggle for group position are ever present in America's racially and ethnically stratified society.

As Jews move up and out of black communities and new immigrants move in, African Americans witness the mobility of other groups and see them realizing the American dream of success. They may not object to immigrants per se, but they do object to the notion that the foreign-born of all backgrounds seem to move effortlessly ahead of them, presumably with government aid, and seemingly at their expense. Imported into interethnic relationships in black communities are beliefs and ideologies about opportunity structure and group position. It is when subordinate groups challenge their position in the ethnic hierarchy that everyday routine breaks down. The fact that boycotts, protests, and riots take place in low-income black neighborhoods normally characterized by civility and routine demonstrates the fine balance between civil relations and racial conflict.

The structural context in which merchants and customers come into contact matters in important ways. In one-on-one encounters between merchants and clients, it links microinteractional processes with social structural outcomes—providing what Anthony Giddens refers to as "structuration."[4] Merchant-customer relations, and interethnic relations more generally, do not exist in a social vacuum. When we view individual interactions within the context of inequality, rising immigration, group position, and group mobility, we find that inner-city poverty and inequality, coupled with the visible presence of upwardly mobile newcomers, provides fertile ground for protest motivations. At times, the balance between civility and conflict tips in favor of protest and intergroup conflict. Business ownership in black communities is one source of contention, because it is a visible and symbolic construction of opportunity and group position. The struggle for group position within an opportunity structure that seems to favor all other racial and ethnic groups over African Americans provides the link between civility and conflict.

This brings us to another important point: boycotts and picket lines often have little to do with the individual merchant per se, and much to do with the symbolism behind Jewish, Korean, and other nonblack businessowners. The resentment of Jews and Koreans stems from different roots; that is, Jews and Koreans are not functional equivalents, as the theory of middleman minorities would lead us to believe. The blacks we interviewed resent Jews because they feel that America is a "Jewish-run society" and that Jews control the nation's leading institutions, from Hollywood to the elite universities to the Fortune 500 companies to the local banks that deny them business loans. Blacks' resentment of Koreans has much more to do with their foreignness, their steadfast reluctance to adopt the mainstream language and norms, the unfair advantages they appear to receive, and their ability to get ahead, seemingly at the expense of African Americans.

Class also shapes merchant-customer relations in a variety of ways. In middle-income black neighborhoods, customers and merchants are more likely to get along on an interpersonal level, but even so, some middle-class blacks object to the presence of out-group merchants in their community. Although the presence of Jewish and Korean retailers in these neighborhoods is unrelated to middle-class blacks' personal or economic well-being, some object to the dominating presence of Jewish and Korean businessowners because they perceive them as outsiders who take opportunities away from blacks as a group. Business ownership in black communities evokes blacks' sense of collective identity, and it is the issue of black control over their own communities that makes black collective identity both salient and contentious. The predominance of nonblack-owned businesses in black neighborhoods is a symbol of black economic subordination to other groups.

Class matters even more in the context of persistent poverty and extreme inequality. When customers are poor, Jewish and Korean merchants, by comparison, appear enormously successful. Poor black customers are the most vulnerable to adopting the view that new immigrant entrepreneurs are little more than "parasites" who take opportunities away from African American businessowners and local residents, regardless of the positive relations they may have with individual merchants. Although immigrant merchants may not directly compete with African American merchants or residents for jobs or profits, low-income residents are more likely to perceive the newcomers as outside competitors who take opportunities away from them. Whether immigrant entrepreneurs (and nonblack businessowners more generally) actually compete with African American entrepreneurs is secondary to the perception that they do.

Frustrated by the infusion of immigrants who barely speak English and appear unfamiliar with American ways and yet are able to open up shops nevertheless, poor African Americans believe the U.S. government must be helping out the newcomers and wonder why such aid has not come their way.[5] It is a common misperception among the low-income black customers we interviewed that small business owners, especially "foreigners" such as Koreans, receive special tax breaks or loans from U.S. banks or government agencies to help them open their businesses. In New York City, where more than one-fourth of the residents are foreign-born, African Americans hold even more tenaciously to this belief than African Americans in Philadelphia, where immigrants make up less than 7 percent of the population. Fallacious as this perception may be, low-income residents are quick to embrace it because they cannot otherwise explain how immigrant merchants are able to accumulate capital and "take over" the businesses in their communities.

In the struggle over "what is" versus "what ought to be," groups constantly jockey for position and try to secure their place in America's racial and ethnic hierarchy. Thus, while merchants make considerable investments to keep the business routine in order, their efforts cannot preclude the rise of protest motivations and the outbreak of intergroup conflict.

Beyond Black and White

Today's multiethnic America is far different from the America of the past. To borrow an overly used but apropos cliché, America is no longer black and white. The post-1965 waves of immigration unquestionably changed the face of America's urban landscape. Representing 11 percent of the total U.S. population, today's immigrants have a discernible presence in urban America as businessowners, domestic workers, computer programmers, and engineers. A mixed lot, the new urban immigrants are far more diverse in terms of their skills and national origins than their European predecessors who arrived on America's doorstep a century ago. Today, 80 percent of post-1965 immigrants hail from the Americas and Asia; a mere 13 percent originated in Europe.[6] Although America's ethnic landscape has become far more multiracial and multiethnic, research in the field of race and ethnic relations has not kept pace with the nation's vastly changing demographic landscape.

According to Census Bureau projections, by the year 2050 America's Hispanic and Asian populations will triple, reaching 24 percent and 12 percent of the United States population, respectively. Although the white population will increase by 9 percent, its share of the total population will decline from 72 to 53 percent, while the African American share of the total population will increase only slightly, from 13 to 15 percent. Given the growing numbers of immigrants from a variety of ethnic backgrounds, research should continue to examine how immigrant newcomers interact with and forge relations with native-born populations.

To date, the scholarly debate on race and ethnic relations has stayed for the most part within a binary racial framework. Relatively few studies in the field of race and ethnic relations go beyond the traditional black-white framework to examine interethnic relations among racial and ethnic minorities. African Americans, Jews, and Koreans are all numerical minorities in America, and in one sphere or another, they are also status minorities. Although native-born, African Americans occupy one of the lowest rungs in America's ethnic hierarchy in terms of median household income, poverty level, and residential segregation. Jews are a religious minority, and anti-Semitism—whether overt or not—remains prevalent to this day in America. And Koreans, a predominantly immigrant group, bear the stigma of foreignness and face anti-immigrant bias. Within these groups differences abound, yet all three find themselves in black urban neighborhoods, negotiating issues of race, status, opportunity, and group position. Future research should focus on the multiracial and multiethnic complexities of America's changing landscape.

Striving for the American Dream

Immigrants who are new to the country and its system of racial and ethnic stratification do not foresee that their role as merchants in the black community will be laden with such import, symbolism, and contention. They arrive in the United States with grand hopes of making a better life for themselves and realizing the American dream of success. Running a small retail business in an inner-city neighborhood may not be what they had in mind. Many Korean immigrants, for example, educated and trained to be white-collar professionals, regard self-employment as a real sign of downward mobility. However, given the obstacles they face in the primary labor market, their loose command of the

English language, and their inability to transfer their credentials, immigrants often turn to self-employment as an alternative to working in relatively low-salaried jobs. Entrepreneurship thus offers a ladder for upward mobility and success, given the limited options immigrants have in the primary labor market.

Often, for economic reasons, the foreign-born set up shop serving the minority poor, where they are exposed to persistent poverty and its consequences—welfare dependency, teenage pregnancy, single motherhood, unemployment, and drugs.[7] Making their adjustment even more difficult is the fact that the foreign-born often migrate from ethnically homogeneous countries and have little understanding of the nuances of America's racial and ethnic order.

Real and identifiable symbols of the American dream are ever present for the newly arrived—in their relatives who have paved the way before them, and in the stories of glamorous professional athletes and entertainment stars who come from humble origins. Popular figures who have "made it" impress upon all—the recently arrived and the native-born, poor and affluent alike—that the dream works. Everyone, regardless of their station in life, has a shot at getting ahead and making it. In black, urban America, the American dream is constructed not only by sensational media images at the national level but also at the local level. In their own communities, it is the Jewish and Korean entrepreneurs who seem to have seized and attained the American dream—and so easily—something seemingly beyond the grasp of poor African Americans.

Jewish, Korean, and now Asian Indian and Middle Eastern immigrants are doing what African Americans have long dreamed of but found impossible to accomplish—setting up shop and operating the businesses in black communities. With comparatively fewer class and ethnic resources and less social capital upon which they can draw, native-born blacks have historically been and continue to be unable to compete with foreign-born businessowners on a level playing field. Jews, Koreans, and other nonblacks have historically dominated and continue to dominate the retail niche in black communities.

A crucial consequence of the historical presence of nonblack entrepreneurs in black communities is that African American customers have become accustomed to dealing with outsiders for business purposes. Both because they are used to dealing with other ethnic groups and because Jewish and Korean merchants can afford to offer credit and lower prices, African American customers are more likely to patronize Jewish- and Korean-owned stores over their black-owned counterparts. African American retailers find that race can also inflect their interactions with coethnic customers. Ready-made stereotypes about the inferiority of black-owned businesses are available for black customers to refer to when they have negative experiences with coethnic merchants. While race may protect black retailers from boycotters, it can serve as a disadvantage in business. African American merchants claim that blacks' reluctance to patronize black-owned stores has to do with in-group criticism and self-hatred, but customers retort, it's all about getting the best deal, regardless of who is doing the selling.

The nation's inner cities may provide a route to realizing immigrant dreams, but it is also here that the foreign-born are forced to reconcile their dreams with American realities. The immigrant dream was abruptly shattered on April 29, 1992. In the Los Angeles riot, Korean businessowners suffered devastating losses totaling $400 million in property damage. Koreans now refer to this unforgettable turning point in their American lives as Sai-I-Gu, referring to the month and day that the riots began. The worst domestic uprising of the century was framed as the culmination of black-Korean conflict—placing the blame on two minority groups. And only a few years later, in 1995, Harlem's businessowners had a scare of their own. Roland Smith, a disgruntled neighborhood resident, entered Freddy's, a Jewish-owned clothing store, and set it ablaze, trapping and ultimately killing seven of the store's employees. Once again the media and the public were quick to frame the dispute as interminority conflict, this time black-Jewish, giving it a context that has a rich, complex history and pushing emotional buttons on all sides of the tragic event. The LA riot and the firebombing of Freddy's became wake-up calls for businessowners in the inner cities, forcing them to acknowledge America's pluralistic society, its ethnic order, and the meaning of opportunity denied for the nation's poorest native-born minorities.

It has often been stated that merchant-customer relations in poor inner-city neighborhoods are the principle sources of black-Jewish and black-Korean conflict. However, the fact that the majority of merchant-customer interactions are civil demonstrates that merchant-customer relations are *not* the source of hostility that leads to intergroup conflict. Imported into intergroup relationships is the struggle over who gets ahead versus who *should* get ahead, and who moves up versus who is left behind. The rise of protest motivations and the outbreaks of boycotts, violence, and riots are symptoms of larger structural problems that plague the nation's inner cities, not the result of antagonistic merchant-customer relations.

In his classic study *The Poor Pay More*, David Caplovitz noted that "the consumer problems of low-income families cannot be divorced from the other problems facing them. Until society can find ways of raising their educational level, improving their occupational opportunities, increasing their income, and reducing the discrimination against them—in short, until poverty itself is eradicated—only limited solutions to their problems as consumers can be found."[8] This was true in the 1960s when Jewish merchants predominated in poor black neighborhoods, and it still rings true today, with a new legion of immigrants dominating the businesses in these communities. Jewish and Korean merchants are not the first groups to experience interethnic conflict with poor black residents, and they will undoubtedly not be the last unless the nation is willing to confront and address the structural problems that plague poor black communities—persistent poverty, unemployment, extreme inequality, and their spiraling consequences.[9] These problems are even more glaring as poor blacks witness a succession of newcomers move up and out of their neighborhoods. So long as these conditions remain a part of the normal scene in America's inner cities, outbursts of conflict and the threat of conflict must also be accepted as part of the normal scene.

Public Policy Recommendations

Aside from attacking the roots of the problem—namely poverty, inequality, and their consequences—there are certainly less ambitious measures that can be taken to ameliorate tensions and perhaps help minimize the potential for protest motivations. I offer three policy recommendations. Two have to do with dispelling some of the myths about immigrant entrepreneurs. The third involves aiding existing African American entrepreneurs, as well as those who wish to start a business of their own.

The first myth to dispel is the commonly held belief that immigrant entrepreneurs receive special government or bank loans to help them to start their businesses. Most of the African American customers we interviewed firmly believe that immigrant storeowners receive preferential treatment in this respect and resent the notion that the government helps all groups—regardless of how recently arrived—before it helps them. However, none of the Jewish or Korean storeowners in our sample had received bank or government loans to help them start their businesses. In fact, African American merchants were far more likely to have benefited from such resources. Twenty percent of the African American merchants I interviewed had started their business using a bank or government agency loan. Dispelling this commonly held myth would make African Americans realize that the U.S. government and financial institutions do not make special concessions for other groups, even those who are newly arrived. Second, it is important to disaggregate the common misperception that immigrant entrepreneurs compete with African American entrepreneurs, thereby impeding African American business development. This would greatly change the way immigrant businessowners are perceived in the black community, since perceptions—whether based in truth or not—can have very real consequences.

The media, through television news and print, could easily dispel both of the myths. Articles could be published in black newspapers, such as the *New York Amsterdam News,* and also in the mainstream press. Dispelling these myths would not be a difficult task, and the rewards would be improved interethnic and interracial relations between the immigrant and American-born populations. In addition, the media could make efforts to depict some of the positive features of everyday life in black communities, rather than focusing strictly on conflict and controversy. Positive media images would help dispel the enduring myth that black communities are fraught with racial warfare.

My third recommendation is that we promote policies that would aid African American entrepreneurs. Business ownership has been a route to upward mobility for many ethnic groups—Italians, Jews, Koreans, Middle Easterners, and Asian Indians, to name just a few. As I have discussed, business ownership in black communities holds a significance beyond the dollars it generates in profit. Because of the symbolism behind black business ownership—that of black control of black neighborhoods—efforts should be made to give African Americans real opportunities to buy and operate the retail stores in their communities. To start, when storeowners decide to sell their business, they should be required to advertise the sale beyond their own ethnic networks, thereby giving African Americans equal opportunity to learn about the sale from the beginning. This would give aspiring African American entrepreneurs, and even those already in business, a fair shot in bidding for businesses they wish to purchase. However, given the lack of capital in African Americans' networks, advertising more broadly would not do enough. To increase the number of African American entrepreneurs, not only do we need to provide opportunities, but we also need to offer realistic means of taking advantage of those opportunities. Therefore, the U.S. government needs to commit to supporting the Small Business Administration in allocating substantial loans to African American entrepreneurs and potential entrepreneurs.

While the Merchants' Program in the late 1960s and early 1970s was successful in turning over Jewish-owned businesses to African Americans, the program was not successful in following up with the African American storeowners. The Merchants' Program was a grand idea in theory, and it could be tried again. However, it would work only with strong economic backing from the Small Business Administration, not just at the start-up phase when buying the businesses, but also at later stages in helping to keep the businesses afloat under new African American ownership. Other groups have access to resources in their coethnic networks to help them through slow periods or see them through unforeseen emergencies, but African Americans do not.[10] To have more successful African American–owned businesses in black communities, African American businessowners need to have a pool of credit readily available at competitive interest rates.

Financial commitments are only one part of the equation. For something like the Merchants' Program to succeed, it would also require a serious commitment on the part of the African Americans willing to take over the businesses. More critically, it would require changing the perception of black customers, who associate black business-ownership with inferior goods, substandard service, and higher prices. Asking black customers to patronize black-owned stores solely on the basis of racial solidarity is not the kind of business strategy that will improve the lot of African American retailers. In the end, black customers are no more willing to pay more for the same goods than the next consumer. So long as the perception remains that nonblack-owned businesses are superior to black-owned businesses, African American storeowners will find themselves at a competitive disadvantage. With an increase in the number of African American–owned businesses, African American merchants could gain coethnic advantages such as lower prices for combined orders from suppliers, which would translate into lower retail prices. Structural advantages such as these would help African American entrepreneurs. African American merchants must become a familiar sight in black communities. In the end, the presence of a hundred African American–owned stores that were formerly Jewish- and Korean-owned would do more for intergroup relations than a hundred interracial and interfaith meetings.

However, African American entrepreneurial growth should not be confined to black communities. Both Jews and Koreans serve multiethnic populations and thrive in black, white, immigrant, and coethnic neighborhoods alike. While these two groups serve customers beyond their ethnic boundaries, this has not been the case for African Americans. Blacks have been largely unable to open businesses in other neighborhoods and have consequently operated under an "economic detour."[11] Unlike other ethnic groups that have used self-employment as a vehicle to upward mobility by serving coethnics and noncoethnics alike, blacks have been unable to exercise this option, and the black-owned business operating beyond the boundaries of a black neighborhood is still a rarity. If African Americans are to succeed in self-employment, they must not be confined to serving only their own. Setting up shop in nonblack neighborhoods will not be an easy task, given the uniquely high levels of residential segregation for blacks and the discrimination that blacks often face outside of black neighborhoods. Hence, changing blacks' perceptions of African American business-owners is only part of the problem. The other more fundamental part is changing nonblacks' perceptions of African American business-owners and African Americans more generally.

One final note of caution. Small business ownership in the retail niche is only one source of employment for African Americans, and considering the expansion of government and corporate sectors, it is not necessarily the most promising.[12] While business ownership will benefit a few African Americans, it certainly cannot create jobs for all (or even most) unemployed blacks. Yet because black business owner-ship in black communities holds meaning beyond the number of jobs it creates or the dollars these businesses generate, we cannot over-look its significance. However, unless the Merchants' Program—or something like it—is accompanied by a vigorous assault on racial, residential, educational, employment, and other barriers that place blacks in subordinate positions, black business ownership will have rel-atively little impact on the economic position of African Americans as a whole.[13] Without a commitment to forcefully attack these larger structural problems, small business ownership alone can have little im-pact in creating a more equitable distribution of the nation's income and wealth. If normalcy in our nation's inner cities consists of inferior education, inadequate housing, chronic unemployment, and persis-tent poverty, then boycotts, firebombings, and riots, while rare, must also be accepted as part of normal life in urban America.

Appendix:
Notes on Methodology and
Tales from the Field

I started graduate school in the fall of 1992, only months after the Los Angeles riot that took place in April of that year. When I entered the doctoral program in the Department of Sociology at Columbia University, I knew from the outset that I would study race and ethnic relations among minority groups. People often say that one's first project is autobiographical, and this is certainly true in my case. As the daughter of Korean immigrants who once owned a small business in a low-income black neighborhood, I felt very close to this topic, particularly after the LA riot. As I read the newspaper accounts concerning the riot and black-Korean conflict more generally, I quickly became frustrated by the slew of articles that highlighted only cultural and linguistic differences, ignoring the context in which the groups came into contact.

When I began researching the topic of black-Korean relations I soon realized that studies of merchant-customer conflict were not new. In fact scholars, journalists, and community leaders had addressed the same issues in the 1960s, but at that time the focus had been on black-Jewish tension. Essays such as James Baldwin's classic "Negroes Are Anti-Semitic Because They're Anti-White" and Herbert Gans's "Negro-Jewish Conflict in New York City," and books such as Gertrude Selznick and Stephen Steinberg's *The Tenacity of Prejudice* and Gary T. Marx's *Protest and Prejudice* vividly describe the conflict between black customers and the Jewish shopkeepers who served them. I decided to meet with representatives of the Jewish Community Relations Council (JCRC) in Philadelphia to learn more about black-Jewish relations from a historical perspective.

The representatives of the JCRC were kind enough to direct me to their archives, which were housed at the Balch Institute for Ethnic Studies in Philadelphia. When I started digging into the archival material, I found that problems involving Jewish merchants in the inner cities, such as exploitation of the black community, draining the community of its resources, failing to contribute back to the community, and not hiring from within, were as contentious in the 1960s as they were three decades later. The main difference is that Jewish merchants predominated in low-income black communities then, while today, in a tale of ethnic succession, Korean immigrants have largely succeeded them. However, black-Jewish relations and tensions are not simply issues of the past. In December 1995, the firebombing of Freddy's, the Jewish-owned clothing store in West Harlem—and the media's framing of it as a racially and ethnically charged event—made it evident that black-Jewish conflict still pushed emotional buttons on both sides. Thus, I decided to compare black-Jewish relations and black-Korean relations in predominantly black communities.

I realized that to understand the effects of race and ethnicity on merchant-customer relations, I needed to hold race constant, which is why I added African American merchants to the sample. No other study to date had examined merchant-customer relations in black communities from a comparative framework. Furthermore, none has looked at the question of intrablack relations, particularly vis-à-vis black-Jewish and black-Korean relations. This comparative framework became a powerful tool in my effort to understand the effects of race and ethnicity on merchant-customer relations. In addition, because previous research had focused on merchant-customer relations only in low-income neighborhoods, I varied the class composition and included middle-class black neighborhoods in my sample. The comparison of low- and middle-income neighborhoods enabled me to study the effects of class as well as the intersection of race and class on merchant-customer relations.

I also decided to compare two cities: New York and Philadelphia. I chose New York because it leads the country in its percentage of foreign-born residents, while Philadelphia lags far behind in the number of immigrants it attracts. Furthermore, while boycotts of Korean- and Jewish-owned stores proliferated in New York City in the 1990s, Philadelphia was immune to this type of collective action. Philadelphia was also interesting because, compared with New York, it was relatively underresearched, even though it has a rich history of black-Jewish relations and a contemporary history of black-Korean relations. Comparing Philadelphia with her northern sister New York provided an opportunity to study the effects of immigration on race and ethnic relations.

The design of the study enabled me to investigate the central question this book seeks answer: What are relations like between Jewish, Korean, and African-American merchants and their black customers in both low-income and middle-income communities? The specific research questions that guide this study include: How are civility and routine maintained each day, and what efforts do merchants make to maintain them? How do differences in race, ethnicity, class, and nativity affect merchant-customer relations? Why is intergroup conflict between blacks and Jews and blacks and Koreans more prominent in New York than in Philadelphia? And, finally, how do we reconcile everyday civility with racial conflict?

Choosing Research Sites

The first research site I picked was West Philadelphia, a low-income black neighborhood. I initially chose this neighborhood as a fieldwork site for Herbert Gans's class in field methods, and I chose this site in particular because my parents once owned a store in the neighborhood. Because I was apprehensive about gaining entry into an unfamiliar business community, I chose my first site based on prior connections in order to facilitate the entry process. Although many of the stores had changed ownership since my parents sold their business, the connection, however distant, proved fruitful in my conversations with the local Jewish, Korean, and African American merchants, as well as with some of the African American street vendors on the block.

I chose West Harlem as the second low-income community not only because of its historical significance but also because the firebombing of Freddy's in December 1995 had made it evident that black-Jewish tension was still a poignant issue in the neighborhood. About the significance of West Harlem for black Americans, a Jewish merchant remarked, "If it happens anywhere, it's going to happen in Harlem. It's the heartbeat of black America." It was evident that West Harlem would be a pivotal research site.

The third low-income neighborhood I chose was East Harlem, which I selected after reading David Caplovitz's classic, *The Poor Pay More*.[1] Caplovitz had written extensively on the exploitative business practices of Jewish merchants in the East Harlem furniture district. He highlighted the high-pressure sales tactics and the exorbitant credit payments to which poor residents were subjected because they did not have the funds to purchase their furniture with cash nor did they have credit cards. I was curious to know whether merchant-customer relations had changed since Caplovitz published *The Poor Pay More* in 1967.

Although I had been to West Harlem on several occasions, I had never been to East Harlem, and therefore I had little idea what the business community was like. I was not even sure whether the large business community still existed that Caplovitz had written about decades ago. Because I did not know exactly where to go and was a little nervous about entering a low-income neighborhood for the first time, a friend of mine, Manny (a Puerto Rican man who grew up near East Harlem), offered to show me around. After a bus and subway ride to reach our destination, we walked along the major avenues, entered the stores and browsed to get a sense of the merchandise, the storeowners, and the employees. Whenever we entered the stores, Manny began conversing with the Latino employees in Spanish, which gave me an opportunity to look around the store. After my initial visit to East Harlem with Manny, I felt comfortable in the neighborhood and knew that I would have no problems getting by on my own.

Although choosing three low-income black neighborhoods to study was a relatively simple task, selecting middle-income neighborhoods was more difficult, since many middle-income black neighborhoods do not have the long commercial shopping strips that are characteristic of low-income communities. One of the reasons for the absence of these commercial districts is that middle-class residents either have cars or can easily afford the transportation cost to travel to larger shopping centers that cater to a wider clientele. Hence, finding a middle-class neighborhood with a shopping strip became a challenge.

Since a sizable portion of New York's middle-class African Americans live in Queens, I decided to scout out an appropriate middle-class neighborhood there with a commercial strip. I initially decided on Flatbush because of the much-publicized boycotts of Korean-owned fruit and vegetable markets there in the early 1990s. However, after visiting the site and then examining the Census Bureau data, I realized that Flatbush had a much higher proportion of foreign-born black residents than African Americans, which made the site significantly different from the three low-income black neighborhoods that I had chosen to study. I decided to look for other middle-class black neighborhoods that had a relatively smaller percentage of foreign-born blacks.

It was an African American undergraduate student at Columbia who suggested Jamaica Avenue in Queens. She was familiar with the neighborhood because she had grown up there, and she described its well-trafficked commercial strip, where businessowners were from a variety of racial and ethnic backgrounds. She was kind enough to meet me on Jamaica Avenue one morning and gave me a tour of the neighborhood's business district and side streets so I could familiarize myself with the area. I now had my first middle-class black neighborhood and fourth research site.

I still needed to find a middle income black neighborhood in Philadelphia that had a large commercial strip, and I was not sure how to go about locating a suitable site. My colleague John Skrentny put me in touch with Tom Sugrue at the University of Pennsylvania, who is familiar with Philadelphia and the Mount Airy community. I could not have asked for a more enthusiastic guide. Tom devoted an afternoon to giving me a tour of Mount Airy, and he helped me locate a commercial strip in East Mount Airy that met all of my specifications. The main shopping strip in Mount Airy features many retail stores and a mix of Jewish, Korean, and African American businessowners, among others, who cater to black customers. At last, I had second middle-class black neighborhood and my fifth and final research site.

Gaining Entry

Entering a new research site can be intimidating, especially when the field researcher is not familiar with the neighborhood or the respondents whom she is studying. This was certainly the case for me. When I decided to embark on a comparative study of merchant-customer relations in five predominantly black neighborhoods, I feared that the merchants would not be interested in speaking with me about their experiences. Furthermore, because I planned to compare three groups of merchants, African Americans, Jews, and Koreans, I wondered to what extent my own race, ethnicity, nativity, and gender would inhibit the merchants from agreeing to an in-depth interview. I was not sure whether they would be interested in speaking with me, whether they would speak with me even if they were interested, how long they would be willing to speak with me, or whether they would answer the numerous questions I had for them. It takes courage to approach complete strangers and ask them to participate in a study, but field researchers quickly learn to overcome their fear of rejection.

I entered each business and asked the person standing behind the register if I could speak with the owner. If the person behind the register was not the owner, she directed me to him or her. I introduced myself to the merchants and then handed them my business card, which indicated my name, title, institutional affiliation, and telephone number. The merchants took the card, studied it, and then studied me. If the owner looked skeptical, I immediately elaborated, "I'm interested in questions like why you decided to go into business, when and how you started your business, and what you think of the community, questions like that." To my surprise and delight, the vast majority of the merchants agreed to be interviewed.

Gaining access to the merchants in the five communities was a "multistaged process." As Charles Bosk notes in his study of surgical training teams, "Entrée was not something negotiated once and then over and done with . . . The most important thing that field-workers must keep in mind is that entrée is not a single event but a continuous process."[2] For the most part I was successful in gaining entry with the merchants, but there were some who refused to speak with me. Those who refused were a small minority, and in fact I can count the number of rejections on one hand. I soon discovered that the key to gaining entry with the merchants was building a favorable rapport with each of them from the outset.

Gaining entry also meant overcoming suspicions in the field. I had not anticipated that some of the merchants, vendors, and residents would be suspicious of me. Some even questioned whether I secretly worked for a government agency such as the CIA or the Internal Revenue Service. I always carried my student ID and driver's license in case anybody requested to see these forms of identification, but almost nobody did. However, one afternoon in West Philadelphia, after I had finished conducting an interview with a Korean merchant, she suggested that I speak to an African American vendor nearby. She said that he had been in the community for a few years and in the past had acted as a broker between her and some of the customers with whom she had disputes. I approached him and introduced myself as a student at Columbia University doing a project about West Philadelphia. He immediately inquired, "Do you have an ID?" I answered, "Yes I do. Just let me find it." My wallet was buried at the bottom of my backpack, and I was fumbling, trying to fish it out from underneath my books, tape recorder, and notepad. Before I could get it out, he said, "You should always carry your ID. I don't know who you are. You say you're a student, but who knows. Someday, somebody can come to me and arrest me for some bombing in Oklahoma or something and they'll say that they have proof because this girl was taping our conversation and she was secretly CIA." Surprised by his comment, I asked, "Do I look like I work for the CIA? Why would anyone think that?" An African American man standing beside the vendor chimed in, "You come here and just ask people questions. They don't know you. You better be careful." I looked at him and asked, "Careful of what?" He looked away and did not answer.

I presented my ID to the vendor, who examined it very closely with the customer standing beside him. They scrutinized the picture and noted that I looked older in the picture and wondered whether my ID was fake. I explained that the picture had been taken three years before, when I'd had longer hair. After scrutinizing the ID for a few more seconds, the vendor handed it back to me as two customers approached his table. While he was busy assisting his customers, I noticed that each time he made a sale, he recorded the amount very neatly on a notepad. I asked him, "Do you keep track of everything?" He responded, "You have to. See, when you want to borrow money from the bank, they want to know why they should lend it to you. You have to show them that you're worth it. You have to record everything." After this initial observation and exchange, he slowly warmed up to me, and we began talking more about his business. The interview flowed from there.

By far, the majority of the merchants I approached were congenial and willing to speak with me at length about their business, their experiences, and their perceptions. The majority of the merchants were extremely gracious with their time and attention. Given how busy they were throughout the day—attending to customers, ordering stock, replenishing their shelves with merchandise, and ringing up sales—I was surprised by how many storeowners were willing to speak with me for hours, patiently answering my probing questions. And when I returned to their store with follow-up questions, the merchants continued to be gracious with their time and attention.

Although I gained a great deal of knowledge from speaking with the storeowners, the exchanges were not completely one-sided. Many times I felt that I played the role of a therapist (like the hairstylists in the sample) as I listened to the merchants speak at length about their lives. I came to realize that the interview process offered them a way to speak freely about themselves to someone who was genuinely interested in their experiences. Because they were gracious in answering all of my questions, I, in turn, tried to be as generous with my attention, listening when they digressed and talked about other issues that concerned them, even when they had nothing to do with my research. This was one minor way in which I could "give back" to my respondents, who had willingly given so much to me.

Building Rapport

Laura Nader had this to say about rapport:

> Rapport, pure and simple, consists of establishing lines of communication between the anthropologist and his informants in order for the former to collect data that then allows him to understand the culture under study. As Audrey Richards . . . illustrates, rapport may have nothing to do with being reasonable or pleasant in the field, or liking and admiring the people with whom one works, although Geertz . . . seems to suggest that it does. Rapport refers to the ability to cope with a field situation in such a way that work is possible.[3]

And Robert K. Merton, in the classic article "Insiders and Outsiders," writes, "Different situations activate different statuses which then and there dominate over the rival claims of other statuses."[4] Upon taking up the task of interviewing seventy-five businessowners, I wondered to what extent my own race, ethnicity, class, and gender would prove advantageous or disadvantageous when I conducted interviews with the African American, Jewish, and Korean merchants. As I began speaking with them, I found myself activating and deactivating certain aspects of my identity in order to build rapport with each interviewee. As Ruth Horowitz articulates, "Identities are not fixed, but are affirmed and changed continually."[5] Furthermore, the process of changing and affirming identities is a dialectical one; the merchants also assigned certain statuses and values to my identity, based on my physical characteristics as a relatively young, Korean, female and the fact that I was a graduate student.

With each merchant, I attempted to evoke a sense of fictive kinship based on certain aspects of my status set, and this proved instrumental in the field.[6] Consequently, I was often (although not always) perceived as an "insider," however distant, allowing the respondents to feel comfortable and speak candidly with me about their experiences. Establishing this sense of kinship was not always a simple or straightforward task, because it involved constant negotiation—pushing certain statuses into the foreground while keeping other facets tucked away.

Negotiating Race and Ethnicity

Coethnicity

With the Korean merchants, I evoked a sense of fictive kinship based on our shared ethnic background. Many of the Korean merchants placed me in the role of a daughter because they felt that I resembled their children—second-generation Koreans—in age, English-language fluency, and inability to speak Korean well or at all. When I introduced myself to the Korean merchants in English, they would often ask me in Korean whether I speak Korean. I would respond in my limited Korean, "I speak only a little." My poor accent and elementary grammar were immediate cues that I did not speak the language well enough to converse with them in Korean. Often they would respond in English, "Like my children."

I had wondered to what extent my not speaking Korean would be a disadvantage in the field, but it proved to be a hindrance in only one case, with a Korean merchant who sold handbags and accessories on Jamaica Avenue in Queens. I walked into the store and asked whether I could speak with the owner. When the woman standing behind the register identified herself as the owner, I proceeded to give her my entry script, yet when I finished, she did not respond at all. The Korean merchant just stared at me for a few seconds, not saying a word. Then she asked in a confused tone of voice, "You Korean?" to which I replied, smiling, "Yes I am," believing that our shared ethnicity would soften her up and make her willing to speak with me. I could not have been more wrong in this case. She then asked in Korean, "You're Korean, and you don't speak Korean?" Having already anticipated that I may have to justify to some of the Korean merchants why I do not speak Korean, I explained that I had come to the United States when I was only three years old. I said that because both of my parents had worked while I was growing up, I was raised in American-operated daycare centers and schools and with English-speaking babysitters and teachers. Although I could understand Korean a little, I could not speak Korean.

The woman was dissatisfied with this response, and she berated me in Korean for more than ten minutes for not being able to speak the language. She told me that she made certain that her children learned Korean, and she was gravely concerned that the second-generation Koreans were coming of age without knowledge of the Korean language. She began interrogating me in a serious and disparaging tone of voice. How I could become a leader of the Korean community without speaking Korean? How could I become a professor responsible for teaching college students without understanding or speaking Korean? What kind of message am I sending to today's second generation? I did not want to lose her as a respondent, so I stood there and patiently waited for her to finish her lecture. When she stopped, I tried to calmly answer her, explaining that because I had grown up in the United States in a largely white neighborhood, without Korean friends or extended kin, I was not able to retain the Korean language.

Still dissatisfied, the merchant began shooting questions at me about my personal life. Where was I from? What do my parents do? Why did my parents not teach me Korean? What kind of parents allows their children to grow up without speaking Korean? Why was I still in school? Why had I not graduated yet? Did I go to church? Was I married? Did I have a boyfriend? Was my boyfriend Korean? I knew that the answer to the last question was consequential. Given how strongly this woman felt about retaining the Korean language, I suspected that she would feel even more strongly about interracial and interethnic dating practices. Every fieldwork instinct told me to lie and tell her that I was dating someone who is Korean, but at that moment I had lost my patience with her. I was so fed up with her remarks about my not being able to speak Korean, her criticisms of my personal life, and, most of all, her criticisms of my parents, that I decided to be candid, even if my candor would cost me a respondent. I told her the truth, that my boyfriend was not Korean. She gasped and then adopted a grave tone, stating that she believes that Koreans should date only other Koreans. How could I not date a Korean? Couldn't I find a nice Korean boy? What was wrong with me?

At this point, I had completely lost all patience with this woman, so I interrupted her ranting and said, "You know what? Why don't we just forget about the interview." I packed up my tape recorder and note-pad, picked up my book bag from the floor, and just walked out. Sheer frustration overwhelmed me. As I walked out the door, I heard her yell in Korean, "Come back," but I could not bear to face her and subject myself to that type of attack again. I kept walking and never looked back.

As this incident illustrates, fieldwork is not easy. Researchers must sometimes put themselves in uncomfortable situations for the sake of getting their data. But each researcher must decide when enough is enough. After fifteen minutes of feeling like a punching bag for this merchant, I had reached my breaking point. Researchers must make their own decisions about their tolerance thresholds. How long is one willing to go along with the scenario, and at what point does the ha-rassment—whatever its form—become so overbearing that one feels the need to exit the situation? Part of my decision to leave stemmed from frustration, but I also realized that this woman would have been very difficult to interview. I suspect that even if she had agreed to speak with me, she would not have taken my questions seriously, espe-cially considering how she felt about my not speaking Korean and my dating someone who is not Korean. I weighed these considerations and decided that the costs outweighed the benefits in this particu-lar case.

Although most of the other Korean merchants understood why I did not speak Korean, a few were less accepting. The Korean storeowners were also very curious about my upbringing, asking questions about my family, my childhood, and my education. Our shared ethnicity seemed to give them license to ask me anything they wanted. They seemed perfectly at ease inquiring about my personal life—whether I was married, dating, and, more specifically, whether I was dating a Korean. When I mentioned that I was dating someone who is not Korean, several of the Korean storeowners bluntly inquired, "You can't find a Korean boy?" Others invited me to their church, where they assured me I would make many new friends with other second-generation Koreans and perhaps even meet "a nice Korean boy."

Most of the time I did not feel uncomfortable answering their questions, since none of the questions was too personal. Moreover, because I asked my respondents many detailed questions about their lives and took up hours of their time, I felt the least I could do in return was respond to the questions they had for me. Shared ethnicity can evoke a sense of affinity or closeness to which coethnics feel immediately entitled.

Many of the Korean merchants viewed me as a young daughter, and they were often protective of me—telling me what streets to avoid while walking alone, making sure that I ate while in the field, and often buying me lunch to ensure that I did. Never did I hear so many comments about my appearance and my weight. The Korean merchants would constantly ask me, "Did you eat? You have to eat more." One Korean owner of a fast food restaurant in West Philadelphia commented that he would never hire me, because he felt that I was "too skinny" and needed to look "more healthy" to work in the food business. After offering this unsolicited opinion, he walked behind the counter and pulled out a Hershey's chocolate bar and handed it to me. He said, "You take this. You need to gain weight."

I patiently listened to the merchants' advice, not because I enjoyed receiving it but because they seemed to enjoy giving it. Perhaps they got a great deal of satisfaction from treating me as a daughter, in part because they could not be home to care for their own children, given their grueling work schedule. Although I did not ask to be placed in the daughter role, I did not find it offensive nor did it inhibit me from doing my research, aside from that one scolding incident. Both Korean men and women, particularly those in their fifties or sixties, easily adopted a parental role with me.

Moreover, some of the Korean merchants, particularly those in New York, would take the opportunity to talk to me about Columbia University or college more generally, asking my advice about the admissions process for undergraduates: mean SAT scores, high school grades, and what extracurricular activities I felt were important. They viewed me as a resource who could help them guide their children through the increasingly competitive college admissions process. I also became a resource for the Korean merchants who were trying to understand their own second-generation children, many of whom had adopted "American" cultural traits. As first-generation immigrants, the merchants struggled to understand and grasp the cultural differences that divided them and their American-born children. Some expressed dismay that their children did not speak Korean and did not take school as seriously as they would have liked. Many of them wished that their children would date coethnics and were perplexed when their children dated "Americans" (using the term "American" synonymously with "white" when they spoke of interracial dating). For first-generation Korean immigrant entrepreneurs, I often acted as a "cultural broker" between them and their native-born children.

The Immigrant Experience

With non-Koreans I used a different strategy to evoke a sense of fictive kinship. With Jewish merchants, it was my immigrant background. Often the Jewish merchants noted parallels between the Jewish and Korean immigrant experience, and these then became the most salient features of my status set in creating the trustworthy bond between fieldworker and respondent. Jewish storeowners would make claims such as, "Koreans are doing things the way Jews used to do them," or "See, Koreans and Jewish people are hard-working people. You know why we're successful? Because we're go-getters. You want to become something, you go out and get it, and that's what brings us satisfaction."

Many immigrant storeowners and managers felt comfortable expressing their conviction of the superiority of immigrants compared with native-born Americans, perhaps because people assumed that I too, as a Korean, believed this to be true. Most of the immigrant storeowners and managers assigned certain values to my identity when speaking with me by using pronouns such as *we* when articulating their

perceptions, suggesting that they too were feeling a sense of fictive kinship. For instance, when expressing his preference for foreign-born
employees, the sales manager of a large Jewish-owned furniture store
explained, "*You, me, and people who come from outside,* because *our* way of
living is so hard, *we* were taught that *we* have to work hard for what *we*
want. Don't wait for handouts. That's a big difference. It's very simple.
Everybody knows it, but only a few want to admit it because it's not po-
litically correct."

While the majority of the Jewish merchants identified with my immigrant background, one Jewish merchant classified me as a nonimmigrant. He was the only one who held a negative opinion of the U.S.
immigration laws, even though, ironically, all of his employees were
foreign-born. He commented, "The immigration laws in my opinion
in this country are awful. I think it's gotten to the point we're over-
saturated. I think *you and I* are going to be a total minority in New
York, and I think that's going to happen very, very soon. I don't think
it has that far to go." I never refuted their classification of my status as a
foreign- or a native-born American, nor did I express disapproval of
their perceptions. If their classification of me as "one of us" made it
easier for the merchants to candidly voice their views, I did not intend
to correct them.

Perhaps most interesting was the way in which my boyfriend's ethnicity proved to be advantageous in building rapport with some of the
Latino employees, in particular José, the Ecuadorian manager of a
Jewish-owned furniture store in East Harlem. When I first walked into
the furniture store and introduced myself to José, he asked me where I
live in New York. When I explained to him that I live with my boyfriend, José asked about his ethnic background, and I mentioned that
he is half-Ecuadorian. José's eyes lit up, and he said, "I don't believe
it. You know I'm Ecuadorian too." When he asked, "What city is he
from?" I replied, "Well, he was born here, but his mother's family is
from Quito." José then told me that he is from Guayaquil. We spoke
for about ten minutes about Ecuador, since I had just spent two weeks
of my summer there. From that point on, José was always warm and
welcoming toward me and allowed me to sit in the back of the store for
hours at a time, observing the interactions between the sales associates
and customers. While in the field, my ethnicity and identity proved to
be far more flexible than I had imagined, with merchants emphasizing
certain elements of my status and ignoring other facets altogether.

Panminority Identity

Of the three groups, I was most apprehensive about how the African American merchants would perceive me, especially since I planned to ask questions about the comparatively low rate of African American entrepreneurship. In this case, I tried to evoke a sense of "panminority" identity based on our shared experience as nonwhites in a predominantly white society. Panminority identity arises when different minority groups feel a heightened sense of their joint status vis-à-vis a more dominant racial or ethnic group. In contrast to panethnicity, panminority identity is the development of solidarities among minority ethnic groups *across* different racial and ethnic categories. By illustration, panethnicity involves Chinese, Japanese, and Koreans identifying under the category "Asian," whereas panminority identity entails African Americans, Asians, and Latinos collectively identifying as racial and ethnic minorities. Clearly, panminority identity does not emerge at all times but surfaces under certain conditions. Hence, with African American merchants, I placed my ethnicity and nativity in the background and instead emphasized our shared status as racial minorities.

Panminority identity surfaced prominently when the African American merchants relayed instances in which they dealt with discrimination in their professional and private lives. For example, when one African American merchant said that white women "all act like airline stewardesses," putting on a "plastic smile" in order to "disarm" him when he gets into an elevator with them, I asked, "You don't think that possibly they're just smiling at you to be friendly? I tend to smile at people when they get in the elevator with me." I wanted to push him to think about whether he believed the white women really felt threatened by him. He answered, "No, I don't think so, because I don't know you, I just met you, but you can just tell you come from a different sort of culture, a different kind of understanding." Later when the merchant spoke about the difficulty he faced working in a predominantly white corporate setting in New York City, he said, "It's a double standard. We have to learn how to accept their culture and try to identify with it. *And I'm quite sure you have the same experience.*" Similarly, another African American businessowner relayed some of his experiences with discrimination and the difficulties associated with trying to fit into a white-dominated society. He explained, "It's hard sometimes, the food you eat, or how you talk to each other. I can have a conversation with you, and with you, I feel comfortable. But if I talk to a white person, you know, they'll say, what is he talking about?"

However, evoking a sense of panminority identity did not work with all the African American merchants. In fact, one African American beauty salon owner reacted to my racial identity as an Asian and wanted nothing to do with me. I entered the salon in West Harlem and asked the hairstylist closest to the door whether I could speak with the owner. The stylist said nothing but motioned to an elderly woman who was curling a woman's hair at the station diagonally across from hers. When I introduced myself to the owner, I told her that I was interested in studying the businesses in the neighborhood. After I delivered my usual entry script, she immediately retorted in a confrontational tone, "Now I have some questions for you. You're probably going to be sorry that you came in here." And then she paused. I told her that whatever she had to say, I wouldn't be sorry that I had come in there. She began by telling me that she lives in Flushing and asked, "How did Flushing become all Asian? When I say Asian, it covers Chinese and everything, because people say all blacks look alike, I say all Asians look alike. I can't tell the difference. I was shocked by all the stores! On both sides of the street are Asian! Now how did this happen?" I asked, "What kinds of stores are you talking about?" Annoyed by my question, she exclaimed, "It doesn't matter, they're all Asian!"

I looked at her, not sure whether she wanted me to respond and not really sure how to do it, and she continued, "People say they have associations." I tried to answer her honestly by replying, "Well, I think a lot of Koreans and other Asians help each other in terms of getting money together and starting a business. Families will help each other." She cut me off and interjected, "I think they offer more money to the landlords and kick out whoever's doing business. Now when you offer someone more money, they can't turn that down." Visibly upset by Flushing's Asian business community, she refused to listen as I explained that I had never heard of Asians offering more money to landlords to get their businesses or anything of the sort.

Since she felt that there are too many Asian-owned businesses, I asked, "What percentage of the businesses on 125th Street do you think should be black owned?" She answered, "Seventy-five percent of the businesses should be black owned, at least. This is a black neighborhood. Asians come in, they're buying up all these stores, and they leave at night with their black cases full of money. They leave their garbage out and don't give anything back to the community." She was growing even more visibly agitated and began speaking more loudly and aggressively, "I'm not gonna stand here and just let them take over Harlem like they did Flushing! I think people should pay attention to it. And you have Al Sharpton up here preaching to a group of young men. He should be encouraging them to open up their own businesses!"

I wanted to ask her more questions, but before I had the chance, she looked at me and blankly stated, "Well, as you can see, I'm busy with a customer, so you're going to have to leave." I thanked her for sharing her thoughts with me and inquired again, "Would there be a better time for us to talk? Maybe when you're not so busy? I'm really interested in hearing what you have to say." She peered over her glasses and answered, "Look, now I'm trying to be nice here, but I'm really going to have to ask you to leave," and then turned back to her customer, who murmured in agreement, "Mm-hmm." From her tone of voice and her body language, I felt that I should not push the issue any further, so I thanked her again and left.

Since this African American merchant had very strong views about Asian storeowners, I wanted to interview her, so I wrote her a letter stating that I was interested in speaking with her and gave her a number where she could reach me. Needless to say, I never heard from her. In this case, the African American merchant strongly and exclusively reacted to my racial identity as an Asian and placed me in the same category with the Asian businessowners she so strongly resented, making it impossible for me to interview her.

As these encounters demonstrate, identities can be perceived and interpreted in a multitude of ways, and even seemingly fixed categories are not static. My respondents ascribed meanings to my identity, and I, in turn, emphasized and deemphasized certain statuses, depending on the situation. This negotiation process was continuous and dialectical. As Robert K. Merton writes, "Sociologically considered, there is nothing fixed about the boundaries separating Insiders from Outsiders. As situations involving different values arise, different statuses are activated and the lines of separation shift."[7] One's identity does not and should not inhibit scholars from conducting research on outsider groups, since the boundaries that distinguish insiders from outsiders are continuously negotiated, malleable, and in flux. What matters is the way in which the researcher decides to use her identity and the extent to which her respondents accept the identity she adopts.

Negotiating Class

Shulamit Reinharz notes about feminists and class issues:

> Several feminist interviewers have attempted to foster trust by downplaying status differences between themselves and people of lower social status. For these feminist researchers, interviewing requires personal commitment between themselves and the research participant. When "interviewing up," on the other hand, feminists must find ways to increase their status and credibility.[8]

Perhaps the easiest of the negotiations is class. Because I was interviewing merchants, many of whom had businesses in low-income neighborhoods, I made deliberate efforts to downplay my middle-class status. Like the middle-class black shoppers in white neighborhoods who make conscious efforts to wear clothes and accessories that project their middle-class status, I made a conscious effort to convey my student status. First, my wardrobe in the field consisted of jeans with a T-shirt, turtleneck, or plain oxford shirt. I made certain not to wear expensive accessories, and I also carried a backpack rather than a purse. However, my decision to wear a student status was not initially intuitive. Although I knew not to flaunt expensive clothes and jewelry, I was not conscious about dressing down until a conversation I had with Joanne, an African American vendor who sells clothing and accessories in West Philadelphia.[9]

During one of my first visits to the West Philadelphia field site, Joanne asked me, "Where did you get your pants?" I simply answered, "In New York." She then asked, "How much did you pay for them?" I paused for a moment, debating in my mind whether I should tell her the truth. I decided to lie about the cost of the pants and answered, "Fifty. Why do you ask?" She replied, "They sell them for twenty-five now. When they first came out, they were going for fifty." I responded, "I got them a couple of years ago." I felt awkward when Joanne asked me the price of my pants because in fact they had cost much more than fifty dollars, and I had purchased them in an exclusive department store in New York City. I felt that if I had answered her truthfully, it would have further magnified the class difference between Joanne and me. I lied also because I felt guilty that I could afford them, and although I was making an assumption, I guessed that she probably could not. After this exchange, I decided to wear a standard "uniform" of jeans and T-shirts so that I could, to a certain extent, conceal (or at the very least not blatantly reveal) my middle-class status to the merchants and residents in the low-income field sites.

The act of dressing down or dulling the characteristics of one's background is a common strategy employed by fieldworkers to minimize the difference between researchers and respondents. For example, in describing her study of an isolated Indian village in Mexico, Peggy Golde writes, "I wore skirts mid-calf length, blouses with sleeves, and earrings, and occasionally I combed my hair in braids."[10] Similarly, in his classic study of African American streetcorner men, Elliot Liebow describes how he adopted the dress and speech patterns of the people in the field as best he could: "I came close in dress (in warm weather, tee or sport shirt and khakis or other slacks) with almost no effort at all. My vocabulary and diction changed, but not radically. Cursing and using ungrammatical constructions at times—though they came easily—did not make any of my adaptations confusable with the speech of the street."[11]

I soon realized that it was easier to downplay my class in New York than in Philadelphia, because in New York, where most of the city's residents rely on public transportation, I traveled to the field sites on subways and buses. By contrast, in Philadelphia, had I used public transportation to reach my fieldwork sites, I would have wasted a great deal of time shuffling back and forth between the suburban commuter train and the city's elevated train. I stayed in the suburbs and borrowed my parents' expensive car to drive to the field sites, and the car became a visible symbol of my class status. My class was far easier to screen in New York City because I arrived at each of the field sites using mass transit—a status equalizer in New York City because most New Yorkers (rich and poor) use it regularly.

Initially I was so conscious about driving my parents' car that when I began my fieldwork in West Philadelphia, I would park it several blocks away from the commercial strip so the merchants and vendors would not know what type of car I drove. However, this soon proved to be impractical. I had to put money in the parking meter every two hours, and when I parked several blocks away, it would take me at least ten minutes to walk to my car and another ten minutes to walk back to the site—a constant distraction during my work.

Also, after I had gotten to know many of the merchants and vendors in the West Philadelphia shopping district, several of the vendors were kind enough to watch my car and keep an eye on the parking meter when I parked on the main commercial thoroughfare. On many occasions, vendors fed quarters into my meter when time had run out and the transit police were on the prowl. I would have received countless parking tickets had it not been for the generosity of the vendors on the block. I repaid them by buying them coffee, hot chocolate, or soda and by doing small favors such as watching their tables for a few minutes so they could use the restroom.

Negotiating class was not only an external process; it also involved explaining my status as a graduate student collecting data for her dissertation to the merchants, vendors, managers, and employees at the field sites. They were often confused by my presence in these neighborhoods, and many merchants asked, "What is a nice girl like you doing on Jamaica Avenue?" or "What are you doing in West Philly if you go to school in New York?" or "Jennifer, you don't have class today?" They wondered what I was really doing, hanging out on the shopping strips when they thought that I should be in class or at the library. Many of the respondents equated student status with physically being on campus, and it was difficult for them to understand why I was in the field. Moreover, most of the merchants did not understand why I was interested in studying them, since they did not view their lives as fascinating enough for scholarly research.

I found that when I said I was writing a paper about Harlem or West Philadelphia (or whichever research site I happened to be in at the time), they comprehended my research as homework. When I explained that my fieldwork was research for a paper for a class, they understood why I was not at school and no longer questioned my presence in the field. In fact, when I returned to West Harlem to revisit one of the merchants, he immediately inquired, "Jennifer, how did you do on your paper? Did you get an A?" I smiled and answered, "Yes

I did. Thanks for asking," to which he replied, "I knew you would. You look like a real smart girl." Researchers should be prepared for respondents in the field to have little understanding of the nature of fieldwork or graduate study more generally, and should be ready to explain their status.

Negotiating Gender

About feminists and gender, Reinharz notes:

> Feminists conducting field research in mixed-gender settings are vulnerable to a special set of obstacles. Fortunately, much feminist ethnographic writing includes a frank, reflexive discussion of these problems, particularly sexual harassment, physical danger, and sex stereotyping. In a society that is ageist, sexist, and heterosexist, the researcher who is female and young may be defined as a sex object to be seduced by heterosexual males . . . Furthermore, both the men and the women in the field site may conspire unwittingly to put the female observer in the role of a daughter to be protected, a non-sex-object-non-daughter female to be ignored, a nurse/mother who will care for them, a lesbian of limited interest to men, a teacher, or some other conventional stereotype. The fieldworker then must decide if she is willing to "go along" in order to "stay in the field" or if she can find some other way to maintain her study without collaborating in these roles.[12]

Negotiating race, ethnicity, and class were far simpler processes than negotiating gender in the field. Whereas the other identities were normally negotiated at the beginning of the interview and then seemed to decline in significance, gender roles proved far more challenging to firmly establish and manage. As a young woman conducting interviews with mostly middle-aged women and men, I was often consigned to the role of daughter or sex object and consequently dealt with both sex stereotyping and harassment.

Although the daughter role did not particularly bother me or inhibit my fieldwork, the sex object role was much more difficult to negotiate. On several occasions, it impeded my fieldwork, and more important, it often required that I behave in ways that were inconsistent with my own values. The sex object role was difficult because I felt compelled to handle the harassment in passive and nonconfrontational ways in order to avoid losing respondents. I engaged in what feminist ethnographers accurately describe as "interactional shitwork." As fieldworkers, we are dependent on the respondents, who consequently have more liberty than they would have under normal circumstances. In addition, when the fieldworker is female and the respondent is male, there exists the potential for exploitative power dynamics. While conducting the interviews, my main goal was to obtain the best data that I possibly could, even if this meant tolerating it when men asked me out on dates and made sexually suggestive remarks. These were things that I decided I would accept and deal with, so long as the harassment was not overbearing and I did not think I was in a dangerous situation. When placed in the role of sex object, a female researcher needs to decide for herself whether she is willing to "go along," whether she can find another way to navigate the interaction, or whether she will exit the situation altogether.

My first encounter with a merchant who put me in a sex object role was with the Jewish owner of a furniture store in East Harlem. He was in his midsixties and was extremely cordial during our interview. He did not seem to mind my asking him numerous questions and taking up his time. He never looked at his watch during the interview, nor did he excuse himself to help the customers who entered the store. When the interview was over, I asked for his card so that I could write him a thank you note, and I said, "Thanks so much for talking to me." He responded, "I'm only talking to you because you're a pretty girl. See, I'm just a dirty old man." Then he chuckled, pinched my cheek, and added, "You're so cute." I was caught off guard, never having anticipated that one of my respondents would feel at liberty to touch me. I found myself laughing, not because I thought what he said and did was amusing, but because I was surprised and made uncomfortable by his actions and was unsure about how I should react. Although I was grateful that he had agreed to the interview, I was irritated that he had touched my face and annoyed at the thought that he had talked to me because he thought I was "a pretty girl." For the first time I felt the tension between my roles as a researcher and a feminist. As a researcher, my primary goal was to collect data for the project, but as a feminist, I was loathe to subject myself to unwarranted physical contact and comments about my appearance or sexuality.

Other Jewish merchants asked whether I was interested in meeting their sons or nephews, and some asked me out on dates themselves. As Peggy Golde notes, "The perception of biological gender is not isolable but is intertwined with age, marital status, and other attributes."[13] In this case, my gender was interwoven with my relatively young age, my single status, and perhaps even my petite frame, making some of the male respondents feel they could make sexually suggestive remarks toward me or even try to set me up on dates with their sons or nephews.

On another occasion, I was nearing the end of an interview with a Jewish businessowner in Mount Airy when I asked him his age. This is one of my standard interview questions, and normally the merchants answered without hesitation. In this case, however, the man responded by turning the question around and asking me, "How old do you think I am?" I replied, "I really have no idea." He then said, "I'm forty-five, but personally, I feel thirty years old. I go out and have fun. I go to clubs and art museums. I'm enjoying my life, and I don't feel one year more than thirty. To be honest with you, I used to go out and date college girls, and they loved it. I have, in a way, the ability to be fun like a college guy, but more mature and not too old, you know, the best of both worlds." Cognizant that he had probably gone through this long explanation of his age to relay to me that, as a "college girl," I would enjoy going out with him, I anticipated that he would ask me out.

When I finished the interview and turned off the tape recorder, the businessowner asked me whether I would like to have dinner that evening. I declined the invitation, telling him that I was going back to New York that day. Although I had no obligation to fabricate an excuse, I felt that it would be easier for both of us if I politely declined with an excuse rather than just saying "no." The businessowner had spent two hours speaking with me, and I was very grateful for his time and attention. There was no way I could repay him, which is why I felt that the least offensive way of declining his invitation would be the most sensible option. Then he suggested that the next time I come to Philadelphia, I give him a call so that he could take me out to dinner. This time I mentioned that I had a boyfriend, which prompted him to drop the subject altogether.

I soon noticed that if I said that I have a boyfriend, the male respondents backed off, not necessarily out of respect for me, but out of respect for my boyfriend. In other words, the male respondents accorded more respect to another man—real or imagined—than they did to me. Whereas they have no qualms about bothering a single woman, most drew the line at harassing another man's girlfriend.

As surprised as I was when middle-aged and older Jewish business-owners asked me out or made sexually suggestive comments, when the harassment came from coethnics, I was completely bewildered. Because many of the Korean merchants I interviewed were close in age to my parents, I had expected that they would place me in the daughter role. Clearly I was wrong on this count. On one occasion, after I had finished interviewing the Korean owner of a clothing store on Jamaica Avenue, the man lit a cigarette and showed me pictures of his two children. I then asked Mr. Kim for a business card so that I could write him a thank you note, as I always did, and he, in turn, asked for my telephone number. I had given him my business card with my name, institutional affiliation, and telephone number, and I said that he could reach me there if he had any questions. Mr. Kim then told me that he would give me a call. I asked, "Why are you going to call me?" He said, "If you didn't have a boyfriend, I would ask you out," and then proceeded to tell me that he would call anyway. I was not sure how I should respond to him because I did not want him to call me just to ask me out, so I said, "I don't think my boyfriend would appreciate that." He retorted, "If I call you, my wife wouldn't like that, but I think all men playing around." I was caught off guard by this statement, but made a conscious effort not to show it. I shook his hand, thanked him for the interview, and left.

By responding, "I don't think my boyfriend would appreciate that," I took a passive but instrumental approach to relay to him that I did not want him to call me. The boyfriend excuse, however, does not always work. As promised, Mr. Kim called me one week after the interview and told me that he was coming into the city and asked whether I wanted to meet him for lunch. I replied in a grave tone, "I don't think that's a good idea." I was surprised by his call; none of the other respondents had called me before. My voice was cordial but firm, and he never called after that. I tried to react as an interviewer who did not want to offend her respondent rather than as a woman who was irritated by the behavior of a man.

As Shulamit Reinharz notes, "Women in the field are forced to deal with issues of gender in ways that are not always consistent with their own values," and she adds that "feminist ethnographers must always be prepared to deal with the intersection of their behavior and the gender ideology of the setting they are studying."[14] When male respondents made sexually suggestive remarks or continued to ask me out after I had declined their first invitation, instead of responding with the obvious "I'm not interested" cues, I tolerated behavior that under normal circumstances I would have not have accepted at all. Harassment has costs that go beyond discomfort on the part of the researcher. Mr. Kim's harassment impeded my fieldwork because I did not go back to conduct a follow-up interview with him, suspecting that he would mistake my professional interest in him for personal interest. I decided that the few questions I had were not worth the aggravation.

However, none of these experiences prepared me for the following exchange. By far the oddest experience I encountered in the field was with Mr. Park, the owner of a store in West Harlem. Because rent is very expensive on 125th Street in West Harlem, many of the storeowners sublease space in their store to other businessowners to help defray the sky-high monthly rent. In this case, Mr. Park subleased some space to a Korean beauty supply merchant, who would periodically visit with him when she had no customers. I had been interviewing Mr. Park for more than an hour and a half when the woman stopped by and said to him, referring to the length of the interview, "Long time." Mr. Park replied to her, "Why? Young girl, young man, talking each other." Not realizing that I was interviewing Mr. Park, the Korean woman assumed that I was flirting with him, which prompted her to look directly at me and announce, "His wife, she's home. She everyday home, and he play." Mr. Park then replied to her in a joking tone, "I'm going to make a girlfriend. I like her [looking at me], fresh, sexy. We just enjoy, enjoy talking. Not the bad kind, the good kind." He then put his hand over mine, and I immediately pulled it away. I said strongly, "I'm interviewing him," but before I could continue, she turned and walked away. I had not finished the interview, and I wanted to get through it without his touching my hand again, so I picked up my notepad and began scribbling notes to keep my hands out of the way.

I continued asking questions about his business, and then I asked him about his perceptions of Harlem as a community and inquired whether he had ever seen drug use in the neighborhood. He immediately replied, "Oh yeah! Drug people outside, right there," and he pointed to the streetcorner. He stopped talking, stared directly at me, and asked in a horrified tone, "Do you do that? You do that?" I answered, "No, not me." He insisted, "How about a little bit?" I replied firmly, "No." He then asked, "You sure? You look, you look," and then he paused and scrutinized my face and body, so I asked, "I look like what?" He continued, "Let me see here," and with both hands he grabbed my right arm and tried to feel my veins through my shirt. I firmly pulled my arm away, and calmly asked, "Why would you think that I do drugs?" He answered, "You skinny." He then continued, "Don't do that. Never do that. One time try and keep going. I saw one girl, but after six months, she almost died. Very skinny, very sick, broken life. So never, never do that. You sure you don't do that?" I was becoming increasingly impatient at this point but I wanted to reassure him nevertheless, so I simply responded, "No, Mr. Park, I don't do drugs." I do not know what made Mr. Park feel he could touch my hand or arm. Perhaps what was most perplexing about his behavior was that he treated me as both a sex object and a daughter. When he first referred to me as a potential "girlfriend" who is "fresh" and "sexy," he was unequivocally expressing his sexual interest. But then his grave concern about my potential drug use revealed concern for me as a daughter. Mr. Park stereotyped me in two gender roles, but by the end of the interview it was clear that he regarded me more as a sex object.

I spent more than two and a half-hours speaking with Mr. Park, and toward the end of the interview he began telling me that he and his wife do not have a good marriage. I was patient and listened to him complain about his marital problems, since he had given so much of his time to answer all of the questions that I'd had for him. When the interview came to a close, he sincerely stated, "It's nice meet you. It's so nice meet you." I had grown increasingly uncomfortable because Mr. Park had begun speaking to me about his personal life, and he seemed so genuinely pleased to have someone who would listen to him attentively. As I was packing up my tape recorder and my notes, Mr. Park looked again at my business card and asked, "Jennifer, this is your room number or your office number?" I replied, "It's both." He asked, "So what time I can reach you?" I answered, "I have an answering machine, so you can leave a message if you have a question about the interview." With each moment, I grew increasingly uncomfortable, and then Mr. Park did something that completely stunned me.

He walked to the cash register and pulled out a few twenty-dollar bills and placed them in an envelope. Then he handed me the unsealed envelope and said, "Take this. It's for school." I said, "No, Mr. Park, I can't take that." He said, "You know, it's Korean custom. You take it for school, for books." I repeated more firmly, "No, Mr. Park, I can't take your money." He then put the envelope under my tape recorder, and said, "I'm rich. You're a student." I picked up my recorder but pushed the envelope toward him and repeated that I could not take his money. I had no idea what this gesture meant, but I knew that it was inappropriate and wanted to leave the store immediately. It could not have been customary to give money to students, since none of the other Korean merchants had done this. He then asked, "I can call you sometime?" I picked up my bags and said, "Only if you have a question about the interview." He then said, as if he thought I did not understand why he wanted to call me, "Maybe we could go to dinner sometime." I looked at him and said, "I have a boyfriend," but he did not seem to acknowledge my response. I thanked him for his time, and I left as quickly as I could.

I was completely frazzled by Mr. Park's touching my hand and my arm, and particularly by his offering me money. I had no idea what I should make of the last gesture. When I relayed this experience to other Koreans, all of them said that it was peculiar, since he was not related to me and hardly knew me. If he were an uncle, an older cousin, or a close friend of the family, it would have been customary to give me money for school, but this was certainly not a standard practice from a stranger. I began to wonder whether my behavior in some way had elicited this type of response from Mr. Park.

I began to question my behavior in the field more generally. Was I too friendly to the male merchants? I thought perhaps I should not smile so much when I first introduce myself to the storeowners. Perhaps I should wear less makeup, or no makeup at all. Maybe I should dress differently by wearing baggier clothing that would deemphasize my figure. I did all of those things—I tried not to be too friendly, I smiled less, I wore less makeup, and I wore less fitted clothing—but these changes did not seem to matter. I was certain that my behavior or appearance must have something to do with the harassment, and I constantly asked myself what I could do to change the male respondents' behavior. I had reflected on this problem for months before I came to the realization that the problem was not with my behavior, my dress, or my appearance. Rather, it is the nature of in-depth interviewing and fieldwork more generally that can provoke harassment.

As difficult as it was to accept the behavior of some of the male respondents, I began to understand why they overstepped the bounds of a professional interview. Gender relations during an interview are affected by the gender norms of our society. In a male-dominated and heterosexist society, women rarely approach men. When they do, men may assume that it is because the women are interested in them personally. In my case, I not only approached male respondents and asked them to participate in my study, but I also asked many questions about their personal experiences and listened attentively to their answers with genuine interest. I routinely asked follow-up questions and urged them to clarify their statements, making it evident that I was paying close attention to everything they said to me. Unfortunately, some of the storeowners mistook my professional interest in them for personal interest.

In addition, because storeowners who operate small businesses have very routinized workdays, my presence was both a novelty and a curiosity. A woman in the field is what Ann Fischer describes as "a curious phenomenon," elaborating, "the curiosity sometimes, but not always, revolves around the sex role."[15] Since many of the merchants did not find their lives particularly interesting, they did not understand why I was so interested. This only augmented their impression that I was interested in them personally rather than professionally. As a young, female researcher embarking on her first research project, I did not at first understand that I was not responsible for the male respondents' behavior. I now know that my demeanor, style of dress, and overall appearance are not to blame for male sexual harassment in the field. As clear and obvious as this may be as I write it, it was certainly not intuitive in the field.

Multiple In-Depth Interviews

I choose to conduct multiple in-depth interviews rather than single interviews for several reasons. First, multiple interviews allow the researcher to ask additional questions that arise after transcribing the initial interview. Second, they allow for corrective feedback or elaboration when there are inconsistencies in the responses from the first interview. And finally, multiple interviews allow the researcher to understand how thoughts and responses are at times situated in particular circumstances.[16] For these reasons, I interviewed each merchant at least twice.

I taped the interviews, except in a few cases when the merchants objected to my use of a tape recorder. Normally merchants did not mind my recording them after I explained that I would not use real names, and that I was bound by Columbia University to keep all of the interviews confidential. Some of the Korean merchants initially expressed reluctance in allowing me to tape our conversations, not because of issues concerning confidentiality but because they were embarrassed by their English and felt that it was not good enough to be taped. I explained to them that I had no trouble understanding their English, that in my opinion their English was very good, and that it would help me enormously to be freed from taking notes throughout the interview. All but one relented and allowed me to tape them.

I strongly advocate tape recording interviews, for several reasons. First, and most important, it allows the researcher to get exact quotes rather than approximate ones. Even when researchers believe they are writing down exactly what the respondent has said, they must rely on memory, which is never 100 percent accurate. Second, when recording, the researcher is able to pay close attention to the respondent without jotting down notes, and there is no lag between questions, answers, and follow-up questions. In other words, taping interviews allows the researcher to follow the dialogue of the interview with her undivided attention. For this project, I also took on the arduous task of transcribing all of the interviews. Although this was extraordinarily time consuming and often tedious, the benefit of transcribing was that I had virtually memorized my data by the time I had transcribed it. I could readily recall who said what, which made the organizational portion of the data analysis go quickly and efficiently.

Following each first-round interview, I wrote a thank you note to the merchant on university letterhead. I would personalize each note, adding specific details about the interview, so that the merchant would realize it was not a standard letter. I made certain that the respondents had received my thank you letters before I returned to conduct follow-up interviews. Many of the respondents were touched by the letters. They greeted me warmly when I entered their business again, often personally ushering me in, and they gladly answered any follow-up questions. One of the African American merchants that I interviewed on Jamaica Avenue was so moved by the letter that he showed it to some of his neighboring merchants and even to some of his regular customers. I had not anticipated that my letters would generate so much enthusiasm from the merchants. The merchants valued them and appreciated that a researcher had shown genuine interest in their experiences.

Interviewing the merchants was not always simple. They were busy and had to go about their work, and I had to fit the interview into their schedule. It did not take long before I realized that the slower retail days were Tuesday through Thursday. Mondays were usually catch-up days, when merchants worked on their books and placed orders, and Fridays and Saturdays were the busiest sales days, so I normally did not conduct merchant interviews on those days. However, Fridays and Saturdays proved to be excellent days to conduct customer interviews since many of the customers shopped at the end of the work week or on the weekend. Furthermore, Fridays and Saturdays were opportune times to observe merchant-customer interactions.

Participant Observation

I acted as a participant observer while I worked as a bag checker in a clothing store in West Harlem and as a cashier in a sneaker store in West Philadelphia. These positions were invaluable to my research, because they allowed me to observe the daily activities of the merchants and their interactions with customers. In West Philadelphia, my position was easy to acquire because I knew the storeowner before I began my fieldwork. When I first went to interview her, I would stand beside her while she rang up sales and bag the sneakers just to make her job simpler. When she needed to run errands or eat lunch, she asked me to take over the register. Soon, whenever I came to her store she would put me on the register, and I would ring up sales and bag the merchandise. At times, it was so busy that a line of customers would form at the register. On those days I was demoted to simply bagging the merchandise, since I could not the count money and make change fast enough to keep up with the steady flow of customers. Apparently, all of my years of graduate school training had not prepared me to ring up sales, count money, and give change quickly enough for the busiest retail days at this sneaker store.

One day the owner of the store asked me, "Do you get paid for this?" I asked, "You mean, do I get paid for my fieldwork?" She nodded yes. I explained to her that I had a fellowship that gave me a stipend, so I did get paid. She responded, "I feel bad because you work here, and I don't pay you." I reassured her, "I don't mind at all. In fact, it helps me to be here." It was difficult to explain to the owner how working as a cashier benefited my research, but I refused to allow her to pay me.

Working as a bag checker in a clothing store in West Harlem happened by chance. I was interviewing the African American manager of an urban sportswear store during his lunch break. Because there was no back room where the employees could eat lunch, they would eat their meals on a counter placed in the corner of the store close to the entrance. Whoever was eating lunch would also act as a bag checker, taking bags from customers who came in, placing them behind the counter, and then issuing identifying numbers to the customers. Because I was interviewing the manager while he ate lunch, I stood behind the counter with him and watched as he took the customers' bags and gave them numbers. Each time he did this, he would have to stop eating and wipe his hands on his napkin to carry out the exchange, so to be helpful, I started taking the bags from the customers and placing them behind the counter. I then took numbers from the box and handed them to the customers, as I had seen the manager do. Soon, I had taken over the bag checking responsibility altogether to allow him to eat his lunch and answer my questions without interruption. I jokingly remarked, "I should work here. I'm pretty good at this," to which he replied, "You should." After that, every time I went to that store I took my post behind the counter, relieving the other employees of having to check the customers' bags. It turned out to be a perfect place for me to quietly observe the merchants, employees, and customers.

My jobs as bag checker and cashier came about simply because I was trying to be helpful. Ethnographers often try to be helpful in the field, in part because we would like to give something back in exchange for the right and privilege of being an interviewer and observer. Fieldworkers give back in myriad ways. For instance, in his study of sidewalk vendors in New York City, Mitchell Duneier gave back by working for a magazine vendor, watching other vendors' tables when they needed relief, and accompanying vendors to police stations when their merchandise was confiscated.[17] Charles Bosk became an extra pair of hands and a gofer for the surgical training team he observed in a hospital.[18] William Kornblum's willingness to defend the honor of the Boyash gypies in a standoff with Serbian immigrants on the outskirts of Paris became his way of giving back.[19] Other forms of giving back are less visible but no less meaningful, such as Elijah Anderson's vouching for a respondent's identity both on the streets and in "decent" society.[20] Working as a cashier and bag checker not only benefited my research but also offered me the chance to give something back—however small and humble my contribution—for the gift of being an observer in the field.

Interviewing the Customers

I did not know how I would interview the black customers in these neighborhoods. At the time that I designed my study, I did not have the research funds to hire African American research assistants, and I thought that I might have to interview the customers myself. Fortunately, I received a Doctoral Dissertation Improvement Grant from the National Science Foundation as well as a Dissertation Research Fellowship from the International Migration Program of the Social Science Research Council. These sources of funding proved to be invaluable to my research, because they allowed me to hire African American research assistants to conduct the interviews with the black customers.

I felt it was important to hire African American research assistants to conduct the customer interviews because I wanted to know about their shopping experiences with African American, Jewish, and Korean merchants. Obviously I do not believe in the doctrine that only insiders can study insiders, but in this particular case, many of my questions dealt specifically with Korean storeowners, and I feared that my race and ethnicity would bias the customers' responses. I did not want the customers to feel inhibited from speaking candidly about their experiences or views, especially those regarding Korean businessowners and Korean immigrants more generally.

Aside from hiring African American research assistants, the research funds allowed me to pay the customers a monetary thank you of ten dollars for their participation in the study. The customers patiently stayed with the research assistants for thirty to forty-five minutes while being interviewed, and I felt that they should be compensated. Those in low-income communities were especially pleased to receive the money. The customers were randomly approached in public spaces such as libraries, food courts, fast food restaurants, beauty salons, barbershops, and laundromats. These proved to be ideal sites for locating residents who frequented the businesses on a regular basis.

Interviewing customers in beauty salons, barbershops, and laundromats turned out to be a particularly fruitful strategy. In beauty salons and barbershops, clients normally had to wait to get their hair styled, so the research assistants would interview the customers while they waited for their turn. Laundromats also proved to be advantageous because the customers had to wait while their clothes were in the washer or dryer, and they welcomed the diversion of being interviewed. My research assistants proved to be very resourceful in locating the best sites to conduct interviews. While I suggested interviewing local residents in fast food restaurants and food courts, they suggested the beauty salons, barbershops, laundromats, and public libraries.

Striving for Balance

Once, before I gave a talk about my research at another university, a white graduate student approached me and asked in all seriousness, "You did your fieldwork in Harlem and you're still alive?" I realized that people who have never set foot in communities like West Harlem and West Philadelphia have little idea what these communities are really like. With this book, while I seek to provide a portrait of merchant-customer relations in five black communities in New York City and Philadelphia, more important, I wish to emphasize that daily life in these neighborhoods is best characterized by civility rather than racial warfare.

Fieldwork "puts us directly in touch with the human dimensions of social life."[21] It allows us to experience those dimensions, describe them, analyze them, and, finally, write about them. I have tried to present a "full-length portrait" of merchant-customer life in these communities instead of a snapshot of conflict.[22] The merchants and residents in the communities I studied are not heroes or saints, nor are they the prejudiced and violent characters that the media often purports them to be. In painting this portrait, I endeavored not to gloss over the unfavorable aspects of merchant-customer life. My goal was to remain true to my data and to allow the data to motivate the analysis as I struggled to achieve balance in each section and chapter of this book. I sincerely hope the merchants and customers of these communities feel that I have justly portrayed them.

Notes

1. Introduction

1. Heon Choel Lee, "Black-Korean Conflict in New York City: A Sociological Analysis," Ph.D. diss., Columbia University, 1993; Claire Jean Kim, "The Racial Triangulation of Asian Americans," *Politics and Society* 27 (1999): 105–138; Claire Jean Kim, *Bitter Fruit: The Politics of Black-Korean Conflict in New York City* (New Haven, Conn.: Yale University Press, 2000).
2. "Black" refers to a generic category that includes African Americans, West Indians, and Africans. When I am able to make ethnic distinctions, I do so.
3. Peter Noel, "Koreans Vie For Harlem Dollars," *New York Amsterdam News,* July 4, 1981; Von Jones, "Blacks, Koreans Struggle to Grasp Thread of Unity," *Los Angeles Sentinel,* May 1, 1986; Itabari Njeri, "Cultural Conflict," *Los Angeles Times,* November 8, 1989; *New York Post,* "Scapegoating New York's Koreans," editorial, January 25, 1990.
4. Itabari Njeri, "Kimchee and Grits," *CommonQuest: The Magazine of Black-Jewish Relations* 1 (1996): 39–45.
5. Paul Ong and Suzanne Hee, *Losses in the Los Angeles Civil Unrest April 29–May 1, 1992* (Los Angeles: University of California, Los Angeles, Center for Pacific Rim Studies, 1993).
6. For a detailed review of the events preceding the fire at Freddy's, see Philip Kasinitz and Bruce Haynes, "The Fire at Freddy's," *CommonQuest: The Magazine of Black-Jewish Relations* 1 (1996): 24–34.
7. *New York Times,* December 9, 1995, p. A1.
8. Connie Kang, "Mourners Remember Beloved 'Mama,'" *Los Angeles Times,* February 4, 2000, p. B1.

9. For a discussion of the importance of focusing on the everyday, the mundane, and the local, see Harvey Sacks, "Notes on Methodology," in *Structures of Social Action,* ed. J. Maxwell Atkinson and John Heritage (New York: Cambridge University Press, 1984), pp. 21–27.

10. Douglas W. Maynard and Steven E. Clayman, "The Diversity of Ethnomethodology," *Annual Review of Sociology* 17 (1991): 387; see also Harold Garkinkel, *Studies in Ethnomethodology* (Englewood Cliffs, N.J.: Prentice-Hall, 1967), and Harold Garfinkel, "Ethnomethodology's Program," *Social Psychology Quarterly* 59 (1996): 5–21. See also John Heritage, *Garfinkel and Ethnomethodology* (New York: Polity Press, 1984).

11. For an elaboration on group position theory, see Herbert Blumer, "Race Prejudice as a Sense of Group Position," *Pacific Sociological Review* 1 (1958): 3–7; Lawrence Bobo and Vincent Hutchings, "Perceptions of Racial Group Competition: Extending Blumer's Theory of Group Position to a Multiracial Social Context," *American Sociological Review* 61 (1996): 951–972; Lincoln Quillian, "Prejudice as a Response to Perceived Group Threat: Population Composition and Anti-Immigrant and Racial Prejudice in Europe," *American Sociological Review* 60 (1995): 586–611.

12. See also Mitchell Duneier, *Sidewalk* (New York: Farrar, Straus and Giroux, 1999); Mitchell Duneier and Harvey Molotch, "Talking City Trouble," *American Journal of Sociology* 104 (1999): 1263–1295; Elaine J. Hall, "Smiling, Deferring, and Flirting: Doing Gender by Giving 'Good Service,'" *Work and Occupations* 20 (1993): 452–471; William Foote Whyte, *Human Relations in the Restaurant Industry* (New York: McGraw-Hill, 1948).

13. Albert E. McCormick and Graham C. Kinloch, "Interracial Contact in the Customer-Clerk Situation," *Journal of Social Psychology* 126 (1986): 551–553.

14. Whyte, *Human Relations in the Restaurant Industry.*

15. Robin Leidner, *Fast Food, Fast Talk* (Berkeley: University of California Press, 1993); see also Martin B. Tolich, "Alienating and Liberating Emotions at Work: Supermarket Clerks' Performance of Customer Service," *Journal of Contemporary Ethnography* 22 (1993): 361–381.

16. Barbara A. Gutek, *The Dynamics of Service* (San Francisco: Jossey-Bass, 1995).

17. The relationship between a cabdriver and his fare is a prime example of a service encounter. See Fred Davis, "The Cabdriver and His Fare: Facets of a Fleeting Relationship," *American Journal of Sociology* 65 (1959): 158–165.

18. Hall, "Smiling, Deferring, and Flirting"; Katherine S. Newman, *No*

Shame in My Game (New York: Knopf and Russell Sage Foundation, 1999); Greta Foff Paules, *Dishing It Out* (Philadelphia: Temple University Press, 1991).

19. Arlie Russell Hochschild, *The Managed Heart* (Berkeley: University of California Press, 1983).

20. Whyte, *Human Relations in the Restaurant Industry,* p. 94.

21. Boas Shamir, "Between Service and Servility: Role Conflict in Subordinate Service Roles," *Human Relations* 33 (1980): 741–756.

22. For excellent analyses of how structural forces can affect individual interactions, see Duneier, *Sidewalk,* and Duneier and Molotch, "Talking City Trouble."

23. For a discussion of merchant-customer disputes, see Moon H. Jo, "Korean Merchants in the Black Community: Prejudice among the Victims of Prejudice," *Ethnic and Racial Studies* 15 (1991): 395–410; Pyong Gap Min, *Caught in the Middle: Korean Merchants in America's Multiethnic Cities* (Berkeley: University of California Press, 1996); In-Jin Yoon, *On My Own: Korean Businesses and Race Relations in America* (Chicago: University of Chicago Press, 1997).

24. Lucie Cheng and Yen Le Espiritu, "Korean Businesses in Black and Hispanic Neighborhoods: A Study of Intergroup Relations," *Sociological Perspectives* 32 (1980): 521–534; Herbert J. Gans, "Negro-Jewish Conflict in New York City," *Midstream* 15 (1969): 3–15; Ronald N. Jacobs, "Civil Society and Crisis," *American Journal of Sociology* 101 (1996): 1238–72; Kim, *Bitter Fruit;* Paul Ong, Gaeyoung Park, and Yasmin Tong, "The Korean-Black Conflict and the State," in *The New Asian Immigration in Los Angeles and Global Restructuring,* ed. Paul Ong, Edna Bonacich, and Lucie Cheng (Philadelphia: Temple University Press, 1994); Gertrude J. Selznick and Stephen Steinberg, *The Tenacity of Prejudice: Anti-Semitism in Contemporary America* (New York: Harper and Row, 1969); Ronald Weitzer, "Racial Prejudice among Korean Merchants in African American Neighborhoods," *Sociological Quarterly* 38 (1997): 587–606; Yoon, *On My Own.*

25. Edna Bonacich, "A Theory of Middleman Minorities," *American Sociological Review* 38 (1973): 583–594; Min, *Caught in the Middle.*

26. Nancy Abelmann and John Lie, *Blue Dreams: Korean Americans and the Los Angeles Riots* (Cambridge: Harvard University Press, 1995).

27. Ivan Light and Edna Bonacich, *Immigrant Entrepreneurs* (Berkeley: University of California Press, 1988); Gary T. Marx, *Protest and Prejudice* (New York: Harper and Row, 1967); Selznick and Steinberg, *The Tenacity of Prejudice.*

28. William Petersen, "Success Story, Japanese-American Style," *New York*

Times Magazine, January 9, 1966; "Success Story of One Minority in the U.S.," *U.S. News and World Report,* December 26, 1966; "Asian Americans: A 'Model Minority,'" *Newsweek,* December 6, 1982; David Bell, "America's Greatest Success Story? The Triumph of Asian Americans," *New Republic,* July 1985, pp. 24–31.

29. Heon Cheol Lee, "Black-Korean Conflict in New York City"; Min, *Caught in the Middle.*

30. Jennifer Lee, "Retail Niche Domination among African American, Jewish, and Korean Entrepreneurs," *American Behavioral Scientist* 42 (1999): 1398–1416; Light and Bonacich, *Immigrant Entrepreneurs.*

31. U.S. Bureau of Census, 1990 Census of Population and Housing (Washington, D.C.: U.S. Department of Commerce, Bureau of the Census).

32. Susan Olzak, Suzanne Shanahan, and Elizabeth H. McEneaney, "Poverty, Segregation, and Race Riots," *American Sociological Review* 61 (1996): 590–613.

2. The Ghetto Merchant Yesterday and Today

1. Claude McKay, *Harlem: Negro Metropolis* (New York: E. P. Dutton, 1940), p. 16.

2. Calvin Goldscheider and Alan S. Zuckerman, *The Transformation of the Jews* (Chicago: University of Chicago Press, 1984), p. 158.

3. Stephen Steinberg, *The Ethnic Myth: Race, Ethnicity, and Class in America* (Boston: Beacon Press, [1981] 1989).

4. Steven J. Gold, "Continuity and Change in Inter-ethnic Conflicts: Relations between Immigrant Entrepreneurs and Their Customers through the Twentieth Century," unpublished manuscript, Michigan State University; Nancy Foner, *From Ellis Island to JFK: New York's Two Great Waves of Immigration* (New Haven, Conn., New York: Yale University Press and Russell Sage Foundation, 2000).

5. Lenora E. Berson, *Case Study of a Riot: The Philadelphia Story* (New York: Institute of Human Relations Press, 1966), pp. 23–24.

6. Harold L. Sheppard, "The Negro Merchant: A Study of Negro Anti-Semitism," *American Journal of Sociology* 53 (1947): 96–99; Robert G. Weisbord and Arthur Stein, *Bittersweet Encounter: The Afro-American and the American Jew* (Westport, Conn.: Negro Universities Press, 1970), chap. 3.

7. Lunabelle Wedlock, *The Reaction of Negro Publications and Organizations to German Anti-Semitism* (Washington, D.C.: Howard University Press, 1942), p. 126, quoting from the *Philadelphia Tribune,* July 26, 1934.

8. Roi Ottley, *New World A-Coming* (New York: Arno Press and The New York Times, 1968), p. 115; Weisbord, and Stein, *Bittersweet Encounter*, chap. 3.

9. Sheppard, "The Negro Merchant."

10. St. Clair Drake and Horace R. Cayton, *Black Metropolis* (Chicago: University of Chicago Press, 1945), p. 448.

11. Dominic J. Capeci, Jr., *The Harlem Riot of 1943* (Philadelphia: Temple University Press, 1977), p. 37.

12. Wedlock, *The Reaction of Negro Publications and Organizations to German Anti-Semitism*, pp. 136–137.

13. Roger Waldinger, "When the Melting Pot Boils Over: The Irish, Jews, Blacks, and Koreans of New York," in *The Bubbling Cauldron: Race, Ethnicity, and the Urban Crisis*, ed. Michael Peter Smith and Joe R. Feagin (Minneapolis: University of Minnesota Press, 1995), pp. 265–281.

14. Harold Orlansky, *The Harlem Riot: A Study in Mass Frustration* (New York: Social Analysis, 1943).

15. Weisbord and Stein, *Bittersweet Encounter.*

16. Berson, *Case Study of a Riot*, p. 46.

17. "White Withdrawal: Ghetto Merchants Shy Away From Civic Ties in Areas They Serve," *Wall Street Journal*, August 16, 1966.

18. James Baldwin, "Negroes Are Anti-Semitic Because They're Anti-White," in *Black Anti-Semitism and Jewish Racism*, ed. Nat Hentoff (New York: Richard W. Baron, 1969), p. 5.

19. L. D. Reddick, "Anti-Semitism among Negroes," *Negro Quarterly* 1 (1942): 116.

20. Roi Ottley, *New World A-Coming* (New York: Arno Press and The New York Times, 1968), p. 125.

21. David Caplovitz, *The Poor Pay More: Consumer Practices of Low-Income Families* (New York: Free Press, 1967).

22. Berson, *Case Study of a Riot*, pp. 42–43.

23. Roi Ottley, *New World A-Coming*, p. 125.

24. Dick Gregory, *Nigger: An Autobiography* (New York: Washington Square Press, 1964), p. 35.

25. Gary T. Marx, *Protest and Prejudice: A Study of Belief in the Black Community* (New York: Harper and Row, 1967), p. 161.

26. Robert M. Fogelson, *Violence as Protest: A Study of Riots and Ghettos* (Westport, Conn.: Greenwood Press, 1971), p. 94; Weisbord and Stein, *Bittersweet Encounter*, pp. 43–44.

27. See Berson, *Case Study of a Riot;* Joseph Boskin, *Urban Racial Violence in the Twentieth Century* (Beverly Hills, Calif.: Glencoe Press, 1969); Capeci, *The Harlem Riot of 1943.*

28. Sol and Shirley Kolack, "Who Will Control Ghetto Businesses?" *National Jewish Monthly,* July–August 1969 pp. 7, 28–31.

29. See Berson, *Case Study of a Riot,* p. 41.

30. E. L. Quarantelli and Russell R. Dynes, "Looting in Civil Disorders: An Index of Social Change," *American Behavioral Scientist* 11 (1968): 7; Berson, *Case Study of a Riot,* p. 40.

31. See Boskin, *Urban Racial Violence;* Fogelson, *Violence as Protest;* Orlansky, *The Harlem Riot.*

32. Kolack and Kolack, "Who Will Control Ghetto Businesses?" 1969.

33. Howard Aldrich and Albert J. Reiss, Jr., "The Effect of Civil Disorders on Small Business in the Inner City," *Journal of Social Issues* 26 (1970): 187–206.

34. Kolack and Kolack, "Who Will Control Ghetto Businesses?" p. 7.

35. Max Geltman, "The Negro-Jewish Confrontation." *National Review,* June 28 (1966), p. 623.

36. Kenneth B. Clark, *Dark Ghetto: Dilemmas of Social Power* (New York: Harper and Row, 1965), p. 29.

37. Ibid.

38. Weisbord and Stein, *Bittersweet Encounter,* pp. 82–83.

39. Center for Community Studies of Temple University and Jewish Community Relations Council of Greater Philadelphia, *Survey of Jewish Businessmen Operating in Selected Inner-City Areas of Philadelphia,* unpublished study, Philadelphia, 1969; Theodore R. Mann, "Jews in the Inner City," paper presented before the National Jewish Community Advisory Council, Cleveland, 1970.

40. Data about the Merchant's Program can be found in the JCRC archives, held at the Balch Institute for Ethnic Studies in Philadelphia.

41. Aldrich and Reiss, "The Effect of Civil Disorders on Small Business," pp. 205–206.

42. Waldinger, "When the Melting Pot Boils Over," pp. 275–279.

43. In-Jin Yoon, *On My Own.*

44. Ku-Sup Chin, In-Jin Yoon, and David Smith, "Immigrant Small Business and International Economic Linkage: A Case of the Korean Wig Business in Los Angeles, 1968–1977," *International Migration Review* 30 (1996): 485–510.

45. George J. Borjas and Stephen G. Bronars, "Consumer Discrimination and Self Employment," *Journal of Political Economy* 97 (1989): 581–605; George R. La Noue and John C. Sullivan, "Deconstructing the Affirmative Action Categories," *American Behaviorial Scientist* 41 (1998): 913–926.

46. Roger Waldinger, *Still the Promised City?* (Cambridge, Mass.: Harvard University Press, 1996).

47. Ivan Light, *Ethnic Enterprise in America* (Berkeley: University of California Press, 1972); Ivan Light and Edna Bonacich, *Immigrant Entrepreneurs* (Berkeley: University of California Press, 1988).

48. When I asked Korean merchants about their funding sources, I made certain to ask them to differentiate between funds obtained through a rotating credit association and loans from family members or friends.

49. Timothy Bates, "An Analysis of Korean-Immigrant-Owned Small-Business Start-Ups with Comparisons to African-American- and Non-Minority-Owned Firms," *Urban Affairs Quarterly* 30 (1994): 227–248.

50. James S. Coleman, "Social Capital in the Creation of Human Capital," *American Journal of Sociology* 94 (1988): 95–121.

51. Nazli Kibria, *Family Tightrope: The Changing Lives of Vietnamese Americans* (Princeton: Princeton University Press. 1993).

52. Steve Gold, "Patterns of Economic Cooperation among Israeli Immigrants in Los Angeles," *International Migration Review* 28 (1994): 114–135; see also Steve Gold, "Chinese-Vietnamese Entrepreneurs in California," in *The New Asian Immigration in Los Angeles and Global Restructuring*, ed. Paul Ong, Edna Bonacich, and Lucie Cheng (Philadelphia: Temple University Press, 1994), pp. 196–226.

53. Elaine Krasnow Ellison and Elaine Mark Jaffe, *Voices from Marshall Street: Jewish Life in a Philadelphia Neighborhood 1920–1960* (Philadelphia: Camino Books, 1994); Alfred H. Katz and Eugene I. Bender, *The Strength in Us* (New York: New Viewpoints, 1976); Ewa Morawska, *Insecure Prosperity: Small-Town Jews in Industrial America, 1890–1940* (Princeton: Princeton University Press, 1996).

54. For a thorough description of coethnic training systems, please refer to Thomas Bailey and Roger Waldinger, "Primary, Secondary, and Enclave Labor Markets: A Training Systems Approach," *American Sociological Review* 56 (1991): 432–445.

55. Waldinger, *Still the Promised City?* p. 256.

56. David Caplovitz, *The Merchants of Harlem: A Study of Small Business in a Black Community* (New York: Columbia University, Bureau of Applied Social Research, 1969).

57. Nathan Glazer and Daniel Patrick Moynihan, *Beyond the Melting Pot: The Negroes, Puerto Ricans, Jews, Italians, and Irish of New York City* (Cambridge, Mass.: MIT Press, 1970), pp. 30–31.

3. The Significance of Small Business and the Nature of the Niche

1. Daniel S. Hamermesh and Frank D. Bean, eds., *Help or Hindrance? The Economic Implications of Immigration for African Americans* (New York: Russell Sage Foundation, 1998); George J. Borjas, "The Economics of Im-

migration," *Journal of Economic Literature* 32 (1994): 1667–1717; Ivan Light and Carolyn Rosenstein, *Race, Ethnicity, and Entrepreneurship in Urban America* (New York: Aldine De Gruyter, 1995); Frank D. Bean and Stephanie Bell-Rose, eds., *Immigration and Opportunity: Race, Ethnicity, and Employment in the United States* (New York: Russell Sage Foundation, 1999); Roger Waldinger, *Still the Promised City?* (Cambridge, Mass.: Harvard University Press, 1996).

2. "Retail niche" refers to a line of business in the retail sector in which ethnic groups concentrate or specialize. For example, in the sampled neighborhoods, Koreans dominate the urban ethnic sportswear retail niche, Jews the furniture niche, and African Americans, the hair styling niche.

3. Ivan Light and Angel A. Sanchez, "Immigrant Entrepreneurs in 272 SMSA's," *Sociological Perspectives* 30 (1987): 373–399; Kenneth Wilson and Allen Martin, "Ethnic Enclaves: A Comparison of the Cuban and Black Economies in Miami," *American Journal of Sociology* 88 (1982): 135–160.

4. In their study of black and immigrant self-employment competition, Robert W. Fairlie and Bruce D. Meyer analyze immigration and black self-employment in ninety-four of the largest U.S. metropolitan areas, using 1980 and 1990 census microdata. They find that immigration has no effect or only a small negative but statistically insignificant effect on black male and female self-employment. They propose an alternative explanation, that "recent immigrants may primarily displace the self-employed among earlier immigrant cohorts or crowd out self-employed blacks in certain cities, industries, or neighborhoods where they congregate, but we find no evidence of a substantial overall effect." See Robert W. Fairlie and Bruce D. Meyer, "Does Immigration Hurt African American Self-Employment?" in *Help or Hindrance? The Economic Implications of Immigration for African Americans,* ed. Daniel S. Hamermesh and Frank D. Bean (New York: Russell Sage Foundation, 1998), pp. 185–221.

5. Roger Waldinger, "The 'Other Side' of Embeddedness: A Case Study of the Interplay of Economy and Ethnicity," *Ethnic and Racial Studies* 18 (1995): 555–580.

6. Jennifer Lee, "Striving for the American Dream: Struggle, Success, and Intergroup Conflict among Korean Immigrant Entrepreneurs," in *Contemporary Asian America,* ed. Min Zhou and James V. Gatewood (New York: New York University Press, 2000).

7. The concept of an "evolutionary retail chain" diverges theoretically from Roger Waldinger's concept of "ethnic musical chairs." Whereas

Waldinger refers to ethnic groups succeeding one another in the retail trade altogether, the concept of an evolutionary retail chain refers to the process by which ethnic groups succeed one another in particular retail niches or lines of business. As older, more experienced entrepreneurs penetrate more capital-intensive industries, they leave room for newer groups to occupy the abandoned retail niches. Roger Waldinger, *Still the Promised City?* p. 260.

8. Jennifer Lee, "Retail Niche Domination among African American, Jewish, and Korean Entrepreneurs: Competition, Coethnic Advantage and Disadvantage," *American Behavioral Scientist* 42 (1999): 1398–1416.

9. Timothy Bates and Michael Woodard argue that although "traditional lines of black enterprise" may be common in inner-city neighborhoods, today's African American entrepreneurs are entering new "emerging lines of business" that are far more capital- and skill-intensive and serve a racially diverse clientele, including corporations and the government. Timothy Bates, *Race, Self-Employment, and Upward Mobility: An Illusive American Dream* (Baltimore: Johns Hopkins University Press, 1997); Michael Woodard, *Black Entrepreneurs in America: Stories of Struggle and Success* (New Brunswick, N.J.: Rutgers University Press, 1997).

10. Waldinger, "The 'Other Side' of Embeddedness."

11. Woodard, *Black Entrepreneurs in America,* p. 69.

12. Roger Waldinger, "Black/Immigrant Competition Re-Assessed: New Evidence from Los Angeles," *Sociological Perspectives* 40 (1997): 365–386, p. 383.

13. Roger Waldinger argues that instead of entering self-employment, African Americans have found better opportunities for employment and mobility in the public sector. See Waldinger, *Still the Promised City?*

14. Miliann Kang, "Manicuring Race, Gender and Class: Service Interactions in New York City Korean-Owned Nail Salons," *Race, Gender and Class* 4 (1997): 143–164.

15. Ibid., p. 161.

16. Arlie R. Hochschild, *The Second Shift: Working Parents and the Revolution at Home* (New York: Viking, 1989).

17. Saskia Sassen, "The Informal Economy," in *Dual City: Restructuring New York,* ed. J. Mollenkopf and M. Castells (New York: Russell Sage Foundation, 1991), pp. 79–101.

18. Laura Zigman, "Living Off-Center on Purpose," *New York Times,* December 12, 1996, C6.

19. U.S. Department of Labor, *Consumer Expenditure Survey, 1993* (Washington, D.C.: U.S. Government Printing Office, 1995). See also Bart Landry, *The New Black Middle-Class* (Berkeley: University of California

Press, 1987); James Rauch, "Trade and Networks: An Application to Minority Retail Entrepreneurship," working paper (New York: Russell Sage Foundation, 1996).

20. David Caplovitz, *The Poor Pay More: Consumer Practices of Low-Income Families* (New York: Free Press, 1967), p. 13.

21. Robert S. Lynd and Helen Merrill Lynd, *Middletown in Transition* (New York: Harcourt, Brace and Co., 1937), p. 26.

22. Barbara A. Gutek, *The Dynamics of Service* (San Francisco: Jossey-Bass, 1995).

23. Almost all of the furniture salespeople in the black neighborhoods I studied are men. During my many months of fieldwork in East Harlem, I met only one female sales associate who worked in a furniture store in this neighborhood.

24. Fred Davis similarly notes that the encounters between cabdrivers and their fares are random and fleeting. See Fred Davis, "The Cabdriver and His Fare: Facets of a Fleeting Relationship," *American Journal of Sociology* 65 (1959): 158–165.

25. Robin Leidner makes a similar argument about the nature of fast food workers and their customers. One of the greatest challenges of fast food service is handling the steady flow of customers while maintaining the standards of service required for the job. See *Fast Food, Fast Talk: Service Work and the Routinization of Everyday Life* (Berkeley: University of California Press, 1993).

26. Kathryn Neckerman, Prudence Carter, and Jennifer Lee, "Segmented Assimilation and Minority Cultures of Mobility," *Ethnic and Racial Studies* 22 (1999): 945–965.

27. Miliann Kang, "Manicures or Mangoes: A Comparative Study of Customer Relations in Korean-Owned Nail Salons and Grocery Stores," paper presented at the annual meeting of the Eastern Sociological Society, Philadelphia, March 1998.

28. Difficulties in customer management are not unique to Jewish or Korean merchants. Black and Latino fast food workers, for example, must also carefully negotiate customer interactions, working by the mantra that regardless of how rude or offensive a customer, he or she is always right. See Leidner, *Fast Food, Fast Talk* and Katherine Newman, *No Shame in My Game* (New York: Knopf and Russell Sage Foundation, 1999).

4. Life on the Street

1. For examples of past research on black-Korean and black-Jewish relations, see Lucie Cheng and Yen Le Espiritu, "Korean Businesses in

Black and Hispanic Neighborhoods: A Study of Intergroup Relations," *Sociological Perspectives* 32 (1989): 521–534; Moon Jo, "Korean Merchants in the Black Community: Prejudice among the Victims of Prejudice," *Ethnic and Racial Studies* 15 (1992): 395–410; Pyong Gap Min, *Caught in the Middle: Korean Merchants in America's Multiethnic Cities* (Berkeley: University of California Press, 1996); Gaeyong Park, "Use and Abuse of Race and Culture: Black-Korean Tension in America," *American Anthropologist* 98 (1996) : 492–499; Ronald Weitzer, "Racial Prejudice among Korean Merchants in African American Neighborhoods," *Sociological Quarterly* 38 (1997): 587–606; In-Jin Yoon, *On My Own: Korean Businesses and Race Relations in America* (Chicago: University of Chicago Press, 1997).

2. Douglas W. Maynard and Steven E. Clayman, "The Diversity of Ethnomethodology," *Annual Review of Sociology* 17 (1991): 387.

3. See Harold Garfinkel, "Ethnomethodology's Program," *Social Psychology Quarterly* 59 (1996): 5–21; Richard A. Hilbert, "Ethnomethodology and the Micro-Macro Order," *American Sociological Review* 55 (1990): 794–808; Harvey Sacks, "Notes on Methodology," in *Structures of Social Action,* ed. J. Maxwell Atkinson and John Heritage (New York: Cambridge University Press, 1984), pp. 21–27.

4. Moon Jo, "Korean Merchants in the Black Community"; Pyong Gap, *Caught in the Middle;* In-Jin Yoon, *On My Own.*

5. Barbara A. Gutek, *The Dynamics of Service* (San Francisco: Jossey-Bass, 1995).

6. Albert E. McCormick and Graham C. Kinloch, "Interracial Contact in the Customer-Clerk Situation," *Journal of Social Psychology* 126 (1986): 551–553.

7. Marx, *Protest and Prejudice,* p. 161.

8. Elijah Anderson, *Streetwise* (Chicago and London: University of Chicago Press, 1990), p. 61.

9. Erving Goffman, *The Presentation of Self in Everyday Life* (Garden City, N.Y.: Doubleday and Co., 1959).

10. William Foote Whyte, "When Workers and Customers Meet," in William Foote Whyte, ed., *Industry and Society* (New York: McGraw-Hill, 1946), pp. 132–133.

11. Gordon W. Allport, *The Nature of Prejudice* (Cambridge, Mass: Addison-Wesley, 1954). See also Lee Sigelman and Susan Welch, "The Contact Hypothesis Revisited: Black-White Interaction and Positive Racial Attitudes," *Social Forces* 71 (1993): 781–95; Lee Sigelman et al., "Making Contact? Black-White Social Interactions in an Urban Setting," *American Journal of Sociology* 101 (1996): 1306–1332; Christopher G. Ellison and

Daniel A Powers, "The Contact Hypothesis and Racial Attitudes among Black Americans," *Social Science Quarterly* 75 (1994): 385–400.

12. See also Weitzer, "Racial Prejudice among Korean Merchants in African American Neighborhoods."

13. The level of racial segregation in housing is not unique to inner-city merchants. John Logan's research of residential patterns reveals segregation indices of .83 and .89 for African Americans with respect to whites and Asian ethnic groups in New York City. See John R. Logan, "Still a Global City: The Racial and Ethnic Segmentation of New York," working paper (New York: Russell Sage Foundation, 1996). Similarly, Douglas Massey and Nancy Denton's pathbreaking study of black-white segregation records extremely high levels of segregation in New York City and Philadelphia—.82 and .77 respectively. With the segregation index ranging from 0 to 1 (with 0 indicating complete integration and 1, complete segregation) African Americans are extremely segregated from both whites and Asians.

14. For an elaborate discussion of the class heterogeneity within middle-class African Americans' networks, see Mary Pattillo-McCoy, *Black Picket Fences* (Chicago: University of Chicago Press, 1999).

15. *Fictive kinship* is an umbrella term used to refer to "people within a given society to whom one is not related by birth but with whom one shares essential reciprocal social and economic relations," Signithia Fordham, *Blacked Out: Dilemmas of Race, Identity, and Success at Capital High* (Chicago: University of Chicago Press, 1996, p. 71). For examples of the use of fictive kinship, see Elliot Liebow, *Tally's Corner* (Boston: Little Brown and Co., 1967); Carol Stack, *All Our Kin: Strategies for Survival in a Black Community* (New York: Harper and Row, 1974).

16. For a notable exception, see Miliann Kang, "Manicuring Race, Gender and Class," *Race, Gender and Class* 4 (1997): 143–164.

17. Arlie Hochschild defines emotional labor as "unpaid labor of a highly interpersonal sort" that involves nurturing, managing, adapting, and cooperating to others' needs. See *The Managed Heart* (Berkeley: University of California Press, 1983), p. 170.

18. For a discussion of gender as an interactional resource, see Susan Ehrlich Martin, "Police Force or Police Service? Gender and Emotional Labor," *Annals of the American Academy of Political and Social Science* 561 (1999): 111–126.

19. Ibid.

20. Jennifer Lee, "Business as Usual," *CommonQuest: The Magazine of Black-Jewish Relations* 1 (1996): 35–38.

5. How Race Polarizes Interactions

1. Robert K. Merton "Self-fulfilling Prophecy," in Robert K. Merton, *Social Theory and Social Structure*, 2nd ed. (New York: Free Press, [1948] 1968).
2. I supplemented the data from the seventy-five merchant and customer interviews we conducted, with participant and nonparticipant observation. Working as a bag checker in a store in West Harlem and as a cashier in West Philadelphia were invaluable experiences, because I was able to observe the daily lives of the merchants and their interactions with their customers.
3. This differential in perception and evaluation among black customers suggests a follow-up study to see whether Jewish and Korean customers also exhibit a similar perceptions in relation to in-group and out-group merchants.
4. Merton, "The Self-fulfilling Prophecy," p. 482.
5. Robert M. Fogelson, *Violence as Protest: A Study of Riots and Ghettos* (Westport, Conn.: Greenwood Press, 1971), p. 94; Gertrude Selznick and Stephen Steinberg, *The Tenacity of Prejudice* (New York: Harper and Row, 1969), p. 127.
6. Philip Kasinitz and Bruce Haynes, "The Fire at Freddy's," *Common Quest: The Magazine of Black-Jewish Relations* 1 (1996): 24–34.
7. Eric Yamamoto, *Interracial Justice* (New York: New York University Press, 1999), p. 180.
8. Selznick and Steinberg, *The Tenacity of Prejudice*, pp. 127–130.
9. Henri Tajfel and John C. Turner, "The Social Identity Theory of Intergroup Behavior," in *Psychology of Intergroup Behavior*, ed. Stephen Worchel and William G. Austin (Chicago: Nelson-Hall Press, 1986).
10. Roy G. D'Andrade, "Cognitive Anthropology," in *New Directions in Psychological Anthropology*, ed. Theodore Schwartz, Geoffrey M. White, and Catherine A. Lutz (New York: Cambridge University Press, 1992), p. 52.
11. Susan T. Fiske and Shelley E. Taylor, *Social Cognition* (Reading, Mass.: Addison-Wesley, 1984).
12. BFOQ (bona fide occupational qualification) is the term used in Title VII of the Civil Rights Act of 1964, which legally exempted some types of difference-conscious hiring.
13. *Spanish* is used as a generic term by most merchants to refer to Latino groups such as Mexicans, Central Americans, and Puerto Ricans.
14. Harry J. Holzer and Keith R. Ihlanfeldt, "Customer Discrimination and Employment Outcomes for Minority Workers," *Quarterly Journal of Economics* 113 (1998): 835–867; see pp. 845–847.

15. Prudence Carter, "Balancing 'Acts': Issues of Identity and Resistance in the Social and Educational Behaviors of Minority Adolescents" Ph.D. diss., New York: Columbia University, 1999; William Labov, *Language in the Inner-City: Studies in the Black English Vernacular* (Philadelphia: University of Pennsylvania Press, 1972).

16. Paul DiMaggio and Hugh Louch, "Socially Embedded Consumer Transactions," *American Sociological Review* 63 (1998): 619–637.

17. Jennifer Lee, "Business as Usual," *Common Quest: The Magazine of Black-Jewish Relations* 1 (1996): 35–38.

18. Gaeyoung Park, "'No Tension, But . . .': Latino Commentary on Koreans and the South Central Aftermath," paper presented at the Paul F. Lazarsfeld Center for the Social Sciences, Columbia University, March 1998.

19. The practice of race-based hiring was also used in government employment in the sixties; federal officials prompted the hiring of blacks because they believed that the all-white police forces used to control black rioting in urban neighborhoods exacerbated racial tensions. See John D. Skrentny, *The Ironies of Affirmative Action* (Chicago: University of Chicago Press, 1996).

20. Examples of studies that examine employers' hiring preferences include Harry J. Holzer, *What Employers Want: Job Prospects for Less-Educated Workers* (New York: Russell Sage Foundation, 1996); Philip Kasinitz and Jan Rosenberg, "Missing the Connection: Social Isolation and Employment on the Brooklyn Waterfront," *Social Problems* 43 (1996): 180–196; Kathryn M. Neckerman and Joleen Kirschenman, "Hiring Strategies, Racial Bias, and Inner-City Workers," *Social Problems* 38 (1991): 433–447; Katherine S. Newman, *No Shame in My Game: The Working Poor in the Inner City* (New York: Alfred A. Knopf and Russell Sage Foundation, 1999); Roger Waldinger, *Still the Promised City? African-Americans and New Immigrants in Postindustrial New York* (Cambridge, Mass.: Harvard University Press, 1996). Studies that focus on the high employment rates of immigrant groups include Robert Aponte, "Urban Employment and the Mismatch Dilemma: Accounting for the Immigration Exception," *Social Problems* 43 (1996): 268–282; Sherri Grasmuck and Ramón Grosfoguel, "Geopolitics, Economic Niches, and Gendered Social Capital among Recent Caribbean Immigrants in New York City," *Sociological Perspectives* 40 (1997): 339–363.

21. Interestingly, immigrant employers and immigrant employees both felt comfortable expressing their belief that immigrants work harder than native-born Americans, perhaps because they assumed that I too, as an Asian American, must be an immigrant who holds similar beliefs. Most

immigrant storeowners and managers ascribed certain values to me by using pronouns such as "we" when articulating their perceptions about the differences between native- and foreign-born people. This fictive kinship gave me an insider status that allowed immigrants to speak freely about what they perceive as the different "work ethic" or the "immigrant mentality."

22. Employers in the hotel and restaurant industries also find that a sense of entitlement typifies much of the difference in work ethic between African Americans and Latino immigrants. "The entitlement theme and the frequency and force with which it was sounded suggested that a preference for employing immigrants and an aversion to hiring blacks might be rooted in employers' perceptions of the different expectations of the two groups." Whereas African Americans expect to move into better-paying jobs with opportunities for mobility, Latino immigrants are far less demanding. Roger Waldinger, *Still the Promised City?* p. 280.

23. See Newman, *No Shame in My Game;* William Julius Wilson, *When Work Disappears: The World of the New Urban Poor* (New York: Alfred A. Knopf, 1996).

24. Christopher Jencks explains that employers are biased against African Americans from the inner city because they have a strong "distaste for ghetto culture" and are hesitant to hire "assertive workers from an alien culture they don't understand." (*Rethinking Social Policy: Race, Class, and Underclass* (Cambridge, Mass.: Harvard University Press, 1992), pp. 128–129.

25. For a discussion of "dual frames of reference," see Min Zhou, "Progress, Decline, or Stagnation? The New Second Generation Comes of Age," in *Strangers at the Gates: New Urban Immigrants in Urban America,* ed. Roger Waldinger (Berkeley: University of California Press, 2001); Min Zhou *Chinatown: The Socioeconomic Potential of an Urban Enclave* (Philadelphia: Temple University Press, 1992).

26. Aponte, "Urban Employment and the Mismatch Dilemma"; Holzer, *What Employers Want.*

27. Nelson Lim, "On the Back of Blacks: Immigrants and the Fortunes of African Americans," in *Strangers at the Gate: New Urban Immigrants in Urban America,* ed. Roger Waldinger (Berkeley: University of California Press, 2001).

28. Newman, *No Shame in My Game.*

29. James E. Rauch, "Trade and Networks: An Application to Minority Retail Entrepreneurship," working paper (New York: Russell Sage Foundation, 1996); U.S. Department of Commerce, *1992 Survey of Minority-*

Owned Business Enterprises (Washington, D.C.: U.S. Government Printing Office, 1996); Mitchell L. Moss, "Harlem's Economic Paradox," *New York Times,* December 13, 1995, p. A-23.

30. Alejandro Portes and Saskia Sassen-Koob estimate that between 1970 and 1980, New York City lost nearly half a million jobs, and in manufacturing alone, there was a 35 percent decline. "Making It Underground: Comparative Material on the Informal Sector in the Western Market Economy," *American Journal of Sociology* 93 (1987): 30–61; also see Barry Bluestone and Bennett Harrison, *The Deindustrialization of America: Plant Closing, Community Abandonment, and the Dismantling of Basic Industry* (New York: Basic Books, 1982); Harry J. Holzer, "The Spatial Mismatch Hypothesis: What Has the Evidence Shown?" *Urban Studies* 28 (1991): 105–122; William Julius Wilson, *The Truly Disadvantaged* (Chicago: University of Chicago Press, 1987).

31. At the same time, the larger employers, subject to Equal Employment Opportunity Commission regulations that require periodic reports on the numbers of blacks and other groups that are hired, can present to the government data showing that they may indeed employ many "blacks." Affirmative action regulations do not distinguish between American-born and foreign-born blacks.

32. Harry Holzer notes that the importance of networks "appears to be relatively greater in sectors in which fewer cognitive and social skills are required for work, and perhaps where more basic issues of personal behavior (for example, lack of absenteeism) are of relatively greater concern to employers"; see *What Employers Want,* p. 52. See also Mark S. Granovetter, *Getting a Job: A Study of Contacts and Careers* (Cambridge, Mass.: Harvard University Press, 1974); Newman, *No Shame in My Game;* Waldinger, *Still the Promised City?*

6. The Coethnic Disadvantage of Serving Your Own

1. St. Claire Drake and Horace R. Cayton, *Black Metropolis* (Chicago: University of Chicago Press, [1945] 1993), p. 440.

2. Ibid., p. 441.

3. Ibid., p. 445.

4. Ibid., p. 446.

5. Susan T. Fiske and Shelley E. Taylor, *Social Cognition* (Reading, Mass.: Addison-Wesley, 1984).

6. See John Sibley Butler, *Entrepreneurship and Self-Help among Black Americans: A Reconsideration of Race and Economics* (Albany: State University of New York Press, 1991); David Caplovitz, *The Merchants of Harlem: A Study of Small Business in a Black Community* (New York: Columbia University,

Bureau of Applied Social Research, 1969); Drake and Cayton, *Black Metropolis*.

7. Jennifer Lee, "Retail Niche Domination among African American, Jewish, and Korean Entrepreneurs: Competition, Coethnic Advantage and Disadvantage," *American Behavioral Scientist* 42 (1999): 1398–1416.

8. Howard Aldrich and Albert J. Reiss, Jr., "The Effect of Civil Disorders on Small Business in the Inner City," *Journal of Social Issues* 26 (1970): 205.

9. Robert K. Merton, "The Self-Fulfilling Prophecy," in Robert K. Merton, *Social Theory and Social Structure* (New York: Free Press, [1948] 1968), p. 482.

10. Ibid.

11. Ibid., p. 483.

12. Ibid.

13. W. E. B. Du Bois, *The Philadelphia Negro* (New York: Schocken Books, [1899] 1967).

14. Katherine Newman, *Falling from Grace: The Experience of Downward Mobility in the American Middle Class* (New York: Vintage Books, 1988), p. 125.

15. Jennifer Lee, "Entrepreneurship and Business Development among African Americans, Koreans, and Jews: Exploring Some Structural Differences," in *Transnational Communities and the Political Economy of New York City in the 1990s*, ed. Héctor R. Cordero-Guzmán, Robert C. Smith, and Ramón Grosfoguel (Philadelphia: Temple University Press, 2001).

16. Butler, *Entrepreneurship and Self-Help among Black Americans*.

17. Kenneth Clark, *Dark Ghetto: Dilemmas of Social Power* (New York: Harper and Row, 1965), p. 28.

18. Ibid., p. 29.

19. Harold Sheppard, "The Negro Merchant: A Study of Negro Anti-Semitism," *American Journal of Sociology* 53 (1947): p. 97; Robert G. Weisbord and Arthur Stein, *Bittersweet Encounter: The Afro-American and the American Jew* (Westport, Conn.: Negro Universities Press, 1970), p. 42.

20. Sheppard, "The Negro Merchant," p. 97.

21. Herbert Blumer, "Race Prejudice as a Sense of Group Position," *Pacific Sociological Review* 1 (1958): 3–7. See also James R. Kluegel and Eliot R. Smith, *Beliefs about Inequality: Americans' Views of What Is and What Ought To Be* (New York: A. de Gruyter, 1986).

22. Howard Schuman and colleagues make a parallel argument about blacks' objection to the symbolism behind Ronald Reagan. Although Reagan may not have directly affected the individual lives of many blacks, they still opposed Reagan as a political figure because he threatened blacks as a group. See Howard Schuman, Charlotte Steeh, and Lawrence Bobo, *Racial Attitudes in America: Trends and Interpretations* (Cambridge, Mass.: Harvard University Press, 1985).

23. Paul Sniderman and Thomas Piazza note that blacks are at least as likely as whites to hold negative views of blacks. For example, they found that 34 percent of white respondents describe blacks as lazy, while 39 percent of the black respondents feel the same. "Indeed, when it comes to judgments of whether blacks as a group exhibit socially undesirably characteristics, whenever there is a statistically significant different between views of blacks and whites, it *always* takes the form of blacks expressing a more negative evaluation of other blacks than do whites." See Paul Sniderman and Thomas Piazza, *The Scar of Race* (Cambridge, Mass.: Harvard University Press, 1993), p. 45.

7. From Civility to Conflict

1. Harold Garfinkel, "Ethnomethodology's Program," *Social Psychology Quarterly* 59 (1996): 5–21; Douglas W. Maynard and Steven E. Clayman, "The Diversity of Ethnomethodology," *Annual Review of Sociology* 17 (1991): 385–418.
2. Herbert Blumer, "Race Prejudice as a Sense of Group Position," *Pacific Sociological Review* 1 (1958): 3–7; Lawrence Bobo and Vincent Hutchings, "Perceptions of Racial Group Competition: Extending Blumer's Theory of Group Position to a Multiracial Social Context," *American Sociological Review* 61 (1996): 951–972; Lincoln Quillian, "Prejudice as a Response to Perceived Group Threat," *American Sociological Review* 60 (1995): 586–611; Eric Yamamoto, *Interracial Justice* (New York: New York University Press, 1999).
3. For excellent examples of studies that demonstrate the way in which structural processes produce certain modes of interaction, refer to Mitchell Duneier, *Sidewalk* (New York: Farrar, Straus and Giroux, 1999); Mitchell Duneier and Harvey Molotch, "Talking City Trouble," *American Journal of Sociology* 104 (1999): 1263–1295; Elaine J. Hall, "Smiling, Deferring, and Flirting," *Work and Occupations* 20 (1993): 452–471; William Foote Whyte, *Human Relations in the Restaurant Industry* (New York: McGraw-Hill, 1948).
4. Nancy Abelmann and John Lie, *Blue Dreams* (Cambridge, Mass.: Harvard University Press, 1995); In-Jin Yoon, *On My Own* (Chicago: University of Chicago Press, 1997).
5. Susan Olzak, Suzanne Shanahan, and Elizabeth H. McEneaney, "Poverty, Segregation, and Race Riots: 1960 to 1993," *American Sociological Review* 61 (1996): 590–613.
6. Pyong Gap Min, *Caught in the Middle* (Berkeley: University of California Press, 1996).

7. Max Weber, *The Protestant Ethic and the Spirit of Capitalism,* trans. Talcott Parsons (New York: Charles Scribner's Sons, 1958); Seymour Martin Lipset and William Schneider, "The Bakke Case: How Would It Be Decided at the Bar of Public Opinion?" *Public Opinion* (March/April 1978): 38–44.

8. Seymour Martin Lipset, *American Exceptionalism: A Double-Edged Sword* (New York: W. W. Norton, 1996), p. 287.

9. Herbert McClosky and John Zaller, *The American Ethos: Public Attitudes toward Capitalism and Democracy* (Cambridge, Mass.: Harvard University Press, 1984).

10. Lipset, *American Exceptionalism,* p. 115.

11. Paul M. Sniderman and Edward G. Carmines, *Reaching beyond Race* (Cambridge, Mass.: Harvard University Press, 1997); Paul M. Sniderman and Philip E. Tetlock, "Symbolic Racism: Problems of Motive Attribution in Political Analysis," *Journal of Social Issues* 42 (1986): 129–150.

12. Donald R. Kinder and David O. Sears, "Prejudice and Politics: Symbolic Racism versus Racial Threats to the Good Life," *Journal of Personality and Social Psychology* 40 (1981): 414–431. Seymour Martin Lipset and William Schneider made a similar argument, contending that while whites may be willing to endorse "special consideration" based on race and gender, they draw the line at policies that propose quotas and absolute preference, since set-asides violate the traditional concept of equality of opportunity. Lipset and Schneider, "The Bakke Case."

13. Lipset, *American Exceptionalism,* p. 133.

14. Jennifer Hochschild, *Facing Up to the American Dream* (Princeton: Princeton University Press, 1995); Kay Lehman Schlozman and Sidney Verba, *Injury to Insult: Unemployment, Class, and Political Response* (Cambridge, Mass.: Harvard University Press, 1979).

15. Lipset, *American Exceptionalism,* p. 133.

16. Seventy percent of whites and 63 percent of blacks agree with the statement, "Hard work is the most important factor in getting ahead." See Schlozman and Verba, *Injury to Insult,* p. 167.

17. Hochschild, *Facing Up to the American Dream,* chap. 4.

18. Michael Dawson, *Behind the Mule: Race and Class in African American Politics* (Princeton: Princeton University Press, 1994), p. 61.

19. Lawrence D. Bobo, Michael C. Dawson, and Devon Johnson, "Enduring Two-Ness," *Public Perspective,* May/June 2001: 12–16.

20. John Skrentny, *The Ironies of Affirmative Action* (Chicago: University of Chicago Press, 1996).

21. Sniderman and Carmines, *Reaching beyond Race,* p. 138.

22. Jon Rieder, "Trouble in Store," *The New Republic*, July 2, 1990, pp. 16–22.

23. The sense that other groups receive special government benefits that hinder African American economic progress is not new. As Herbert Gans noted in his 1969 study of black-Jewish relations, the presence of Jewish storeowners, landlords, and teachers in poor black neighborhoods led blacks to "easily if inaccurately conclude that they are being held back by *the* Jews." See Herbert J. Gans, "Negro-Jewish Conflict in New York City," *Midstream* 15 (1969): 10.

24. Stock stories are "a conglomeration of group members' selective historical recollections, partial information of events and socioeconomic conditions, and speculations about the future . . . the narratives create social identities for group members. They also influence the dynamics of interracial relations by providing the lens through which group members see and understand other groups." See Eric K. Yamamoto, *Interracial Justice* (New York: New York University Press, 1999), p. 180.

25. Paul M. Sniderman and Thomas Piazza, *Black Pride and Prejudice* (Princeton, N.J.: Princeton University Press, 2002).

26. Vilna Bashi Bobb, "Neither Ignorance nor Bliss: Race, Racism, and the West Indian Immigrant Experience," in *Migration, Transnationalization, and Race in a Changing New York,* ed. Héctor R. Cordero-Guzman, Robert C. Smith, and Ramón Grosfoguel (Philadelphia: Temple University Press, 2001); Nancy Foner, "Race and Color: Jamaican Migrants in London and New York City," *International Migration Review* 19 (1985): 708–727; Philip Kasinitz, *Caribbean New York: Black Immigrants and the Politics of Race* (Ithaca: Cornell University Press, 1992); Mary Waters, "Ethnic and Racial Identities of Second-Generation Black Immigrants in New York City," *International Migration Review* 28 (1994): 795–820, and *Black Identities: West Indian Immigrant Dreams and American Realities* (Cambridge, Mass.: Harvard University Press, 1999).

27. In the preface to *Facing Up to the American Dream,* Jennifer Hochschild defines the "American dream" as "not only the right to get rich, but rather the promise that all Americans have a reasonable chance to achieve success as they define it—material or otherwise—through their own efforts, and to attain virtue and fulfillment through success," p. xi.

28. Edna Bonacich, "A Theory of Middleman Minorities," *American Sociological Review* 38 (1973): 583–594.

29. James Baldwin, "Negroes Are Anti-Semitic Because They're Anti-White," in *Black Anti-Semitism and Jewish Racism,* ed. Nat Hentoff (New York: Richard W. Baron, 1969).

30. Gary T. Marx, *Protest and Prejudice: A Study of Belief in the Black Community*

(New York: Harper and Row, 1967), p. 167; Roi Ottley, *New World A-Coming* (New York: Arno Press, 1968), p. 129.

31. Harold Cruse, *The Crisis of the Black Intellectual* (New York: William Morrow and Co., 1967).

32. Joane Nagel, "Constructing Ethnicity: Creating and Recreating Ethnic Identity and Culture," *Social Problems* 41 (1994): 154.

33. See Mary Waters, "Explaining the Comfort Factor: West Indian Immigrants Confront American Race Relations," in *The Cultural Territories of Race: Black and White Boundaries,* ed. Michèle Lamont (Chicago: University of Chicago Press, 1999), pp. 63–96.

34. On the issue of "distancing," see also Milton Vickerman, "The Responses of West Indians to African-Americans: Distancing and Identification," *Research in Race and Ethnic Relations* 7 (1994): 83–128; Milton Vickerman, *Crosscurrents: West Indian Immigrants and Race* (New York: Oxford University Press, 1999).

35. See Stephen Cornell and Douglas Hartmann, *Ethnicity and Race: Making Identities in a Changing World* (Thousand Oaks, Calif.: Pine Forge Press, 1998).

36. Susan Olzak, *The Dynamics of Ethnic Competition and Conflict* (Stanford, Calif.: Stanford University Press, 1992).

37. Olzak and colleagues define black race riots as "large-scale, violent, crowd events driven by racial grievances in which Blacks were the main instigators." See Olzak, Shanahan, and McEneaney, "Poverty, Segregation, and Race Riots," p. 601.

38. Lawrence Bobo and James Kluegel, "Opposition to Race Targeting: Self-Interest, Stratification Ideology, or Racial Attitudes?" *American Sociological Review* 58 (1994): 443–464; Bobo and Hutchings, "Perceptions of Racial Group Competition"; Quillian, "Prejudice as a Response to Perceived Group Threat."

39. See also Harold L. Sheppard, "The Negro Merchant: A Study of Negro Anti-Semitism," *American Journal of Sociology* 53 (1947): 96–99.

40. Philip Kasinitz and Bruce Haynes, "The Fire at Freddy's," *Common Quest: The Magazine of Black-Jewish Relations* 1 (1996): 27.

41. See also Schlozman and Verba, *Injury to Insult,* chap. 2.

42. Kasinitz and Haynes, "The Fire at Freddy's."

43. Political entrepreneurs galvanize difficult to organize and dispersed citizens to support their cause and policies and serve a variety of functions. See John H. Mollenkopf, *The Contested City* (Princeton: Princeton University Press, 1983); John R. Logan and Harvey Molotch, *Urban Fortunes* (Berkeley: University of California Press, 1987); Mark Schneider

and Paul Teske, "Toward a Theory of the Political Entrepreneur: Evidence from Local Government," *American Political Science Review* 86 (1992): 737–747. At the same time, "ethnic identity entrepreneurs" appeal to an essentialized image of identity, using race and ethnicity as the basis for affiliation. See Barbara B. Lal, "Ethnic Identity Entrepreneurs: Their Role in Transracial and Intercountry Adoptions," *Asian and Pacific Migration Journal* 6 (1997): 385–413.

44. The mainstream media was not swayed by the boycotters' perspective, however, and instead framed the conflict as one between greedy, spiteful, and opportunistic blacks against an industrious model minority. See Claire Jean Kim, "The Racial Triangulation of Asian Americans," *Politics and society* 27: 105–138.

45. In his 1992 survey of blacks in New York, Pyong Gap Min found that only 27 percent supported the 1990–1991 boycotts of Korean-owned fruit and vegetable markets. See Pyong Gap Min, *Caught in the Middle* (Berkeley: University of California, 1996), p. 97.

46. Heon Choel Lee, "Black-Korean Conflict in New York City," Ph.D. diss., Columbia University, 1993.

47. Mollenkopf, *The Contested City;* Schneider and Teske, "Toward a Theory of the Political Entrepreneur."

8. Shopping While Black

1. Moon H. Jo, "Korean Merchants in the Black Community: Prejudice among the Victims of Prejudice," *Ethnic and Racial Studies* 15 (1992): 395–410; Heon Choel Lee, "Black-Korean Conflict in New York City: A Sociological Analysis," Ph.D. diss., Columbia University, 1993; Pyong Gap Min, *Caught in the Middle: Korean Merchants in America's Multiethnic Cities* (Berkeley: University of California Press, 1996); Ronald Weitzer, "Racial Prejudice among Korean Merchants in African American Neighborhoods," *Sociological Quarterly* 38 (1997): 587–606.

2. Paul M. Sniderman and Thomas Piazza, *The Scar of Race* (Cambridge, Mass.: Harvard University Press, 1993), pp. 177–178.

3. John B. McConahay and Joseph C. Hough, Jr., "Symbolic Racism," *Journal of Social Issues* 32 (1976): 38.

4. Sniderman and Piazza, *The Scar of Race*, chap. 2.

5. For discussions about the nature of racism today, see Seymour Martin Lipset and William Schneider, "The Bakke Case: How Would It Be Decided at the Bar of Public Opinion?" *Public Opinion* March/April (1978): 38–44; David O. Sears, Carl P. Hensler, and Leslie K. Speer, "Whites' Opposition to 'Busing': Self-Interest or Symbolic Politics?"

American Political Science Review 73 (1979): 369–384; David O. Sears et al., "Self-Interest versus Symbolic Politics in Policy Attitudes and Presidential Voting," *American Political Science Review* 74 (1980): 670–684; Donald R. Kinder and David O. Sears, "Prejudice and Politics: Symbolic Racism versus Racial Threats to the Good Life," *Journal of Personality and Social Psychology* 40 (1981): 414–431.

6. Philomena Essed, *Understanding Everyday Racism* (Newbury Park, Calif.: Sage Publications, 1991), p. 2.

7. Joe R. Feagin, "The Continuing Significance of Race: Antiblack Discrimination in Public Places," *American Sociological Review* 56 (1991): 106.

8. Ellis Cose, *The Rage of a Privileged Class* (New York: HarperCollins, 1993); Essed, *Understanding Everyday Racism;* Feagin, "The Continuing Significance of Race"; Joe Feagin and Melvin P. Sikes, *Living with Racism: The Black Middle-Class Experience* (Boston: Beacon Press, 1994).

9. Feagin and Sikes, *Living with Racism,* p. 48.

10. Edmund S. Phelps, "The Statistical Theory of Racism and Sexism," *American Economic Review* 62 (1972): 659–661. Researchers have shown that the practice of statistical discrimination occurs frequently in the hiring process. For instance, Braddock and McPartland demonstrate that in the absence of information about individual job candidates, employers use race and ethnicity to predict skills and attitudes about work, consequently discriminating against minority applicants. Moreover, Kirschenman and Neckerman show that race, class, and space interact and affect employers' views of black men from the inner city, whom they perceive as dishonest, uneducated, and unstable. See Jomills Henry Braddock and James M. McPartland, Jr., "How Minorities Continue to Be Excluded from Equal Employment Opportunities: Research in Labor Market and Institutional Barriers," *Journal of Social Issues* 43 (1987): 5–39; Joleen Kirschenman and Kathryn M. Neckerman, "'We'd Love to Hire Them, But . . .': The Meaning of Race for Employers," in *The Urban Underclass,* ed. C. Jencks and P. Peterson (Washington, D.C.: Brookings Institution, 1991), pp. 203–232.

11. Gary S. Becker, *The Economics of Discrimination* (Chicago: University of Chicago Press, 1957).

12. Cose, *The Rage of a Privileged Class.*

13. Elijah Anderson, *Streetwise: Race, Class, and Change in an Urban Community* (Chicago: University of Chicago Press, 1990).

14. Cose, *The Rage of a Privileged Class,* p. 41.

15. Jennifer Hochschild, *Facing Up to the American Dream* (Princeton: Princeton University Press, 1995).

16. Ibid., p. 216.

17. See also Nancy Foner, "Race and Color: Jamaican Migrants in London and New York City," *International Migration Review* 19 (1985): 708–727; Philip Kasinitz, *Caribbean New York: Black Immigrants and the Politics of Race* (Ithaca, N.Y.: Cornell University Press, 1992); Milton Vickerman, *Crosscurrents: West Indian Immigrants and Race* (New York: Oxford University Press, 1999).

18. Mary C. Waters, "Explaining the Comfort Factor: West Indian Immigrants Confront American Race Relations," in *The Cultural Territories of Race: Black and White Boundaries,* ed. Michèle Lamont (Chicago: University of Chicago Press, 1999), pp. 63–96; Mary C. Waters, *Black Identities: West Indian Immigrant Dreams and American Realities* (Cambridge, Mass.: Harvard University Press, 1999).

19. Waters, "Explaining the Comfort Factor," p. 84.

20. Feagin and Sikes, *Living with Racism.*

21. Anderson, *Streetwise.*

22. Hochschild, *Facing Up to the American Dream,* p. 124.

23. William Julius Wilson, *The Declining Significance of Race* (Chicago: University of Chicago Press, 1978).

24. For an insightful discussion on the way race affects the life chances of middle-class blacks, see Mary Pattillo-McCoy, *Black Picket Fences* (Chicago: University of Chicago Press, 1999). For detailed analyses of how wealth affects the life chances of blacks and whites, see Dalton Conley, *Being Black, Living in the Red* (Berkeley: University of California Press, 1999), and Melvin L. Oliver and Thomas M. Shapiro, *Black Wealth/White Wealth* (New York: Routledge, 1995).

25. Sniderman and Piazza, *The Scar of Race,* pp. 177–178.

26. Henri Tajfel and John C. Turner, "The Social Identity Theory of Intergroup Behavior," in *Psychology of Intergroup Behavior,* ed. Stephen Worchel and William G. Austin (Chicago: Nelson-Hall Press, 1986).

27. Douglas S. Massey and Nancy A. Denton, *American Apartheid* (Cambridge, Mass.: Harvard University Press, 1993).

28. Raymond S. Franklin, *Shadows of Race and Class* (Minneapolis: University of Minnesota Press, 1991), p. 118.

9. Conclusion

1. Herbert J. Gans, "Negro-Jewish Conflict in New York City," *Midstream* 15 (1969): 10.

2. Robert K. Merton, "The Self-fulfilling Prophecy," in Robert K. Merton, *Social Theory and Social Structure* (New York: Free Press [1948] 1968).

3. Herbert J. Gans, *Deciding What's News* (New York: Pantheon, 1979);

Pamela E. Oliver and Daniel J. Myers, "How Events Enter the Public Sphere: Conflict, Location, and Sponsorship in Local Newspaper Coverage of Public Events," *American Journal of Sociology* 195 (1999): 38–87.

4. Anthony Giddens, *The Constitution of Society* (Berkeley: University of California Press, 1984).

5. Jonathan Rieder, "Trouble in the Store," *New Republic* 203 (1990): 16–22.

6. Roger Waldinger and Jennifer Lee, "Immigrants in Urban America," in *Strangers at the Gates: New Immigrants in Urban America,*" ed. Roger Waldinger (Berkeley: University of California Press, 2001).

7. William Julius Wilson, *The Truly Disadvantaged* (Chicago: University of Chicago Press, 1987).

8. David Caplovitz, *The Poor Pay More: Consumer Practices of Low-Income Families* (New York: Free Press, 1967), p. 192.

9. See also James H. Johnson and Melvin L. Oliver, "Interethnic Minority Conflict in Urban America: The Effects of Economic and Social Dislocations," *Urban Geography* 10 (1989): 449–463.

10. Jennifer Lee, "Entrepreneurship and Business Development among African Americans, Koreans, and Jews: Exploring some Structural Differences," in *Migration, Transnationalism, and Race in a Changing New York,* ed. Héctor R. Cordero-Guzmán, Robert C. Smith, and Ramón Grosfoguel (Philadelphia: Temple University Press, 2001).

11. John Sibley Butler, *Entrepreneurship and Self-Help among Black Americans: A Reconsideration of Race and Economics* (Albany: State University of New York Press, 1991).

12. Roger Waldinger, *Still the Promised City?* (Cambridge, Mass.: Harvard University Press, 1996).

13. See also Robert M. Fogelson, *Violence as Protest* (Westport, Conn.: Greenwood Press, 1971).

Appendix

1. David Caplovitz, *The Poor Pay More: Consumer Practices of Low-Income Families* (New York: Free Press, 1967).

2. Charles L. Bosk, *Forgive and Remember: Managing Medical Failure* (Chicago: University of Chicago Press, 1979), p. 194.

3. Laura Nader, "From Anguish to Exultation," in *Women in the Field: Anthropological Experiences,* ed. Peggy Golde (Berkeley: University of California Press, [1970] 1986), p. 113.

4. Robert K. Merton, "Insiders and Outsiders: A Chapter in the Sociology of Knowledge," *American Journal of Sociology* 78 (1972): 25.

5. Ruth Horowitz, "Getting In," in *In the Field: Readings on the Field Research*

Experience, ed. Carolyn D. Smith and William Kornblum (New York: Praeger, 1989), p. 53.

6. "Fictive kinship" is an umbrella term used to refer to "people within a given society to whom one is not related by birth but with whom one shares essential reciprocal social and economic relations." See Signithia Fordham, *Blacked Out: Dilemmas of Race, Identity, and Success at Capital High* (Chicago: University of Chicago Press, 1996), p. 71.

7. Merton, "Insiders and Outsiders," p. 28.

8. Shulamit Reinharz, *Feminist Methods in the Field* (New York: Oxford University Press, 1992), p. 30.

9. All the names that I use in the text are pseudonyms.

10. Peggy Golde, "Odyssey of Encounter," in *Women in the Field: Anthropological Experiences,* ed. Peggy Golde (Berkeley: University of California Press, 1986), p. 80.

11. Elliot Liebow, *Tally's Corner* (Boston: Little, Brown and Company, 1967), p. 255.

12. Reinharz, *Feminist Methods in the Field,* p. 58.

13. Golde, "Odyssey of Encounter," p. 88.

14. Reinharz, *Feminist Methods in the Field,* p. 62.

15. Ann Fischer, "Field Work in Five Cultures," in *Women in the Field: Anthropological Experiences,* ed. Peggy Golde (Berkeley: University of California Press, 1986), p. 274.

16. See Reinharz, *Feminist Methods in the Field,* pp. 36–37.

17. Mitchell Duneier, *Sidewalk* (New York: Farrar, Straus, and Giroux, 1999).

18. Bosk, *Forgive and Remember.*

19. William Kornblum, "Introduction," in *In the Field: Readings on the Field Research Experience,* ed. Carolyn D. Smith and William Kornblum (New York: Praeger, 1989).

20. Elijah Anderson, *A Place on the Corner* (Chicago: University of Chicago Press, 1976).

21. Charles Bosk, "The Fieldworker and the Surgeon," in *In the Field: Readings on the Field Research Experience,* ed. Carolyn D. Smith and William Kornblum (New York: Praeger, 1989), p. 144.

22. See Barbara Myerhoff, *Number Our Days* (New York: E. P. Dutton, 1978).

Index

Acculturation: economic mobility and, 151

Affirmative action, 111–112

African Americans: resentment toward Jews, 25–26, 153–155, 188–189; self-employment and, 33–34, 40–41, 46–47, 133–136; perception of competition with immigrants, 48–49, 70, 157, 189, 194; compensatory consumption, 57–59; inequality of opportunity and, 70; kin networks, 82; lack of social contact with Jews and Koreans, 82; exclusion from service-sector and retail employment, 110–118, 119–120; racial and ethnic meaning of being black, 110–118, 119; employers' biases against hiring, 114–116; critical views of work ethic among, 115–116; wage issues and, 116–118; ambivalence toward immigrants, 130–133; American dream and, 132, 145–147, 191; individualism and, 132, 135, 136; in-group criticism of disunity among, 132–133; mutual cooperation and, 133–134; lack of access to resources and networks, 135–136; collective identity and, 147; belief that government preferentially aids immigrants, 147–150, 188–189, 194; distrust in government, 150; West Indians' sense of superiority over, 150–151; resentment toward upward mobility of other groups, 150–153, 187; resentment toward Koreans, 151–153, 188; autonomy and, 158, 159, 162; problems with American identity and, 158–159; salience of race in daily life, 176–177, 179, 180; limited benefits from small business ownership, 196–197

African American businesses/merchants: in Harlem, 21, 24, 25; street vendors, 22; "Don't Buy Where You Can't Work" campaign and, 24; in Philadelphia, 25; race riots and, 28; turnover of Jewish-owned businesses to, 30–32, 46; starting up, 39–41; bank or government loans and, 40, 149, 194; attitudes toward self-employment, 40–41; impact of ethnic networks on occupational outcomes, 41–42; capital and, 42, 44–46, 136; retail niches occupied by, 46, 52–53, 59–60; exclusion from markets and distributor networks, 54; interethnic competition and, 54–55; merchant-customer relations and, 59, 60–61, 62, 70; social space for clientele and, 62–64; class of customer base and, 65, 66, 67; black customers and, 74, 75, 81–83, 87, 91–92, 121–130; benefits of length of time in business, 75; fictive kinship and, 81–83, 91–92, 129–130; experi-

and, 42, 136; importance to small
businesses, 42–46
Social space, 62–64
Soon Ja Du, 1–2
South Central Los Angeles. *See* Los Angeles
South Korea, 33
Sportswear retail: mass marketing, 56–
57; class of customer base and, 65–
66
Starting up businesses: Korean merchants, 34–37; Jewish merchants, 37–
39; African American merchants, 39–
41
Statistical discrimination, 171, 174
Status shield, 9
Steinberg, Stephen, 199
Stereotypes: anti-Semitic, 24–25; black
stereotyping of Jewish merchants, 24–
25, 94–97, 130–132, 140, 184–186;
Jewish stereotyping of black business
inferiority, 31–32; erosion with length
of time in business, 79–81; black stereotyping of Korean merchants, 94–
97, 130–133, 140, 184, 185; stock stories, 97–100, 149; of African American
work ethic, 111–112, 115–116; of
black businesses by black customers,
122–130; black stereotyping of immigrants, 130–133, 140
Stock stories, 97–100, 149
Street vendors, 22
Streetwise (Anderson), 75–76
"Structuration," 187
Sugrue, Tom, 203
Symbolic racism, 166

Tajfel, Henri, 177
Taxes, 44–45
Teenage customers: retail niches and,
65–66; shoplifting and security measures, 68; treatment by merchants,
85–87
Theft. *See* Robberies/theft
Time on the street: Jewish merchants
and, 75–76; merchant-customer relations and, 75–84; seizing control of
service interactions and, 76–77; comfort level with customers and, 78–79;

erosion of rigid stereotypes and, 79–
81
Turner, John, 177

United House of Prayer for All People,
2, 3
Upward mobility: in Korea, 33; small
business ownership and, 47; American
dream and, 145, 146; African American resentment toward in other
groups, 150–153, 187
U.S. Immigration Act, 23
U.S. population: predictions and trends,
189–190

Vertical integration, 127

Waitresses, 76–77
Waldinger, Roger, 42, 49
Washington, Booker T., 41
Waters, Mary, 174
"Wearing your class" strategy, 171–174,
179
West African blacks, 110
West Harlem: commercial strip in, 12,
15; median household income in, 12;
black entrepreneurship in, 21; presence of immigrant merchants in, 21;
sense of community in, 21; treatment
of elderly black customers in, 86;
treatment of young black customers
in, 87; de-racializing tensions through
black employees, 107–108; black criticism of black-owned businesses in,
122; choice as research site, 201–202
West Indian blacks: preferential hiring
of, 114; perception of "immigrant superiority," 150–151; identity issues,
151; belief in self-reliance and individual mobility, 156; American racism
and, 174
West Philadelphia: commercial strip in,
12, 15; median household income in,
12; street vendors in, 22; black anti-
Semitism in, 24–25; Jewish stereotyping of black business inferiority in,
31–32; black community membership
in, 83; female Korean merchants in,
89–90; racialization of conflicts and,